BOER WAR

BOER WAR

THE LETTERS, DIARIES AND PHOTOGRAPHS OF MALCOLM RIALL

FROM THE WAR IN SOUTH AFRICA 1899-1902

COMPILED AND EDITED BY NICHOLAS RIALL

BRASSEY'S • LONDON

Also from Brassey's

Brassey's History of Uniforms Series
World War One: British Army
Dr Stephen Bull
World War One: German Army
Dr Stephen Bull

Brassey's Companion to the British Army
Antony Makepeace-Warne

First English Edition 2000

UK editorial offices: Brassey's, 9 Blenheim Court, Brewery Road,
London N7 9NT

A member of the Chrysalis Group plc

Library of Congress Cataloging in Publication Data
Available

British Library Cataloguing in Publication Data
A catalogue record for this book is available from the British Library.

Frontispiece caption:
"The West Yorkshires will Advance!" The infantry would make twenty or so miles each day, followed by slowly plodding ox-drawn wagons

ISBN 1 85753 266 X

Printed in Spain

CONTENTS

ACKNOWLEDGEMENTS

My grandfather died when I was sixteen and my memories of him are from the viewpoint of a rather awed, somewhat terrified, youngster. He was then white haired with beady, bright eyes that seemed to know everything. A somewhat irascible man who, I felt, was not overly enthusiastic about small boys. Although he spoke of his experiences in South Africa and India – but never of his war service in Flanders – my recollections are minimal. I suspect that the knowledge I have gained of the Boer War in recent years has completely obliterated most of what he had to say. Not that young boys pay much attention anyway.

All of Malcolm Riall's papers passed to me on the death of my father, Arthur Riall, in 1984. The letters were still in the envelopes that Malcolm had addressed home to his parents at the turn of the century and which had not been read since. A huge muddle of paper scattered through many trunks that had spent most of the intervening years in various lofts and attics. The entire collection of papers spans most of Malcolm Riall's service life and runs to over a thousand letters, many diaries and much else besides.

Malcolm Riall's Boer War papers, along with the 600 or so photographs he took, provide an eloquent voice from the past; more evocative by far than any memories of conversations a grandson had. They tell his story, and that of his regiment, a story of battles fought, of trials and tribulations occasioned by long marches, poor rations and extremes of weather in a strange and often hostile country. This book offers selections from Malcolm's written record alongside many of his photographs.

A great many people deserve my thanks for their part in the writing and production of the book. I am especially grateful to Bill Gunston, John Golley and particularly, Michael Pierce, who through their company So Few Ltd enabled this project to get off the ground. Without their endless enthusiasm and support I never would have been able to transcribe the whole of Malcolm Riall's Boer War archive to computer disks, let alone write this book. Also, to Jackie Gibson for her splendid prints of many of Malcolm's photographs.

I have been fortunate in the encouragement, support and advice I have received from many individuals and institutions. In particular, Brigadier J M Cubiss CBE, MC (retired) and Lieutenant Colonel T C E Vines (retired) – past and present curators of the Prince of Wales's Own Regiment of Yorkshire Museum in York together with Mrs R McMoines for permission to explore their large archive of Boer War material written by officers and men of the West Yorkshire Regiment. Mr D L Andrews who provided me with George Crossman's letters and photographs from the Boer War before these were deposited in the Liddell Hart Military Archive at King's College, London. Mrs R Fearns who gave me permission to quote from the diary of her father, Drummer Goodwin. Patricia Methven and Kate O'Brien at the Liddell Hart Military Archive who allowed me access to their Boer War materials. Professor Johan Barnard of Pretoria for his advice and enthusiasm. Dr Angela Smith for her comments on the text. Steven Dance, Meurig Jones and Tony McCabe (all members of the Victorian Military Society) who helped me gain a deeper insight into the Boer War and for their comments on the historical value of Malcolm's photographs. Keith Matthews at the Castle Museum, York, for his comments on the photographs, and lastly, Martin Boyce of Alton who produced many prints from Malcolm's negatives.

This book owes much to the hard work and patience of the editorial team at Brassey's, for which, my sincere thanks.

A note on placenames

There has been a gradual movement in recent literature to utilise African placenames instead of the Afrikaans or British names applied to geographical features and locations across South Africa in the Victorian period. Such a move has been resisted here as this book depends so heavily on the original writings of those who participated in the campaign.

One

AT THE FRONT
DECEMBER 1901

Opposite: The West Yorkshires crossing a trestle bridge over the Little Tugela on their way to participate in the Spion Kop battle. Note the steam traction engines on the sky line.

Kroonstad. 14 December 1901

My Dear Mother,

... As you will see that far from being 'away from all the fighting' as you rather unkindly put it, I am always well up in it, for whenever there is fighting the Brigadier must be there to conduct operations, and where he goes I go too. I have no ardent desire to be at the head of the Advance Guard every day in order to be sniped at I can tell you, still, when the time comes I am no coward, but at the same time I see no use in running unnecessary risks. If I wanted to be shot I should like to have been shot in some big engagement at the beginning of the war and not ignominiously at some unknown fontein or platz out in the bare open veldt.

I must first explain that great stumbling-block of yours – 'my duties as signalling officer'.

You must understand first of all how a Column marches, fights, camps etc. We will say there are 700 fighting men, 4 field guns, 1 pom-pom, 1 maxim gun to each regiment (i.e. 2 in all), about 150 Regimental ox or mule waggons and about 100 smaller vehicles (Cape carts, wagonettes, scotch carts, etc) all with their own drivers etc.

The Advance, Flank and rear Guards are split up into two portions, one right ahead and well extended and the other, say, 500 yards behind in support of it. The pom-pom goes with the Support to the Advance Guard but, if the Brigadier desired it, the pom-pom would be sent to the Rear Guard, or the Flank Guards. If a party (or 'push' as old Bethune would call it) were sent out from the 400 men in Reserve to go on some little expedition away from the main Column and Convoy, the pom-pom might be sent too or perhaps two guns ordered out. Well then, close behind the Advance Guard comes the Main Body consisting of 2 guns and 400 men, the other 2 guns staying behind the Convoy to help the Rear guard in case of accidents. The Brigadier with his ADC, Signalling Officer, and 3 or 4 Orderlies careers about wherever he pleases in the Column, but, as a General rule, he is to be found at the head of the guns with the main Body.

You were right enough when you asked if I was away on hill-tops working helios. I frequently am,

MALCOLM RIALL WITH HIS HELIOGRAPH

though 'tops of mounds or kopjes' describes them better than 'hill-tops'. The Brigadier will say 'Riall!' 'Yes Sir'. 'Call up the Advance Guard and tell Col A... to do so and so' 'Very good Sir'.

'Pte L ..., bring up the 5-in helio and set it on the Advance Guard', 'Right Sir'. Then we all halt, the helio is put down and the Advance Guard is called up, and when our light is answered the message is sent and if necessary we wait for an answer to come back, then we move on again. For taking messages short distances the ADC and Orderlies are used or if the day is cloudy probably I might be sent.

When there were 3 or 4 Columns working in the Division General Elliot used to take it in turns to go with different Columns and when he was not with our Column (which was generally the case as he and Colonel Bethune did not exactly hit it off) I had to try and keep touch with the Columns on our right and left and more particularly with the Column that General Elliot was with in case he had any fresh orders to send to my Brigadier. To do this I would have to climb the highest point near our line of march, whether alongside the road or away on the flanks, and search the countryside round for traces of these Columns. Burning farms were a great assistance to me, as a Column's route could be fairly easily traced by them. Once found and given plenty of sun the rest was easy, but on a cloudy day or with a bad signaller sending or very long messages to get through, the work was sometimes extremely hard, as the Flank Guards or Rear Guard would be perpetually catching me up and I would be left behind and then when too far behind have to pack up (with the chance of losing the station at the other end, as they might have to move on too), rush on myself and start once again. Fortunately I am a fairly good signaller myself and if there was any difficulty I would take a turn at the instrument and could generally rely on getting the message through...

By the time he wrote this, Malcolm Riall had been in South Africa for nearly two years and in the Army for only six months longer. This is his story written mostly in his own words, and it begins in Aldershot back in the late summer of 1899.

Two

THE ORIGINS
OF THE WAR

Historians have suggested a range of reasons that contributed to the coming of war between Great Britain and the two Boer republics – the Transvaal under the premiership of President Paul Kruger and the Orange Free State under President Steyn – but it has to be said that the matter remains controversial.

The greatest difficulties surrounded the gold mines at Johannesburg and the diamond mines at Kimberley which had attracted huge numbers of non-Boers to run them – both Europeans and natives. The Boers, it may be remembered, had trekked out of the British controlled Cape Colony and Natal to found their republics and run them free of British interference and in a manner that suited their Bible-based culture. The discovery of the huge treasures beneath their lands destroyed any hope the Boers entertained of continuing their way of life unhindered. In an attempt to prevent the unwelcome 'diggers', the *uitlanders* as the Boers called them, exerting too much influence on the Boer republics, the immigrants were heavily taxed and denied any voting rights. The mine owners, Cecil Rhodes and Albert Beit among them, were in addition very active in South African politics – indeed Rhodes was for a time Prime Minister of the Cape Colony. They, like the uitlanders in the Boer republics, wanted Britain to take over the running of the two countries.

Rhodes was determined to achieve a dream, the creation of a railway line from Alexandria in Egypt to Cape Town which ran entirely across a landscape governed by Great Britain, and it was a dream which in the 1890s was coming closer to reality. However, the Boer republics stood in the way and Rhodes wanted something done. He was fortunate with the arrival in South Africa of a new British high commissioner, Sir Alfred Milner, who shared Rhodes' vision. Both were supported in secret by the secretary of state for the colonies – Joseph Chamberlain – who was prepared to see the expansion of the British Empire where there was a strategic necessity for it.

Chamberlain was concerned by the growing influence of Germany, and, indeed, by the increasingly hysterical Emperor Wilhelm II of Germany, who viewed any political or diplomatic rebuff by Britain, however slight, as a personal rebuff. It was no coincidence that the Boers were armed with vast quantities of weaponry from German manufacturers such as Mauser and Krupp – although the Boers also bought huge quantities of British armaments as well. It was also German industry that created the telegraph network across the Boer republics – the metal bases of the telegraph poles still stride across the Boer landscape bearing their German manufacturer's imprint. Germany herself did not pose a serious problem to Britain's military might in the late 1890s – especially as far as the Royal Navy was concerned – but Chamberlain was well aware that the future held greater threats.

Ultimately, it was the excuse of safeguarding the interests of the uitlanders and those of the coloured and Indian communities in the Transvaal that were used as the public reasons for looking to war as a means of resolving the issue. President Kruger was confronted by Milner with a series of demands which effectively required the granting of the franchise to the immigrant populations and a diminution of the level of taxation on the uitlanders – and which, in turn, would ultimately cause the end of Boer domination in the republics.

Kruger knew he could not win in this situation and, believing that the British were determined to have the Boer republics by either diplomacy or war, he elected to deliver an ultimatum which required the British to either reduce the level of their forces in Natal or else face a state of war.

We might consider two other strands on the path to conflict. The newspapers and popular magazines such as *Punch* and the *Illustrated London News* were beating a drum of patriotic fervour which strongly supported the popular view that Britain ought to invade the Boer republics and bring them under the Union Jack. Secondly, there was a feeling of 'unfinished business' within the British Army with regard to the Boers by whom the British had been beaten, indeed hugely embarrassed, at Majuba back in 1881. They had something to wipe off the slate.

Aldershot 1899

The principal Army base in England in 1899 was at Aldershot in the north-east corner of Hampshire and about an hour's railway journey from London. The military town, so-called to mark it out from civilian Aldershot, comprised the two main camps: North Camp and South Camp, which spread across a level plain of several square miles. Away to the east were the extensive rifle ranges of Ash, Pirbright and Bisley, while to the west lay the rolling heathlands running for mile after mile northwards from Farnham which were used for manoeuvres. It was in Aldershot that the troops of General Redvers Buller's Army Corps were stationed. Malcolm Riall's own unit, the 2nd Battalion The West Yorkshire Regiment, formed one of the four infantry line regiments belonging to Major-General Henry Hildyard's 2nd (English) Brigade.

THE OFFICERS, 2ND BATTALION, THE PRINCE OF WALES'S OWN (WEST YORKSHIRE REGIMENT) 20 OCTOBER 1899. THE REGIMENT WAS USUALLY REFERRED TO AS THE WEST YORKSHIRES OR, VERY OCCASIONALLY, PWO. MALCOLM RIALL IS SECOND FROM RIGHT IN THE BACK ROW.

When, in February 1899, Malcolm Riall presented himself for duty at Talavera Barracks, the home of the West Yorkshires in Aldershot, the battalion was occupied with preparing for a summer season on the rifle ranges and out on the training areas. However, they were without the presence of their commanding officer, Colonel Walter Kitchener, the younger brother of (the then) General Herbert Kitchener. Both men were on campaign in the Sudan, Herbert as commander-in-chief and Walter as commander of the transport. That campaign culminated with the battle of Omdurman which raised Herbert Kitchener to superstar status in the eyes of the British public. The two men returned to England in the summer of 1899 where they were fêted, wined and dined and treated as heroes. As far as the officers and men of the West Yorkshires were concerned their colonel was the best, and they would follow him wherever he led them. This was very much a 'crack' regiment full of self-belief; well disciplined and highly trained, and led by officers who were well-regarded by their men.

That summer of 1899 was very much a time of hard work and hard play for Malcolm Riall and his brother officers. For Malcolm there were various tests to be passed – in horsemanship, in the gymnasium and on the parade square – before he could be fully accepted as a subaltern in the West Yorkshires. Additionally, having acquired an interest in signalling whilst at the Royal Military College at Sandhurst, Malcolm was undergoing further and more extensive training in all aspects of signals work as it pertained to the workings of an infantry formation, through it would seem he had little to do with field telegraphy or field telephones. Night exercises, forced marches of varying distances, endless hot summer days out on the ranges, riding both horse and bicycle around the district to visit friends at Sandhurst and his old school, Charterhouse, games of croquet, visits to the theatre, mess nights and long evenings playing cards or billiards – it was a busy, almost hectic life for Malcolm and his fellow officers. In late May, Malcolm, resplendent in full dress uniform, attended a levee at St James' Palace and spent his afternoon shopping in town. Without doubt they followed the developments in South Africa in the newspapers and speculated on what the outcome would be; in mid-June Malcolm noted in his diary that the regiment was to form part of the 1st Army Corps just after mentioning that he had found a jay's nest with four fresh eggs in it. This mixture of nature notes alongside descriptions of his military life is a thread that runs through all of Malcolm's writing during the war.

Malcolm's diaries, letters and photographs

The collection of letters, diaries and other papers, along with the vast numbers of photographs, provide an eloquent voice from the past and offer a personal view of the war that most accounts and biographies cannot achieve. Malcolm offers no clues within any of his writings as to exactly why he took so much trouble to keep up his diary – there are entries for virtually every single day he spent in South Africa – other than to suggest, as he did very obliquely in a letter to his mother, that some day he might contemplate writing an account of his activities in the Boer War. His letters were intended, as he wrote, '…so that you may see what part I play in all this…'.

It is clear that once mobilisation had begun Malcolm began to take greater care in writing up his diary; where previously his entries were quite erratic, from October 1899 onwards he was very particular about keeping a daily record. Once in South Africa Malcolm seems to have made a conscious decision to keep a daily record in a scrap notebook, or on loose-leaf pages or any other writing material that came to hand, and transfer these entries into his Cambridge Pocket Diary from time to time. This ensured that his formal diary was kept safe and his notebook diary could be put at hazard if need be. In the event both sets of diaries survived. As regards his letters home, they would have been no more and no less than was expected of him by his close family and relations – indeed he would have been writing such letters since the tender age of eight, when he first began going away to school at Arnold House in North Wales. From time to time Malcolm recorded in his letters the volume of his personal mail, the letters and packages he received from his family and those he sent: he was quite a correspondent. Eventually he recognised that he could not write regularly to everyone in his family and so he began to send home a general account of his military activities for consumption by all. In effect these were letter-diaries, and enclosed a covering page to his parents. Unfortunately he did not start doing this until the spring of 1900. Before then he wrote many letters to various individual members of his family, in which he described the events leading up to the relief of Ladysmith and, especially, the battle of Colenso. These letters have been lost, but we are fortunate that 81 of his letters as well as several postcards have survived.

One of the last things Malcolm did before leaving for South Africa was to buy a three-guinea Kodak camera at the Junior Army & Navy Stores in Aldershot. The photographs were intended to serve much the same purpose as his letters, and provide his family with a visual record. Malcolm sent the films back to the store in Aldershot where they were processed and printed and then sent on to his family home in Ireland. Eventually, many weeks later, Malcolm would see the prints when they were sent out to him in South Africa. He kept a detailed record of his photographs as he took them and, so well organised was he that he sent back with each film a list of photograph numbers and a description of each shot, retaining the master copy or catalogue amongst his papers. The early Kodak cameras permitted the user to scratch a number on each frame on the 12-frame roll of film: there is a small hatch on the back of the camera and a steel point was supplied on the hatch cover.

At some later date, after 1902 but before 1905, Malcolm assembled the best of the photographs into a set of three albums and annotated each snap with its original number and description. He also compiled a fourth album of what he considered to be his very best work.

Late in 1900 his Kodak stopped working, despite the best efforts of his sergeant to mend it, and he had a second, similar, camera sent out to him. This camera lasted him for many years, and later saw active service on the North-West Frontier of

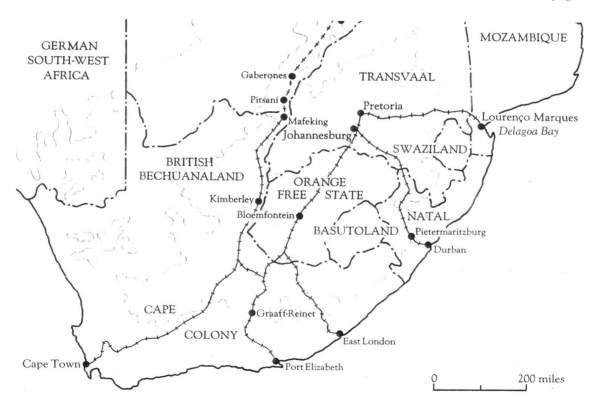

MAP OF SOUTH AFRICA

India; a great tribute to the quality of those early Kodak cameras.

When, in 1984, my grandfather's papers came into my hands, most of the letters were still in their original envelopes, the notebook diaries were wrapped up in a piece of oil-paper that Malcolm must have used on campaign in South Africa, and the other documents were scattered through his other papers. Only the photograph albums had been treated with any sort of care or been looked at in the intervening years. Grandpa appears to have given up any idea of writing a book on the Boer War. Perhaps having seen the huge numbers of books published in the immediate aftermath of the war he felt his would not be worthwhile, and contented himself with leaving behind a marvellous collection of photographs. In his declining years Grandpa devoted himself to researching the family history and exploring the family trees of both the Riall family and those families into which the Rialls married — the task of writing about wars and warfare he was happy to leave to others.

Three

'I BOUGHT A THREE GUINEA KODAK...'

Opposite: Malcolm Riall (right) and some of his brother officers at Spearman's camp

Events moved rapidly that summer and autumn of 1899. The national and provincial papers had for many weeks past been filled with news of the deepening crisis and the possibility of conflict with the Boers in South Africa. With increasing tension between Briton and Boer, coupled with the flight of thousands of *uitlanders* from the Boer republics into the Transvaal, on 9 September the British government stiffened the garrison in Natal by ordering 8,000 more troops to the colony. It was soon clear that the Boers were not going to back down, and on 22 September a newspaper report announced that the Cabinet had decided to send Buller's Army Corps. This 'leak', for such it was, seems to have galvanised the Boers into action: on 28 September the Transvaal mobilised its *commandos*. On 2 October, the Orange Free State followed suit, and by 9 October the Boers were massed along the Natal border. On 11 October the Boers invaded Natal and Great Britain was at war.

Back in England, mobilisation was announced on 7 October – a Saturday – and so nothing much happened in Aldershot until the following Monday. Then, as Malcolm noted in his diary, the regiment was paraded, given a speech by Colonel FW Kitchener on inoculation (against typhoid), and then inoculated by companies. 'I was done 3 o'clock pm, got very shivery and cold after 6, lay down' reads the entry.

The West Yorkshires were fortunate, many other regiments were inoculated whilst they were at sea and thus suffered the after-effects of the injection on top of seasickness. On 20 October the battalion set off from Aldershot: taking trains to Southampton and there boarding ships to Cape Town and Durban via Las Palmas. Malcolm soon had pen to paper,

THE WEST YORKSHIRES ON PARADE AT TALAVERA BARRACKS, ALDERSHOT

On board RMS Roslin Castle 24th October 1899

My dear Mother,

I don't know how you should address a letter to me, the Base of operations is of course the

Depot for everything to be sent on to us but nobody seems to know where the base is to be! Anyway I should think 'West Yorkshire Regiment, South African Field Force, via Cape Town' or something of that sort would turn up after a bit.

We have had a most lovely calm passage up to this, 'the Bay' [Biscay] of course excepted. On Saturday we were well in the middle of the Bay and I and several others retired to our berths and until today I have never felt really at home ~ now I don't mind the sea a bit and have been running about all day on different jobs, but I must say it requires even now a little extra nerve to go down for an hour or two into the men's berths or 'messes' as they call them at the bottom of the ship. They are like furnaces and you want a sense of smell like Father's to withstand the extras as well...

It was a most amusing job escorting the men down to the train for embarkation, most of them were reeling ~ I was looking after the rear of my Company and it was like hustling along a lot of crabs! They were very merry some of them and indeed I hardly blame them, it was of course their last chance of a good bust-up for months.

I hope Father will not be offended at not getting a letter, but of course you all understand that a letter home has to do for all and the person it is addressed to is merely nominal and put on for convenience sake.

I have bought myself a present in the shape of a 3 guinea Kodak and hope to take many pictures which will I hope be good and serve to show you something of the life we live and the scenery we pass through, that is when we get on land once more for there is not much scenery now.

I remain...

His next letter was written in much the same vein, with descriptions of shipboard life together with something of a scare:

...An Officer came over from HMS Niobe about signalling and told me how communication

was kept up between two vessels and the end of it was that I had to stay on board the whole time in case a message should come while the others went ashore. One short message and an answer to it was all that passed! I was very disappointed as you may imagine as of course I wanted to see the place, the people etc. and take a few snap-shots. When the coaling was over I was one mass of coal-dust, but luckily khaki is very easy to wash.

Lying in Las Palmas harbour were some queer craft and amongst others a torpedo boat flying the Brazilian flag, which it was rumoured had been bought by Mr Kruger and which was timed to sail three hours after us. A British man-of-war, HMS Niobe, was lying outside the harbour and her skipper had a long interview with our heads of staff, the General [Hildyard], Colonel Kitchener, etc. the result of which was that when we once got fairly on our way again (and that was not for an hour or so after leaving harbour as a kink had somehow got in the chain of the steering-gear and it required a deal of persuasion to right itself again ~ some said the chief engineer was in Kruger's pay!). Well once we got started we changed our course and after Mess all lights were extinguished. At first we none of us knew about the Brazilian flag and every imaginable rumour was afloat, all were up on deck, some with glasses sweeping the horizon for the lights of possible war-ships, others discussing the question in little knots. Intense excitement prevailed. The men of the watch were given ball ammunition, an officer was told off as a special orderly to the General, who for some time stood grave and motionless peering over the bulwarks into the darkness beyond, then slowly marched up and down the deck deep in conversation with our Colonel. Some slept little or not at all that night. I am afraid I must have been very tired for I slept sound. It was the same all the next day and night, only the Mess was eaten by candle-light instead, and the next day after that again. After that as no war vessel loomed in sight we reverted to the ordinary state of things and now the next thing we expect to see, bar perhaps a homeward bound liner or two, is Table Mountain.

COALING SHIP AT LAS PALMAS

Malcolm's diary and notes show that he spent quite a substantial time on the voyage out to Cape Town working with his signallers, training them up in semaphore and heliograph work. He was sufficiently impressed with progress amongst his men to note in his diary that they sent a 52-word message through four stations, set up around the ship and produced a 47-word answer. He was also encouraged by Colonel Kitchener to get an officers' class going, but his brother officers were not enthusiastic about undertaking this extra work. It is also curious to note that Malcolm was the most junior officer, and the youngest, in the battalion which further emphasises the lack of interest most officers had for the work involved in signalling.

In a letter dated 10 November to his brother Claud, Malcolm observed,

...The Colonel is very keen that everyone in the Battalion should know how to signal by Semaphore and the consequence is that I have been doing nothing but semaphore ever since I came on board. We had rather an ordeal yesterday in the shape of a funeral.

A poor chap got pneumonia rather badly and in spite of all the doctors attending him he died [No 4616 Private W Wiffin died 8 November and was buried at sea the following day]. The burial service took place on the Officers' Upper Deck aft and there were well over 1,000-odd men assembled, four, five and six deep on either side of the deck and in their hob-nailed boots. The ship was rolling her very worst just then and just at the critical moment she gave a terrific lurch, men were sprawling about deck in all directions, I was holding up a flag in one hand, as a signal to an officer on the Bridge to stop the engines, and holding on to a railing with the other for all I was worth.

The original plan had been to ship the Army Corps to Cape Town and then advance against the Boers from there utilising the extensive railway network. Events in Natal had moved so swiftly though that it was necessary to send the troops onwards by sea to Durban. The West Yorkshires had to endure a few more days aboard the Roslin Castle.

9.83 (COPYRIGHT) "THE FIRST OF THE ARMY CORPS TO REACH DURBAN" THE 2ND BAT. 14TH (PRINCE OF WALES OWN) WEST YORKSHIRE REGIMENT - BOER WAR 1899

Four

ALL OVER BY CHRISTMAS

Opposite: The West Yorkshires disembark at Durban

As you will see that far from being 'away from all the fighting' as you rather unkindly put it, I am always well up in it, for whenever there is fighting the Brigadier must be there to conduct operations, and where he goes I go too. I have no ardent desire to be at the head of the Advance Guard every day in order to be sniped at I can tell you still when the time comes I am no coward, but at the same time I see no use in running unnecessary risks. If I wanted to be shot I should like to have been shot in some big engagement at the beginning of the war and not.

Even as mobilisation was taking place back in England, the Boers were streaming across the borders into Natal and the Cape. Their objective was to overrun the British troops in Natal and sweep into the Cape Colony as rapidly as possible before yet more troops arrived from Britain or other parts of the Empire. A half-century later this strategy would be recognised as a *blitzkrieg*. The Boers hoped that by inflicting an early defeat on the British they would be able to force the politicians back to the negotiating table and hammer out another peace settlement – just as they had done back in 1881 in the First Boer War. That campaign had been fought against very small numbers of troops, many of them scattered in small garrisons across the Transvaal, and the Boers had very easily defeated them, culminating with a victory at Majuba, in northern Natal, where Sir George Colley and his small force had been annihilated. 'Remember Majuba' would be a battlecry taken up by the British – though, it has to be said, more by the Press and postcard makers than the troops themselves.

Apart from an initial British success at Talana (20 October) where the Boers were held and driven back, the Boer strategy worked well. By the end of October the Boers had laid siege to Kimberley, Mafeking and, incredibly given the numbers of British troops there – 13,000 including the much needed cavalry – Ladysmith. It had been a dreadful start to the campaign for the British, aside from a brilliant exposition of all-arms fighting by Major-General Ian Hamilton at Elandslaagte. On 21 October Hamilton's infantry, well supported by artillery and cavalry, had driven the Boer advance back and given the British a short breathing space. It was not enough though to halt the Boer advance and, with Ladysmith completely bottled up, the way to the south and the principal port of Natal, Durban, was open, with only minimal numbers of British troops, perhaps 2,000 in all, guarding both the railway line and the port.

The Boers hesitated, taken by surprise by the totality of their success, and yet confronted by the problems of maintaining three substantial sieges in the certain knowledge that British reinforcements were on their way. The younger Boers, among them Deneys Reitz and Louis Botha, were all for riding hell-for-leather to the south, whilst their aged commander, Piet Joubert, is supposed to have told them, 'When God offers you his finger, don't try to take the whole hand'. Their hesitation was probably the defining moment to the campaign, for had the Boers swept south and simply denied the British the use of the railway, and destroyed the railway bridges in doing so, it would have been enough to ensure Ladysmith's surrender and, quite probably, have knocked the will to fight out of the British government.

As it was, on 13 November, Piet Joubert and Louis Botha led a force of some 2,000 men across the Tugela River at Colenso, and having laid dynamite under the road and rail bridges there, they rode south reaching Chieveley on the 14th, having laid demolition charges beneath every rail bridge they came to. But they were too late, the British were coming and, indeed, the advance parties had already arrived.

Major-General Hildyard, his brigade staff and the West Yorkshires arrived at Durban on 12 November and, loaded up into three trains, headed north to Pietermaritzburg where the battalion spent the night. Malcolm's diary records his first impressions of South Africa:

By troop train to Estcourt

November 12, Sunday. *Crossed the bar and arrived in harbour 10 am. Went ashore and posted letters and got stamps. Wired to Pietermaritzburg about some Ordnance stores for Colonel Kitchener. Went to a chemist and got foot powder, spectacles for signallers, pills etc. Left Durban by 3rd train. Railway winds up round the hills in steep gradients & sharp curves. Pretty scenery. Blacks and whites cheering us lustily all the way up along the line… Arrived Pietermaritzburg 7 pm. General Hildyard left for Estcourt but we went into barracks.*

November 13 *Found sleeping in valises on a hard floor not all joy. Woken at 2.30 am. Took my valise myself to railway station but the Company was not there. Returned to barracks & found them all snoring. Bustled all out. Started 5 am in 2 trains… Stopped at Mooi River and talked to some men of Murray's Light Horse. Arrived Estcourt in afternoon and pitched tents by 5 pm. Lunched and dined with the Border Regiment in a tin house they use for their Mess. Slept well, ground very hard.*

Estcourt had become, almost by default rather than for any particular strategic reasons apart from the presence of the railway, the anchor point for the British forces now gathering to repel the Boers. This was a dangerous time for the regiments assembling at the front, fresh from Britain and tired from a long railway journey carried in open trucks. The troops were vulnerable and felt very exposed.

November 14 *Woken up at 3 am by Spry who gave me orders about signalling. Washed in small canvas bath. 8 am went up to HQ Signal station and saw Cayzer (Divisional Signalling Officer). Moved signalling station to a place just in front of railway station. Kept busy all day with messages coming and going. Light bad at times, misty & sun in. I am made Brigade Signalling Officer for the week. Troops all turned out on the alarm sounding to reinforce Outpost line. Camp struck and baggage taken to railway station. Troops returned towards evening and baggage was taken back again, but tents not pitched. A Naval detachment arrives. They put their guns on the hill behind the Railway Station. Armoured train goes out on reconnaissance and returns all right. Small parties of Boers seen on the Colenso road. I have men of Durban Light Infantry & MI orderlies of KRR to help me at Signal Station. Good night. Made a fire and slept beside it. Eucalyptus trees everywhere and sparrows with tails a foot long.*

NOVEMBER, TRYING TO CONTACT THE LADYSMITH GARRISON BY HELIOGRAPH

The greatest problem for the British was the lack of cavalry, most of whom were now stuck in Ladysmith. Without them it was almost impossible to reconnoitre the ground to the north of Estcourt and attempt to discover what the Boers were doing. This problem was further compounded by a lack of adequate maps – the so-called 'blue-print' maps being little more than property maps with the absolute minimum of topographical detail, and such of that as there was was inaccurate. As *The Times* history put it, 'A dense, paralysing mist of uncertainty enveloped all things beyond a narrow radius from the village'. One answer to this difficulty was to use an armoured train to patrol the line northwards from Estcourt which, from about 3 November, the British had done without incident. Then on 15 November, the armoured train sallied forth once more, with amongst her troops the war correspondent of the *Morning Post*, Winston Churchill.

Estcourt Camp, November 16th 1899
My dear Mother,

The news today is that the Boers attacked Sir George White in Ladysmith yesterday and his cavalry settled the first attempt killing about 500 and that the second time he got so much the best of it that he came out after them and is now on his way here [sadly, this was not the case]. We are naturally in great glee. Of course this will all be stale news by the time it reaches you but still it will show you what part we take and how matters really stand.

When we arrived the forces in camp were 3 Regiments of Infantry: The Dublin Fusiliers, The Border Regiment and ourselves, with 2 or 3 Companies of Durham Light Infantry, about the same number of Mounted Infantry, a Naval detachment of about 30 men manning 2 long guns carrying 7 miles or so, and some Imperial Light Horse. The Volunteers are most useful, especially to me as I use them to carry messages and some of them signal fairly well, and they are very keen.

Yesterday our armoured train went out as usual up the line to Colenso but alas it was her last

journey [Actually, not true, as MR shows below]. There were companies of the Dublins and Borderers and a newspaper correspondent went with them too [Churchill]. The Boers laid dynamite and blew up the train and then turned their guns on the poor wounded devils struggling back into the train. One part of the train came back here and the casualties were 1 killed and 2 seriously wounded and several slightly wounded. A Hospital train went out to try and get the wounded but the Boers refused to let us have them without word from General Joubert, but we may get them yet. Amongst others left [behind] was the Newspaper correspondent who they say fought very bravely.

We have got a very nice position here, the Queen's [Regiment] arrived today and we expect the rest of the Division in the next four days, and we feel pretty confident of success if attacked. My job at present is to take it in turns with another chap being Brigade Signalling Officer, a job which entails a good deal of hard work, staying out all day and all night in all sorts of weather. I have got a lift in the world you see and the Divisional Signalling Officer has asked me if I should like to be his assistant. I am of course very keen on the subject, like to see things properly done etc., and that goes a long way.

Friday 17. The post goes tomorrow so I must finish this off today. Troops have been arriving all day and at one time about six trains were waiting outside the station to come in. I was trying to get in touch with Ladysmith this morning from a high hill but the sun only lasted a couple of hours and now it is raining hard. There are some lovely butterflies, a great variety of flowers and flowering shrubs too. I hope you will be able to decipher this, it is rather scribbled,

your affectionate son,

AT WILLOW GRANGE. AN ARMOURED TRAIN ABOUT TO DEPART

as the ships at Durban offloaded the troops and the long strings of cattle-trucks wound their way north to Estcourt and Mooi River. Hildyard's and Barton's brigades were at last assembled and it was time for the British to seize the initiative and advance against the enemy. Later on the 17th the West Yorkshires marched out of Estcourt and, in the cool of the evening, advanced along the railway line to Willow Grange some seven miles away. Malcolm's Diary tells us:

18 November *Took up a position on a hill about 4 am till 2 pm. Went round outposts with Colonel Kitchener, helped to make loopholes for men with rocks, posted my signallers and got them going. Long messages passing to and fro between Colonel Kitchener and Major Spry. Enemy expected from E and SW; kopjes [small hills] to south of position very rocky, covered with iron stones. Scare in afternoon because [Captain] Berney fired on cattle, all left railway station except about 30 men, Pitched camp on south side railway station but did not sleep nearly as well as first night. Only 5 Companies here [Willow Grange] and all out on Outposts. Sighted some Boers at 4.50 pm, fired on them and dispersed them without their returning fire.*

19 November (Sunday) *Did not do very much all day. Were to move Regiment in* afternoon by GOC's orders; 1,000 Boers reported just over the hill 7 miles from Willow Grange. We wanted to attack them with the Mounted Infantry and Cavalry here if Estcourt sent up another Infantry Battalion and a gun. [Boers were in fact effecting a pincer movement around Willow Grange and the force there was in danger of being trapped]. *In evening General Hildyard sent 1 Infantry Battalion and 2 guns to cover our retirement. We are all absolutely sick about it. Kitchener had them sent back and we bivouacked for the night not knowing what was to be done in the morning. Valises & tents all packed away*

Although there were constant reports of Boers in the vicinity, and quite a number of false alarms, it seemed they had not gathered in strength. Every day brought battalion after battalion

due to earlier scare & prepared in case of need to move quickly. Living on 'bouilli' beef, bread and biscuits mostly, Tommy grouses but we find it very good, especially stewed and minced. Some officers have sore feet, all growing huge beards. 2 Naval guns and East Surreys arrive in afternoon to cover our retreat but returned before morning to Estcourt. General Clery in command there with General Barton at Mooi Bridge. Murray's Light Horse disbanded.

This situation highlights a problem that would bedevil the entire campaign to relieve Ladysmith, namely the lack of hard information concerning the enemy's strength, movements and intentions. Whatever the feelings of the West Yorkshires, Hildyard was quite correct to be concerned about splitting his forces into small units which the Boers might easily pick off. Nevertheless he decided that Kitchener was safe enough for the moment. It was only when the divisional commander, Lieutenant-General Clery, arrived that the West Yorkshires and the various mounted infantry units were recalled on the 20th.

20 November *Up at 2.30 am. Battalion left Willow Grange at 3.30 … 7 miles march, blazing hot day. One of the Naval guns here sent a shell into the enemy advance and the Dublin Fusiliers fired a good many long range volleys. Got into Estcourt about 10 pm,.*

21 November *Nothing particular occurred. On duty, HQ just outside our Mess…* Flashlight apparatus for signalling Ladysmith brought up and worked from truck in railway station. [One of the many important contributions made to the campaign by Captain Percy Scott, RN, and his men of HMS *Powerful*.]

OCCUPYING WILLOW GRANGE

The Boers, however, were now between the British forces at Estcourt and the Mooi River, and even if no one was sure of their numbers, some attempt was going to have to be made to shift them. It fell to Hildyard's brigade to undertake the task. The East Surrey, Queens, and the West Yorkshire regiments, supported by a 12–pounder naval gun and 7th Battery RFA (Royal Field Artillery) were given orders to march out and attack the enemy. Malcolm gives a description of his first battle and the events leading up to it in a letter to his father,

Frere Camp, Natal. Thursday December 7th 1899
My dear Father,

It seems ages since I wrote to you. I wrote from Estcourt by the last mail promising a long account of my first fight by this mail so now I can begin. In case the mails have been going wrong I must tell you that from Monday 20th up till Saturday 26th Nov. Estcourt was completely cut off from communications with Maritzburg or Durban or anywhere else. The telegraph lines were cut, the railway line smashed up and even the armoured engine or 'khaki engine' as Tommy calls it did not venture up or down.

I don't know how far I got in my last letter but I will start again from the time we were at Willow Grange station and give you the events leading up to the fight of Bryn Bella or Beacon Hill. Friday evening the 17th Nov we started on a long night march across country to the next station down the line about 6 or 7 miles off. By we, I mean 5 companies of our Regiment and a good proportion of mounted infantry under a Colonel Martyr, a bloodthirsty soldier with two rows of medal ribbons. We slept under the verandas of the railway station at Willow Grange that night and next morning went out on picquet. It is a very pretty little station on the low slopes of a hill and for the few days we were there we had really a very good time. There was a Boer commando reported in the neighbourhood so we had plenty of work to do and frequent alarms which always ended in nothing. Our job was to keep the line clear which we did till Monday morning when we were ordered back to

Estcourt without having fired a shot at them. We were very disappointed as you may imagine. While we were there [Willow Grange] trains preceded by the armoured engine and full of horses and all kinds of baggage kept passing up and down. We officers had our meals etc in the Ladies waiting room which had a lavatory attached so that we were fairly comfortable. We feasted on ration biscuits and bully beef for the most part, nothing much else being forthcoming. We have got a kaffir assistant cook and he has turned out a real treasure, making us mealy cakes, rissoles and quite a variety of things…

As soon as we got back to Estcourt along came the Boers to Willow Grange and began pulling up the railway line very naturally. There we left them until Wednesday evening the 22nd when all the troops available at Estcourt started after them on a night attack. We started about 5 pm and went about 3 miles in the Willow Grange direction and in the sketch on a separate bit of paper you will see a thick blue curved line going round a long hill marked C. In case you cannot get Claud to explain the sketch-map the red wavy lines represent levels of about 80 feet and so that you may distinguish the tops of hills I have put the top levels or contours as they are called in ink as well as red. The blue line I mentioned represents our General line of advance into the sketch, you will then see two longer blue lines in front of the arrow head, these represent the position we took up that night on the side of this long rocky hill. You will see better what I mean by the first diagram on the back of the sketch.

Well, till 12 o'clock we sat on the side of this dreadful hill and shivered. We had no greatcoats and we were out in one of South Africa's very worst thunderstorms and that means a good deal. All the kopjes around here are covered in loose ironstone rocks and what between these and some barbed wire which gave you a shock if you touched it the lightning was playing about us the whole time and at times you could actually smell it after a discharge. As for the hail stones, pigeon-eggs were not in it they were more like owl's eggs and didn't they just hurt. We didn't sleep much that night I can tell you. At 12 o'clock we started and the storm had just about spent itself and the moon came out dimly for a bit, then we went up the valley between D and E leaving a dark track behind us in the long grass, along the line -.-.-. and across the wall twice, still in column of route, then we turned to the right and went up the Hill X in line of 6 Companies; 4 of our companies in the centre, 1 of Queens on the right and 1 of the East Surreys on the left and charged up the hill with fixed bayonets. The Boer camp was on top but their picquets were fast asleep and no one fired on us till we were within a few feet of the top when of course it was too late and with a cheer we took the hill. We had bad luck in not capturing their 12-pdr which afterwards pounded away at us from Hill B as it had only left 40 minutes before we arrived. The camp we suppose to have been Joubert's as he was in charge of the Boer column and we captured all sorts of luxuries like jam, pickles, soap etc. which the average Boer does not get from all accounts. When the Boers left Hill X

they took up position on Hill A and B and at daylight they set the ball a-rolling. Hill X was only large enough to hold 3 companies and 3 of ours went into position and blazed away at the enemy. I forgot to tell you that Colonel Kitchener was in command throughout and it was entirely owing to him that the night attack was so less successful but from this on we had decidedly the worst of it. Our big naval 12-pdr on Hill C could not reach them at all although theirs could easily reach us and as for our battery it was worse than useless in the position it took up. Eventually we had to leave Hill X and it was when we rose up to retire that we suffered most. Our supports did not arrive in time for us to hold on as General Hildyard had forgotten all about them and we were in a bad way. I forget the exact numbers of killed and wounded but it was something like 10 killed and 67 wounded, 1 officer wounded (who has since rejoined us) and 1, poor Major Hobbs, taken prisoner.

your affectionate son

Malcolm's rather dry account is in stark contrast to that of Lieutenant George Crossman who adopted a heroic style of writing that owed much to the *Boys Own* magazine of that time. Crossman might, perhaps, have read too much G A Henty, a historical novelist whose ideas of right and wrong, and of muscular Christianity alongside heroic deeds, did much to influence generations of schoolboys. Crossman had this to say about the battle:

"Moved on silently over open ground. Passed two stone walls. Fairly shivering with cold and funk. Still raining streams and thunder roaring. Came to forming up place. Rain and thunder almost stopped now and moon coming out. 'Lines to follow at 20 yards. When in enemy's position no firing, bayonet only and kill everyone till daylight.' Such our last orders. Said a short prayer for myself and family and then we started. My Company was in the first line in place. I'm H Company. Hill was tremendously steep and we could only crawl along. When within 50 yards of top 'Halt !' Dead Silence. 'Halt ! Who goes dat ?' Enemy's challenge ! Trying to bluff us in broken English. Dead silence. We lay down a moment or so. Bang ! bang bang !! Ugh, it was awful. 'Advance !' sang out the senior man. Up we got and towards the summit. 'Prepare to charge' 'CHAAAAAARGE !'. Bullets whistling all around us, up, up. Should we never get to the top ? 'Hurrah ! Hurrah ! yaaak, ahaaaha!' Heaven help me we were right into them. Ugh ! Lord preserve me from anything again like it. They went at once. Could not stand the bayonet. Never can. We only managed to down about 5 of 'em there and

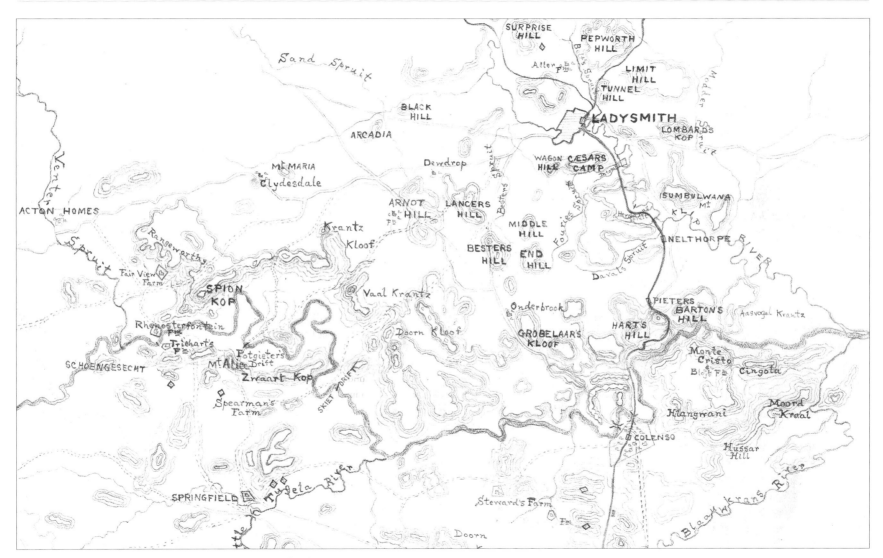

MALCOLM RIALL'S MAP OF THE LANDSCAPE SOUTH OF LADYSMITH SHOWING COLENSO AND SPION KOP

then along the top of the hill till their second line opened fire on us. Down we went and on our faces and lay low. Thank God it was pitch dark. Thousands of bullets sang along over us. Then on again [we went] with another yell and out went the second line of them and down the other side of the hill and the position was ours. Up came [our] second line and we had got the first hill. The first line we met was only the Picquet. The second the Support. Little did we think what was to come. Now we waited and prayed for daylight and counted our loss which was quite small. Only two killed and two or three wounded. Thank heaven it was in the night. Suddenly up came the sun. It rises almost suddenly in these parts and it was broad daylight at once. Then we caught sight of 'em offing it in the distance. Opened long range volleys on 'em. And formed a firing line to fire on them. My Company was placed in reserve now and lay down among the rocks. Some of the dead and wounded were a terrible sight. Enemy now opened fire on us with 12 pounder and Hotchkiss gun. Shells and bullets fairly whistled around. Enemy were about 1,000 to 2,000 strong. This lasted till about 9 am or about 4 hours and then we got orders to retire as we had driven them out of their first position and ascertained their numbers which was really all we wanted. Only we had intended taking their main position but saw it was impossible. Got back to camp about 10.30 or 11 am after as awful an experience as I wish to go through. General was awfully pleased with the Regt. We did all the fighting and had all the losses except about three. We, the 14th, lost 10 killed and 57 wounded [compare MR's figure] and

our second-in-command captured. One subaltern was hit very slightly and will be well in a day or two. Had some narrow escapes personally. One shell went over my head as we were retiring and pitched about 10 yards in front of me luckily without bursting. Awfully glad to get back to Estcourt safe and sound."

So the British infantry marched back to Estcourt, leaving the Boers in possession of the field, more-or-less, while the British mounted infantry and irregular cavalry kept an eye on them. It transpired much later that soon after the battle and just before the Boers held a council of war, Joubert's horse threw him. The Boer commander was seriously injured, indeed he never fully recovered. When Botha and the other Boer leaders gathered, they decided they should send Joubert home and that they should withdraw to the line of the Tugela River – ripping up the railway line and blowing-up railway bridges as they retired.

Even as the Boers retreated the British were once more on the move. This time they advanced in full brigade strength and by late on the 26th had occupied Frere, 10 miles or so north of Estcourt, where, inevitably, they came to a halt because the bridge was down. The weather was now incredibly hot, with the very occasional huge downpour, and there was an insatiable requirement for drinking water. All the original contemporary accounts of this phase of the campaign speak of the difficulties of water supply and the lack of adequate facilities to supply the men in the field with water.

On 30 November the British advance brought them up to the site where the armoured train had been wrecked. Drummer Goodwin has this to say,

THE BROKEN RAILWAY BRIDGE AT FRERE – 1 DECEMBER 1899

November 28 "We saw the bridge that the Boers had blown up and the armoured train which the Boers destroyed when the Dublin Fusiliers were in and two of the trucks being off the line and two left on and we could easily see where the Boer shell had gone through and close to the wreck was the grave of the lads that was killed and the troops decorated it up by stoning it round (placing a kerb stone) and the names of the killed being put in the soil by Boer cartridges it looked splendid."

It is as likely, in fact, that the cartridge cases were British.

As Goodwin said, the grave of those killed in the armoured train ambush was soon decorated with kerb stones and the names of the men picked out with cartridge cases. Within weeks a proper headstone was installed.

The West Yorkshires found themselves just outside Frere 'camped' alongside Howell's Farm – the farmhouse being placed at the disposal of the officers for their officer's mess; at this stage of the campaign the officers maintained the usual gulf between themselves and the men. Whilst individual officers are referred to, normally by surname alone, the names of the men in the ranks hardly ever occur. This should not, however, be taken to mean that the officers did not care for the men under their command, to the contrary, there seems to have been considerable respect and, even some affection, between the officers and the men.

Once the battalion had its position, the men were ordered to dig-in their outposts. The West Yorkshires always dug-in, and if the soil prevented the digging of trenches then they built sangars – stone breastworks. It was a feature of the regiment's life on active service and one which would, in due course, serve to save many of their lives. The point should perhaps be made that not all regiments followed the same practice. In the days that followed, Malcolm was employed on outpost duties alongside his signalling work. He noted on the 28th that he saw the Boers blow up the bridge at Colenso but this must be incorrect, Colenso was too far away to the north, and perhaps he witnessed a bridge near Chieveley being blown. The 30th saw the arrival of the 2nd Battalion The Devonshire Regiment, thereby completing the assembly of the Hildyard's 2nd (English) Brigade. The day before, two 4.7 inch guns from HMS *Powerful* arrived with their crew of bluejackets. They would have a significant role to play in the next fortnight or so.

WRECKED TRUCKS FROM THE ARMOURED TRAIN LYING BESIDE THE RAILWAY LINE

BATTLE FIELD
OF Colenso
15 Decbr 1899.

Five

COLENSO

As you will see that far from being 'away from all the fighting' as you rather unkindly put it, I am always well up in it, for whenever there is fighting the Brigadier must be there to conduct operations, and where he goes I go too. I have no ardent desire to be at the head of the Advance Guard every day in order to be sniped at I can tell you still, when the time comes I am no coward, but at the same time I see no use in running unnecessary risks. If I wanted to be shot I should like to have been shot in some big engagement at the beginning of the war and not.

Opposite: A view of the Colenso battlefield from a Boer gun position

By the early part of December 1899 some 20,000 men had been assembled in the general area around Frere. For the men of the West Yorkshire regiment it was a time spent digging more trenches, carrying out patrols and reconnaissances, forming up in brigade strength and practising attacks against the outpost lines – by day and night – in a series of exercises strongly reminiscent of the Aldershot field days they had participated in a few months earlier. It was a wearying, almost boring, routine carried out during intensely hot days. Little wonder then that the West Yorkshire diarists scribbled, 'Nothing much to note', in their diaries and letters day after day in the first two weeks of December. The numbing heat was accompanied by flies and dust, both got everywhere, so that the khaki army was truly that, the more so as the lack of adequate water supplies prevented anything other than a cursory washing. The arrival of General Buller on 6 December did wonders for the morale of this dusty army, but what they really needed was to come to grips with the Boers and beat them. Meanwhile to the north, the besieged British troops in Ladysmith hung on, kept the Boers out, and became progressively thinner as food supplies dwindled.

of the 7th. This interlude of inaction came to an end on the 11th when, battalion by battalion, brigade after brigade, with guns and cavalry and mounted infantry, Buller's army marched north from Frere, enveloped Chieveley and spread out either side of the Ladysmith road preparatory to bringing battle to the Boers who, by now, were well entrenched on the north side of the Tugela River – not that the British were aware of the fact.

The plan of battle was to engage the Boers with one brigade and artillery directly across the river and, at the same time, send a flanking force of three brigades to cross the Tugela at Potgieter's Drift, a ford some 15 miles upstream of Colenso. This would bring the bulk of Buller's force down on the Boer flank north of the river. Even as Buller's forces were deploying on the Chieveley plain, shattering news came of British reverses elsewhere. In the Cape Colony on 10 December, Lieutenant-General Gatacre had mounted a night attack on the Boers holding the railway junction at Stormberg. His attack miscarried and he lost both the battle and some 600 men. At dawn on the 11th, Lord Methuen's advance at Magersfontein ran into a well-prepared Boer position and this

THE WEST YORKSHIRES ADVANCE TO CHIEVELEY ON THEIR WAY TO THE BATTLEFIELD AT COLENSO

December 3, Sunday *There was a church parade for all not on duty. I was on Inlying Picquet so did not go. About the hottest day experienced yet. Reinforced picquet in evening, saw enemy camp well lit up in distance.*

Then the weather changed again and it rained in torrents, turning the camps into huge quagmires. Fortunately the sun shone fitfully, and while the ground stayed exceedingly damp underfoot, at least the tents and bedding and clothes dried out quickly enough. The brief spell of rain filled the rivers allowing the men a chance of a bath. Drummer Goodwin notes with almost a sense of joy that the West Yorkshires bathed in the river during the night

attack too was beaten off, leaving Methuen wounded and over 200 dead Highlanders littering the field. After such reverses it was imperative that Buller achieved success on the Tugela.

The plans to attack through Potgieter's Drift were abandoned and new orders drafted for what has come to be known as the battle of Colenso. The details of the battle have been described many times and, in view of the limited role played by the West Yorkshires, it is unnecessary to say much here. The plan of action was straightforward enough: Hart's 5th Brigade was to cross the Tugela at Bridge Drift, off to the west of Colenso, while Hildyard's 2nd Brigade was to advance through Colenso and, using the existing road bridge, assault the Boer positions supported by artillery. Lyttleton's 4th Brigade was to support either Hart or Hildyard, leaving Barton's 6th Brigade in reserve. The cavalry and mounted infantry were to take Hlangwane Hill, off to the

Boers arriving at Ladysmith. This was one of many photographs taken by an anonymous professional photographer, who worked amongst the Boers though not necessarily supporting them, who identified himself with an 'S' – for Sniper – on his photographs

east of Colenso, with the object of providing a firing position covering the kopjes across the river. The plan may have been simple enough, but in practice it all went horribly wrong.

Major-General Hart and his guides were soon at cross-purposes, Hart insisted that his route lay in one direction while his guides proposed another, with the result that the 5th Brigade advanced into a loop of the Tugela where, enfiladed on three sides by Boer riflemen dug into the river banks, Hart's men, advancing in close order, were devastated by the Boer fire. Towards Colenso, Hildyard's 2nd Brigade moved off just after 4 am. The brigade was deployed along a 400 yard front in three lines. In the first line: 2nd Queens on the right and 2nd Devons on the left, then in the second line, 800 yards behind: half of the West Yorkshires and brigade headquarters on the right with 2nd East Surreys on the left. The other half of the West Yorkshires brought up the rear, 800 yards further back. The 2nd Brigade was supported by two batteries of field guns, 66th and 14th RFA, under Colonel Charles Long, and 6 naval guns, under the command of Lieutenant Ogilvy, RN. Hildyard's men advanced in open order, using such cover as there was, and were soon in amongst the buildings of Colenso. The field artillery, however, outran the infantry cover, and advancing far too far forwards was soon pinned down by Boer rifle fire, forcing the gunners to abandon their guns and seek cover.

Malcolm's letter describing the battle was lost and his diary offers little, but Drummer Goodwin's account provides a vivid description of the action:

"…the Division advanced in fine style, some of the boys singing and some passing jokes, but when we came in sight of Colenso it looked a terrible position, the hills are terrible high and we had nothing but a long plain to go over and they [the Boers] were well in their trenches. Our naval guns started shelling the enemy and our artillery and infantry moved forward under the fire from the Navals. [Goodwin is incorrect here, the naval guns came into action much later.] The battle got nicely hot the enemy firing their big guns into our infantry who were still advancing and

getting a terrible fire from the enemy but were sticking it well. The sun came out and it was terrible hot and no water."

In fact Colonel Long's advance had been so swift that he even outpaced the naval guns which might have offered sufficient covering fire to protect him. Without the artillery to provide covering fire, or the support from the left flank by Hart's brigade, Hildyard's leading battalions could do nothing about the Boers to their front. At 7 am the attack was called off and Hart's and Hildyard's men began the perilous task of disengaging.

By late afternoon the various units had regrouped and returned to their tented camps around Chieveley, there to tend to their wounded and consider the events of the day. The British casualties amounted to 7 officers and 138 men killed, 43 officers and 719 men wounded, and 21 officers and 199 men missing or captured. Of these, some 500 casualties had been inflicted on Hart's brigade, contrasting with the 40 or so casualties suffered by Hildyard's men. To the late 20th century reader, conditioned by the casualty lists run up in the two World Wars, these numbers seem almost derisory, but it should be remembered that in the second half of the 19th century, in the decades after the Crimean War and Indian Mutiny, there had only been two occasions when casualties in the British Army had exceeded more than 100 men killed. To these numbers had to be added the 2,000 and more men who had surrendered to the Boers elsewhere and were now prisoners-of-war in Pretoria — with Winston Churchill in their midst, though not for long. Churchill's daring escape from prison made the headlines in newspapers across two continents, and provided a solitary gleam of heroism in an otherwise gloomy festive season that saw the British continue their attempts to relieve Ladysmith by year's end..

Amongst West Yorkshires, only one man was wounded — 2nd Lieutenant Ross who was hit by a shell fragment. Ross had just rejoined the battalion having recovered from the wounds he received during the battle for Bryn Bella Hill. Ross seems to have led a charmed life as he was wounded several times more during this campaign, survived the North-West frontier in India

NAVAL 4.7 INCH GUNS BOMBARD THE ROAD BRIDGE AT COLENSO FROM A RANGE OF 13,000 YARDS

and fought through the Great War as well. Malcolm had little to say about Colenso in his diary:

"…Got a few shots and several shells in our direction but did no harm. Ross and 1 man wounded. Devons' lost heavily, Colonel Bullock, Osborne and Bonhom captured and a lot of rank and file [men of the 2nd Devons who managed to get into Colenso village] … The troops behaved well and our guns did a lot of damage. Boer losses not known. Said to be about 2,000."

Malcolm's entry concerning Boer losses probably reflects the general opinion amongst the British that they had inflicted many casualties on the Boers — more as a result of shell fire, and in particular through the use of lyddite, than from rifle fire. For Drummer Goodwin and his comrades of the 2nd West Yorks the day ended with a very welcome issue of rum and a good night's sleep.

They had said at the beginning of the campaign that it would be all over by Christmas. After the various setbacks suffered by the British forces in the middle of December, 'Black Week' as it was dubbed by British politicians and the Press, it was all too clear that the campaign would last a great deal longer than anyone had realised. For Buller's corps the rest of December was spent in the camps alongside the railway line at Chieveley with only the occasional foray by cavalry

MEN QUEUEING FOR WATER IN CAMP AT CHIEVELEY — THE LACK OF LARGE SUPPLIES OF GOOD DRINKING WATER LOCALLY CONTRIBUTED TO BULLER'S DIFFICULTIES

patrols and sporadic bursts of fire from the naval guns who, on 18 December, shelled and destroyed the road bridge at Colenso to prevent the Boers using it to launch an attack. The infantry settled down to man their outpost line. Off-duty they queued for hours to draw their water ration, and played football. On Christmas Day the men were given a huge dinner and took part in the divisional sports day over which General Buller presided. Malcolm spent this, his first Christmas Day in the Army on duty, out with the sentries in the outposts: 'Quiet day in the Platelayers Hut, much annoyed by flies. Divisional Sports but of course did not see it'.

Other officers, however, settled down to cricket and played a series of matches against teams from the other infantry battalions in Hildyard's brigade as well as against the Royal

Navy. They also prepared for a Christmas point-to-point race meeting to be held on Boxing Day. Meantime, in Ladysmith, the British continued to resist the Boers and to get steadily thinner. This interlude of relative peace was brought to an abrupt end some three weeks later when the Boers made a determined attempt to break into the town.

6 January   *Severe fighting at Ladysmith. Heliograph message reported that Boers made a night attack in considerable force but were repulsed on all sides. Alarm sounded at 1.30 pm. All troops went out on a reconnaissance to Colenso. We gave them* [the Boers] *a small show here. It was called a demonstration by Buller. We wanted to know what it was but could not find words to express the funny show. Batteries shelled Boer position and naval guns in rear backed them up… Went out at dark and did a route march in the rain. Not a bad night on the whole.*

This 'demonstration' comprised Buller's response to the urgent request for assistance from Ladysmith's commander Lieutenant-General White. Buller though could do little else as the Tugela River was now in spate, as a result of the heavy rains of the preceding days. As usual, the naval guns were brought into action and shells sent screaming across the river to do who knew what damage amongst the Boer lines. If anything, the sound of the guns firing was a tremendous morale booster for the British troops who had endured inactivity harassed by the heat and flies, and were now suffering floods that were almost on a biblical scale. At least there was now adequate drinking water and water to wash bodies and clothes in.

Buller had to attempt another crossing of the Tugela River and get to grips with the Boers, but the problem remained — where were the Boers weakest? No one truly knew, and Buller returned to his original proposition: to force the Boer right flank and enter Ladysmith along the roads from the west. To achieve this he had the services of the newly arrived 5th Division, under the command of Lieutenant-General Sir Charles Warren. So began the road to Spion Kop and another great British military episode.

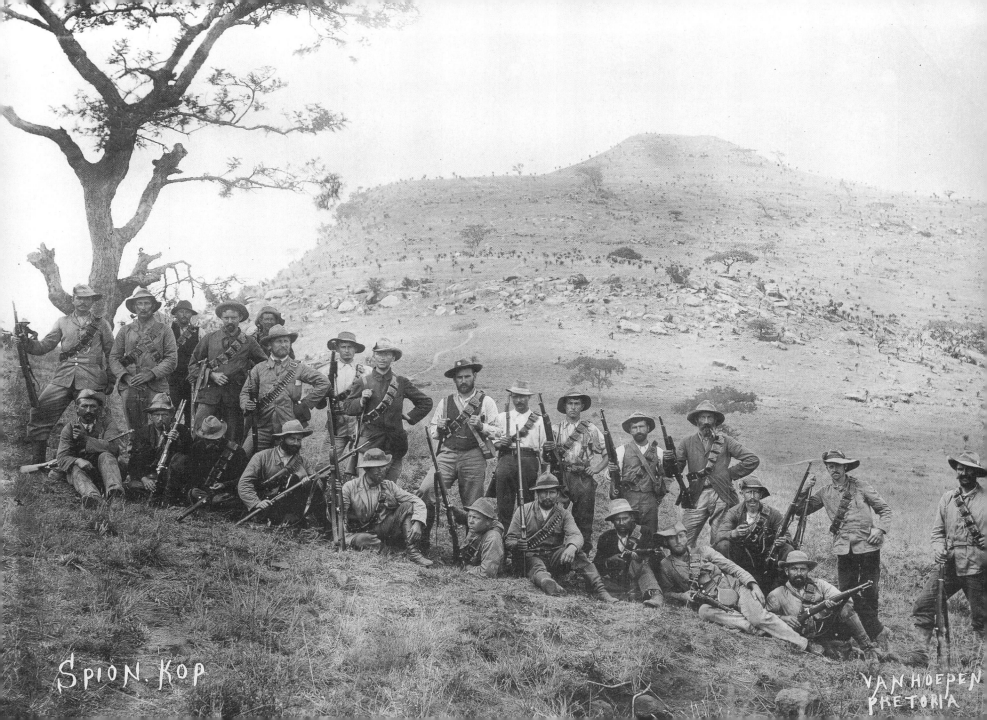

SPION KOP

VAN HOEPEN
PRETORIA

Six

SPION KOP

Opposite: Boers at Spion Kop

On the 10 January, in the torrential rains, Buller's army sallied forth to do battle once more: all five infantry brigades, a single brigade of cavalry, eight batteries of field artillery, ten naval guns and 650 transport wagons, together with, most fortunately, several steam traction engines.

10 January   *Brigade started about 5 am for Pretorius' Farm, Frere. Some regiments got in early in the afternoon but we did not reach camp until 5 pm owing to Naval guns and ox-wagons sticking every few yards in dongas* [dry water courses] *and soft ground and the West Yorks had to drag them out. After taking about five hours to march four miles Battalion ordered to detour via Zietmann's Farm with Naval guns to make use of better roads. Very hot. Saw a good many storks or cranes en route. Transport arrived before us and we pitched tents as soon as we got in.*

11 January   *Stood to arms as usual at 4 am. Started out at 5 am (on breakfast of cocoa and a slice of bread and butter) on a big demonstration from Pretorius' Farm towards Tugela River and Boer positions. We are moving about in skirmishing order. Again very hot. Only our Brigade went out but accompanied by RA and Naval guns. Thorneycroft's MI* [mounted infantry] *and other MI well away on our left. Had a pretty stiff time signalling. Got back about 2 pm rather done. Mail came in about 7.30 with letters from home.* [Battalion War Diary: '4th Brigade pushed on to hold drift; Warren's Division camped at Springfield, Hart's Brigade about 2 miles west of us'.]

12 January   *Cold morning, hot afterwards. Parade at 3 am. Stood to arms as usual at 3.50 am. We formed a transmitting signal station on a high kopje near Doornkop between Chieveley and 2nd Brigade HQ at Pretorius' Farm. 2 or 3 messages come from Ladysmith, one about Stevens the war correspondent laid up with enteric. Some of Sir Charles Warren's Division encamped the other side of this hill. Hart's Brigade and other troops in camp 3 miles west of us.*

At first it all went well, the cavalry seized Potgieter's Drift and Trichardt's Drift, the two fords across the Tugela which gave access to the Boer positions amongst the kopjes overlooking the river. Dominating the whole area from the centre was Spion Kop. As at Colenso, the overall plan was to seize the two drifts, some seven miles apart, which would

ONE OF OUR SIGNAL STATIONS TO CONNECT BULLER WITH CHIEVELEY. 12 JANUARY 1900

THE ROYAL ENGINEERS STEAM TRACTION ENGINES, 15 JANUARY 1900

serve as bridgeheads through which the British forces would pass on their way to attack the Boers dug in on the north banks and hills overlooking the Tugela. Sir Charles Warren was allotted the task of attacking the Boer flank and taking the hills around, and including, Spion Kop, whilst Buller watched from afar. It should have all been relatively straightforward, although the plan of attack did call for speed and decisiveness.

Almost the first difficulty that Warren, and indeed Buller, encountered was the state of the roads. After the weeks of hot, dry weather and lack of water it now rained in torrents, and the entire British force found itself bogged down in, seemingly, one huge morass. The few steam traction engines that there were worked wonders, pulling ox-wagons out of the muddy dongas where spans of up to eighty oxen had failed, but there were not enough of these machines and, besides, as the roads became ever muddier, so the traction engines themselves became stuck. The march from Frere should have taken, at most, four days, in the eventuality it took over a week. Buller was appalled and the Boers were delighted as they stripped men from their eastern positions around Colenso, and reinforced their right flank.

The West Yorkshires had advanced as far as Pretorius's Farm where they set up camp. Their bell tents held 3 officers each whilst the men were packed in 17 to a tent, field kitchens and all. Here the battalion remained for the next four days. With little else to do except mount picquet duties and watch the Boers trekking west, the West Yorkshires held a church parade.

THE WEST YORKSHIRES CROSSING A TRESTLE BRIDGE BUILT BY THE ROYAL ENGINEERS ACROSS THE LITTLE TUGELA ON THEIR WAY TO SPION KOP

14 January, Sunday   *Got back from Picquet too late for Church Parade, but just in time for breakfast. Foraging party went out to farms round about and brought geese, hens, and ducks. Kaffirs keep large flocks of sheep and goats here. These are all colours; white, black, brown and grey are commonest. There are dogs galore; a fox terrier and a collie in the Mess.*

15 January   *Started 6 am for Springfield. Battalion advance guard for Brigade and made a good quick march of it getting in at 11.30, distance 6 or 7 miles. Company wagons arrived about 3 pm* [Battalion War Diary: 'wagons had to detour via Springfield Bridge over Little Tugela River'] *and we pitched tents in a shower of rain. Brigade crossed over a small bridge Spry made over a spruit* [small water course]. *The Little Tugela runs quite close under the camp. Warren and Naval guns about 6 miles ahead of us. Hart's Brigade followed us in the afternoon.*

The Royal Engineers building a pontoon bridge at Trichardt's Drift

And here of course we find the heart of the matter: the British were overloaded with baggage and, the main cause of their delay, the weather, had made it necessary to create bridges across the Little Tugela and Tugela Rivers.

16 January *Company on Inlying Picquet. 4.40 pm camp fell in but tents left standing, valise left behind. Allowed great-coat & 20 lbs kit.* [Battalion War Diary: 'Joined Warren's Force under Mount Alice, marched under cover of darkness about 9 miles in direction of Trichardt's Drift, arrived on heights above drift about 1 pm, and bivouacked at dawn'.] *Marched about 8 or 10 miles and had a long halt, 3 or 4 miles more, passing pontoon section of the Royal Engineers, and then halted in Column for the night. Dark, still night and fairly warm. Coats and kit arrived on wagons and I slept fairly well.*

The next day the battalion formed the advance guard and, with the Royal Engineers and their pontoons, advanced to Trichardt's Drift.

17 January *Up at about 4 am and moved down a big donga to a farm in a bend of the Tugela.* [Battalion War Diary: 'D & H Companies reconnoitre drift at dawn and report all clear. Force marched to drift and RE started to make a pontoon bridge. Boers open fire, killing 1 man of the Devons. Long range volleys from H Company drive off Boers. Guns shell a farm on the other side of the river and neighbouring heights but no Boers there'.] *Some Companies of ours went out in front of the farm and dug trenches in a ploughed mealy patch. Fired on by Boers when the trenches were almost completed. Sappers made 2 very successful pontoon bridges. Boyall led West Yorks across first; half our Battalion went across under Major Fry to farm opposite, half stayed at first farm. Slept on veranda on bench at farm.*

During the night the battalions that composed the Lancashire Brigade passed through the bridgehead and deployed on the plain north of the Tugela River with almost no opposition from the Boers. Following the infantry came the artillery, ammunition wagons and supply wagons, that rolled for the better part of two and half days.

18 January *Woken at 3 am to take fatigue parties to pontoon bridge to assist on drag*

ropes of carts etc. 5 battalions passed during the night. Generals Buller, Warren, Clery, Coke and Hildyard etc. all came down to see the bridge and I could have got excellent photos but spring went wrong. After tea Brigade moved over river and took up night position. All transport across by 10 pm.

Meanwhile, the advance elements of Lyttelton's brigade had waded across the Tugela and had seized the north bank at Potgieter's Drift. The two arms of Buller's assault were safely across the Tugela, the disaster of Colenso had not been repeated. It was now time for Warren to show some dash and get to grips with the Boers. Warren, though, had other ideas. He reckoned that as you had to have practise sessions for cricket and football matches, then you also should for war. And this is what he now did: practise.

19 January *Marched to Venter's Drift. Started about 2 am in the dark and advanced about 3 miles to our left front. Went up road after breakfast in the direction of Acton Homes. The cavalry out in front of us.* [This was Dundonald and his 1,800 or so cavalry who out-flanked the Boers on the west and had found the road open to Ladysmith before being recalled by Warren.] *Retired to opposite side of spruit (using a trestle bridge put up by RE) and lay down for the night. Were issued out with Moconochie rations for the first time. Excellent eating. Balloons and howitzers at Potgieter's drift.*

On the morning of the 20th Warren launched his first assaults. The two veteran brigades from Colenso, Hildyard's 2nd and Hart's 5th, scrambled up the slopes of Rangeworthy Hills, on the west of Spion Kop, their objective being to take the long plateau of Tabanyama which lay just to the north.

20 January *All troops except our Brigade went out early and took up positions on kopje to our right front. Sugar Loaf Hill and other kopjes taken by evening* [along the southern edge of Tabanyama, and known collectively as the Rangeworthy Hills]. *Artillery assisted us with good effect. Watched fight through our glasses. Awfully hot day. East Surreys took Sugar Loaf Hill. West Yorkshires advanced in afternoon and lay all night in a big donga, it rained slightly. Moved forward 4 am to the kopje (Sugar Loaf Hill) the Queens were on. Great deal of sniping all night, built sangars.*

21 January, Sunday *Fight began in real earnest at dawn. Sniping had been going on all night. Sergeant Valette and 4 signallers away on a Divisional Signal Station and one man hit in the thigh early in the action so consequently left rather short. Ran about with messages for the Colonel and with him all day. Got very hot and rather done. Colonel in command of Brigade* [Major-General Hildyard having been given command of the extreme left of the British forces] *but under General Hart's orders. Signallers worked well. Messages for the Generals continually passing. Boyall and a section advanced about 400 yards in front of position and nearly got wiped out. Captain Ryall wounded in three places and died next morning. Battalion retired at dusk as it was impossible to advance against the Boer fire.*

And there was the crux of the matter. It had taken Warren so long to move his force from Frere via Springfield to the banks of the Tugela that Botha and his Boer forces had had time to establish a defensive position along the Tabanyama plateau. The Boers were not that well dug-in, and had Walter Kitchener been permitted by Lieutenant-General Clery to continue pushing against the Boer position, it is conceivable that the Boer line would have collapsed. As it was, all that the British lodged on the edge of the Rangeworthy Hills could do was to hang on as best they could, build sangars from rocks for protection, while Warren called for more artillery support.

Having reached this impasse the various leading battalions were rotated out of the line to feed, wash and rest. Malcolm's diary records:

OFFICERS RELAXING IN CAMP

22 January *...lost my watch by Venter's Spruit. A quiet day. Battalion returned to camp, West Yorkshires only, about 8 am; signallers, maxim gun and all. Bathed, and cleaned up generally had a nice rest. Sun very hot. Strong wind blowing. Battle still going on Spion Kop but West Yorkshires not engaged today.*

23 January *Got up at 5 am, no stand to arms. An easy day in camp. Left camp about 2 pm and relieved Devons on Sugar Loaf Hill.*

That night Major-General Woodgate's column, consisting of three battalions of the Lancashire Brigade and some mounted infantry, was assembled at the foot of Spion Kop. They climbed its steep slopes, before, in the early hours of the 24th, seizing the summit of the hill yelling at the top of their voices, 'Majuba! Majuba!'. Holding the hill had been only 15 Boers. Soon after dawn Woodgate was appalled to see that he had made a massive tactical mistake – he had taken a false crest on Spion Kop. The Boers soon recognised the British error, and from their vantage point overlooking the British position, poured down an annihilating fire, both rifle and artillery. Somehow, all through that long and hellish day, the British troops held on despite the Boer attacks. At one point the Boers even managed to get into the British position and persuaded a number of the British troops to surrender but, in heroic fashion, the Boers were driven back.

Meantime, out on the right flank, Lyttleton's brigade made a flanking attack and took Twin Peaks. The Boer commandos that had held the line here abandoned the position entirely and were all for riding north to Ladysmith before Botha arrived and encouraged them to take

up the fight once again. The British, unaware of the extent of their success on Twin Peaks, but gloomily contemplating events on Spion Kop, elected to abandon the advance on this flank and withdrew. Out on the left flank, where Hart's and Hildyard's men had gained a finger-tip hold on the edge of the Tabanyama, things were going relatively well. Lieutenant George Crossman laconically noted:

"…Came out here at 1 pm yesterday [23 January], relieved Devons, and have been sitting in firing line ever since. Battle very quiet today, lost no one so far. Woodgate's Brigade captured Spion Kop this morning. From here I could watch the attack beautifully with glasses as it is only 2 miles off. This show seems to be going to be a great victory. V. glad !!! The battle has now entered its fifth day. One of the longest on record. Glad I am in it. Have not much time for details as am under fire as I write sitting in my little pile of stones [sangar]. I have personally fired over 100 rounds today. Wonder if I have hit anyone. Hope news of this is not worrying you at home. We have not eaten bread or fresh meat and vegetables for over 9 days now. Continual sound of firing and bullets and shells whistling round gets very tiring to nerves after 24 hours. Awful glad of letters…"

25 January *Same place. Battle here still going on and I am still in the firing line. Awfully sick of it. Boiling hot today. Believe a move of some sort is on tonight. Hope so. Lancashire*

THE BARE NECESSITIES OF LIFE AND THEN SOME. WATER AND SUPPLIES FOR THE WEST YORKSHIRES

Brigade took Spion Kop yesterday but hear they have evacuated it today as useless. Heavy loss of life and wounded. Have been on this hill fighting for over 2 days now and in same place.

In the absence of substantial artillery support and with only two maxim guns to a battalion, there was no chance that Hart's or Hildyard's troops were going to be able to launch a frontal attack across the plateau of Tabanyama without massive loss of life. There would be no suicidal assaults in the Boer War of the sort that would come to characterise the First World War. At the same time, the British on the Tabanyama were dependent on Woodgate holding Spion Kop, this being Buller's 'key in the lock' which would open the door to Ladysmith.

Back on Spion Kop the situation became more and more confusing as British officers were killed and wounded and the men of the various battalions became increasingly muddled together. To add to their troubles there was also confusion over who was in command. Woodgate was mortally wounded and the command was finally given to Colonel Thorneycroft, despite the presence of other officers senior to him, who consequently disbelieved his appointment in the absence of effective communications. At dusk and having consulted his officers, Thorneycroft decided to abandon the position. Spion Kop might be a disaster but it could not be allowed to become a repetition of Majuba. Attempts were made to stop the retreat, by amongst others Winston Churchill, but contact could not be made with Lieutenant-General Warren because there was no oil for the Begbie signal lamps.

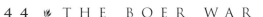

For Malcolm and the West Yorkshires, it was a question of roughing it in real earnest. None of them had been in action and under fire for this length of time before.

24 January *We built up the sangars the Devons had started through the night and firing continued all day but owing to good cover only one man wounded. Spion Kop taken by our people about 1 pm. Mail arrived during night but I got no letters. Machine-guns found very useful. Slept out on hill in the sangars, fight still going on, guns have being going hammer and tongs for the last few days, especially howitzers.*

25 January *Sniping as usual. Colonel Kitchener very uneasy and afraid our hill will be shelled. Made us build up sangars higher and thicker; no more casualties. Several men going sick owing to sleeping out in open and on nights so cold. Casualties in Spion Kop affair said to be very great. Spion Kop taken in early morning and no time to build proper sangars and consequently heavy shelling causes great casualties. Out on hill, sniping when anything seen.*

Thorneycroft's evacuation of Spion Kop, together with the heavy casualties, and the lack of progress elsewhere on the extended battlefield, persuaded Buller that all their efforts had been in vain. It was time to abandon the attempt and look elsewhere for the road to Ladysmith. The troops were to withdraw during the night and return to their tented camps whilst plans for a fresh assault across the river were formulated. Officers and men in

THE ENGLISH MAIL BRINGS THE FIRST ISSUE OF *THE KING*, AN ILLUSTRATED MAGAZINE WHICH PUBLISHED SEVERAL OF MALCOLM'S PHOTOGRAPHS.

Buller's command were bewildered; Field Marshal Lord Roberts, recently arrived in South Africa and now in over-all command, suggested that Buller should go over to the defensive whilst he attempted to beat the Boers in the western theatre of action – by taking Pretoria. In Ladysmith, where the men were now considered by their commander, Lieutenant-General White, to be too unfit to attempt any effort at assisting Buller's attacks, the British hung grimly on and began to slaughter their horses for food.

26 January *Sniping as usual from sangars. No casualties. The men looking miserable and hungry, All in need of clean and dry clothes. Retired from position and crossed river. Very tired.*

Lieutenant Crossman, in his own particular way, saw things rather more esoterically:

"..at 6 pm it started raining and then the fun began. By ten we were absolutely soaked as we had no great coats and little food. It was also awfully cold. The extremes of temperatures here are wonderful, in the day time it sometimes reaches 105 to 110 in the shade and in the night it might go down to 45 degrees. Precisely at 10, the Battalion passed me and I fell in and went on with them. At the same moment a tremendous rifle fire burst out all along the ridge on our right. I was sure the enemy had spotted our retirement and was attacking. As a matter of fact it was the Irish Brigade keeping the Boers awake. This lasted some half hour or so. I might have guessed it, as we had played

the same game, in a lesser degree, twice before. You can't see to aim, but the bullets fly somewhere near the enemy and that is bad enough at night. Our progress was of course painfully slow as there was no road and walking over the rough veldt at night is terribly rough work. At 2 pm we reached the Tugela, which was only five miles, and crossed the pontoon bridge which was taken up as soon as we were over as we were the last Brigade to cross. The men were awfully done up as they had been on the hill fighting for three consecutive days and nights and not a man had more than five hours sleep in all that time. They were falling asleep as they marched…"

Malcolm's rather terse entry informs us:

…Acted as rear-guard to troops. Got an issue of rum just before we marched off for Spearman's Farm. Wagons with tents etc. arrived about 4 pm. Very little water to be had. Sergeant Russell and mess wagon turned up and we soon had a fairly comfortable Mess tent and grub going. Camp a fairly big one. 2 brigades, a good deal of cavalry and artillery.

THE RAILWAY BRIDGE AT FRERE BLOWN UP BY THE BOERS

28 January, Sunday   *Church services held. All indulged in a well-earned rest. Bathing parade by Companies in pools of dried up spruit. Dried ourselves in the sun. Mail came in, I got 2 letters from home. Auction of poor Captain Ryall's kit.*

29 January   *Up at 3 am, camp struck, marched at 6.30 to a camp nearer Spearman's Farm. Waggons followed in about an hour and we soon got settled down. Brigade paraded in afternoon, formed square and Buller spoke to us. Told us our hardships of last ten days had not been in vain, he believed in his heart of hearts that we had found the 'Key to Ladysmith' and would be there in a week. Mentioned our Regiment, Devons and Hampshires as having done good work. Hart's Brigade and ours then gave three cheers for the Queen.*

30 January   *Very hot. Soap and water have no impression at all on the brown stain on one's feet. Draft of 177 NCO's and Men with Major Watts, Captain Tew and young Fryer joined us. Drafts for other battalions in camp also arrived. Awfully cold night, Fresh meat issued again. Ross rejoins Regiment from Hospital at Wynburg* [he had been wounded at Colenso].

As Thomas Pakenham in his history of the war rather neatly put it, victory was not simply to be a question of geography, the right drift or commanding hill, but a question of method. Buller's 19th-century army was learning to fight a 20th-century war. Tents, camp beds, the luxuries of life would all have to be abandoned in favour of lighter loads and mobility. Also, the three fighting arms would have to work more closely together and this called for better signalling. Sadly, it would take a long time for the lessons to be learnt thoroughly.

COPYRIGHT.

Z.22. A BOER CONVOY, OFFICERS AND ATTENDANTS

Seven

VAALKRANTZ AND THE FERRYMAN OF THE TUGELA

Opposite: A Boer convoy in the field. Both sides employed large numbers of natives.

Within days Buller had his army crossing the Tugela River once again. This time the objective was Vaalkrantz, a tangled mass of kopjes a few miles east of Spion Kop. This operation was supposed to have started on 31 January but owing to heavy rain, and the failure of a battery of horse artillery to arrive in time, the assault was postponed until 5 February. Once again, therefore the movements of British brigades were easily seen from the heights overlooking the Tugela – and the Boers were able to reinforce their line.

3 February *Another burning hot day. Warren's Division is really off, tents and all gone. Story going round that the RA [Royal Artillery] were ordered to get their guns on a certain hill which they said was impossible without a road being made. When RE [Royal Engineers] working parties arrived they found two RN 4.7 on top. Delightfully cool in the Mess tent but awfully hot outside.*

This episode is the origin of the RN Field Gun competition.

4 February, Sunday *Awfully hot morning. Church parade at 6.10. Wrote letters to Father, Claud and Edith. Paraded 2 pm, camp struck. 20 lbs kit and maconochies. Reached camp where Lyttleton's Brigade etc were encamped near Potgieter's Drift moving along under the crest-line of Schwartz Kop at dusk* [marshalling area on south side of Tugela]. *Slept well on hillside, kit and greatcoats turning up after dinner.*

5 February *Up about 5 am. Nice morning. Buller's scheme shown us: a feint to be made*

INSPANNING AN OX-WAGON

by *Artillery and Lyttleton's Brigade in direction of Ladysmith road. Main attack to be on hills Vaalkrantz Kop and Doorn Kloof hill to right of this. Feint a complete success, Artillery gradually disengaging and retiring and moving over a pontoon bridge to right. Light Brigade cross Tugela by another bridge to right. Durhams take Vaalkrantz Kop. Our Artillery – Field Howitzers, Naval guns including 5-in playing up wonderfully well. Field batteries came out of action in feint in a wonderful manner. Devons the only regiment of our Brigade to cross Tugela River and they lay along wall by farm up main donga. General Lyttleton's Brigade occupy Vaalkrantz Hill.*

6 February *Sat tight all day on Schwartz Kop. Boers started shelling us almost immediately it was light, a shell burst right in the middle of the Queens who were having their breakfast all together in Quarter column but did not kill a man. Shelling and firing on Vaalkrantz fairly continuous all day.* [Buller was attempting to silence Boer artillery with massive bombardment by his own artillery.] *Buller rather crusty and anxious. Found some trees of jessamin, pressed one or two blooms and some yellow flowers I found in the wood in my notebook. Our Brigade relieved Lyttleton's at dusk and were fired on a good deal… The men employed building sangars during the night.*

7 February *At work until dawn with signals, kept in shelters, a good many shells knocking about and bad smell of corpses. At 9 am Warren came up for a look around…*

It was at this point that Buller had recognised that his troops had stalled on Vaalkrantz.

BOER PRISONERS TAKEN ON VAALKRANTZ WITH WEST YORKSHIREMEN AND A TROOPER OF THE IMPERIAL LIGHT HORSE (ILH).

The sixty-year-old Warren was on a fact-finding mission, to discover the mood of the men and to see for himself what lay on the other side – to the north – of Vaalkrantz. Later that day, back at Buller's HQ, the various general officers gathered for a council of war to answer Buller's question, 'do we advance or withdraw?' Only Warren and Hart were in favour of advancing, the rest advocated retreat. Hildyard was not, as far as we know, consulted on the matter.

…Chilly morning – shelling started almost immediately it was daylight and consequently messages coming and going pretty thick between us and RA and Divisional HQ. Messages continuous until 11 o'clock. Boer guns shell us from both flanks, left worse than right. Long Tom on Spion Kop shelling our rear; Pop-pops [pom-pom] on left and on right. Not much damage done luckily. All of our men well hidden in sangars. Sun very hot towards mid-day and shelling ceases more or less. Moving about hill very difficult and rations unobtainable. Loose stones, rocks and bits of shell flying. All troops retired from hill at 9 pm across pontoon bridge. Pontoon bridge lifted.

Yet again it was a half-hearted attempt on Buller's part. Buller seems to have abandoned all hope of breaking through the Boer lines almost as soon as the leading regiments got stalled on the slopes of Vaalkrantz. The real difficulty, it seems, was simply lack of intelligence: Buller really did not know how well his assault was going and, once bogged down, he was fearful of the rising casualty rates. He preferred instead to withdraw from the battlefield and seek another place to attack. Back at the War Office in London, Field Marshal Lord Wolseley christened Buller 'the Ferryman of the Tugela' because he had crossed and recrossed the river so often. Buller's men, hitherto hugely devoted to Buller, began to think of him as 'Sir Reverse Buller'. Drummer Goodwin captures the mood:

"…It was not long after daybreak when the Boers opened a heavy shell fire, killing some of the men of the Queens Regiment. This continued all day, our regiment being lucky. About 4 pm the [observation] balloon went up and brought some good information down, it noticed the Boers were getting big guns into position ready to surprise us the next day but at night Buller gave orders to retire so we all retired once again, this was breaking the lads hearts to think it was no use once more. But Buller knew that if

we had stopped there the next day there would not have been one of the West Yorks left to tell the tale, so we thought God help the boys in Ladysmith – but all the same we retired that night… we got an issue of rum but a lot of men never got it on account of falling asleep so you see it is every man for himself."

Meanwhile, from Malcolm's diary:

11 February, Sunday
Started about 3 am for Chieveley and did a nice cool march getting in to Blaaukrantz camp about 10 am and had a meal under a big tree on the grass. The Prince sat by and talked to us [Prince Christian Victor who served on Hildyard's staff in the hope that this would keep him safe from Boer bullets]. *Wagons arrived almost as soon as we did. Mimosa thorn in flower and very sweet too. Warm night. Went round to two kraals with Berney and got four chickens, the conductors* [native wagon drivers] *did the bargaining.*

Drummer Goodwin had also appreciated the food and wash:

"troops allowed to bathe this morning this was the first chance of a wash for about ten days, the men are in a filthy condition…our clothes are falling apart what with the privations and campaigning."

"STAND DOWN!" THE WEST YORKSHIRES RELAX IN THE SUN WHILE AWAITING FRESH ORDERS

Eight

ONCE MORE UPON THE BREACH... LADYSMITH RELIEVED AT LAST

Opposite: Grizzled veterans and young lads – some of the occupants of No 1 tent, F Coy

It was now quite apparent to most senior officers that if Ladysmith was to be relieved then the British forces attempting to force the Tugela River would have to employ different tactics. The three-part dramas rehearsed on Aldershot field days – preliminary artillery bombardment, infantry assault and cavalry follow-through would have to go – indeed the whole concept of a field-day action was clearly now erroneous. It was going to take days, perhaps weeks, of continuous fighting to prise the Boers from their positions, and it would require close co-operation and flexibility between the three arms: infantry, artillery and cavalry. Buller had asked at that council-of-war after the assault on Vaalkrantz, 'Where do we attack next ?', to which Lieutenant-General Warren had suggested – Hlangwane. This hill had featured briefly during the Colenso engagement when Lord Dundonald's cavalry screen had attacked the Boers holding the kopje. Buller, contemplating his blueprint map, could find no other answer. They had attempted the centre, Colenso, and the west flank, Spion Kop, there remained only the east flank but with wider objectives.

NAVAL 6 INCH GUN BEING MOVED UP TO THE FRONT ON A RAILWAY TRUCK

In fact, the Boers were spread across a series of kopjes along the southern side of the Tugela, and occupied Hlangwane, Green Hill, Cingolo and Monte Christo. It looked a formidable task. On the 14 February, Dundonald's men advanced once more and swiftly took Hussar Hill which would soon form the firing position for thirty-four pieces of artillery.

14 February *Reveille at 4.30. March 7 am. After a very hot slow dusty march we eventually reached Hussar Hill to the right front of Chieveley, our brigade in support of Warren's Division. Had lunch and then moved off to the right up a donga with steep sides and took up a new position by the Light Brigade (Lyttleton's). Half of the battalion on Outposts in front, half bivouacked in rear. Battalions and brigades all very mixed up. Got water from water holes dug in sand of donga. General Hildyard would not allow lamps to be used with Outposts. Some sort of attack going on all day; guns set grass on fire on Hlangwaini. On Picquet all night, quiet, some guns fire at 2 am.*

15 February *Up about 5 am. Rode out to Outposts on Colonel Kitchener's black pony. Had a hurried breakfast of mutton and bread and then moved further up donga, other half of battalion joining in. Went about 4 miles and the brigade formed up for the night on the side of a woody hill. We apparently form the right of a long line extending back to Gun Hill and Chieveley. Heat intense but plenty of bushes about and water close at hand in dongas. Waggons came up to plain below hill. Rations but not coats issued. Frankum found a nest with 4 eggs which he presented to me.*

16 February *Very warm night, cold towards morning. Orders to move at 6 am. Counter-ordered at last minute. Queens go out on a reconnaissance. Rest of brigade went out later, crossed over hill and moved through thick scrub towards Green Hill. Advanced 300-400*

A Naval 4.7 inch gun, manned by officers and men from HMS Philomel, in an emplacement looking across to Pieter's Hill, 27 February 1900

yards and then retired to our old position. Went down to Blaauwkrantz river in afternoon with Bicknell and Lyster and had a ripping bathe and found some nests. 20 lb kits came up and we had a very good night. Guns bombarded enemy's position.

Malcolm's 'thick scrub' had caused some delay to the deployment of Buller's brigades. Nonetheless, Malcolm's diary does not, at this stage, convey any sense of urgency, as this entry clearly shows. But at last, after faltering and then resuming once more, and after hearing the wonderful news that Major-General John French had got into Kimberley (though he had destroyed most of his cavalry horses in doing so), the British went into action. The advance really got going the next day when Hildyard's 2nd Brigade seized Cingolo Hill. The West Yorkshires formed the firing line supported by the Queens and Devons.

17 February *Lyttleton's Brigade on left and ours on right started about 5 am and made across valley through thick scrub for Cingolo and hill in front of Hlangwane, RA assisting. Queens got up on right end of Cingolo, ILH got round and up, we went straight up and to left. Boers sniped us from top at 2500 yards but did not do much harm. We had about 20 casualties in all. Queens moved along top, and West Yorkshires moved along side half way up,*

ONE OF BULLER'S MANY ARTILLERY PIECES COMING INTO ACTION

shifted all Boers on Cingolo onto Monte Christo (the kopje adjacent to the north-west) and sat tight for the night. Mess came up and we were alright. No greatcoats and rather a chilly night and very damp. Colour Sergeant Armstrong, who had been sniping at Boers at 2500 yards with me, got hit in foot.

The first stage had been an unqualified success, now for the next hill – Monte Christo – on the extreme left of the Boer position:

18 February, Sunday
General advance. Artillery shelling all hills well. Lyddite smashing up top of Monte Christo. We advance with Queens on right, West Yorks in centre and Devons in support and on left. East Surreys in reserve. 3 Companies of West Yorks and 2 Companies of Devons pulled 2 batteries of field artillery up hill into position over enormous rocks. Major Fry with half of the battalion in firing line. Our men advanced up Monte Christo in fine style. Cavalry on right flank. Came up with Berney and few men, opened fire, joined by Porch.

Berney got hit, Porch tied him up and called me to bring another bandage. Directly I got there Porch hit. I tied him up and sent him away and then turned to Berney who was about dead, did what I could for him and covered him up. Hurried up more men into the firing line. Colonel Kitchener arrived and more men. Regiment advanced

THE PONTOON BRIDGE AT TUGELA FALLS

and Boers fled. Opened fire on their laager and then built sangars hurriedly when Boer artillery opened fire. Gretton hit in arm by shrapnel and also good many men. Awful hot fire. 4th Brigade advanced lower down and Boers fled leaving camp etc. Buller sent up special congratulative message to Regiment. West Yorkshires took about 50 casualties. Devons got some ponies. Colonel Kitchener sent me continually running messages and got awfully done. Pop-pop worked busily when we got on top but did not do much damage. Half of the battalion went down hill and slept at the bottom and returned early following morning — no water on top of the hill — a good night.

For Drummer Goodwin it was not a good day, the loss of many men and, particularly the death of Captain Berney, quite distressed him:

"…when we got to the top the bullets were flying in every direction, one of our officers was shot dead at the brow of the hill, Captain T Berney, he was a gentleman every inch of him and it is only Tommy that knows kind officers and when they searched him they found a picture of his wife and child in his breast pocket and it did seem hard a few of the boys was blown to pieces so you can see we were in a tight… we fought like heroes, Colonel Kitchener keeping to the front and they would follow him anywhere no matter what danger was in view…"

It had been an expensive day for the West Yorkshires, one officer and four men killed with two officers and 40 men wounded. The next day Buller's troops took Hlangwane and the Boers fled north across the river. On the 19th the leading infantry companies of the 5th Brigade entered the village of Colenso and the next day some of Thorneycroft's mounted infantry splashed across the Tugela. It had been just nine weeks since that fateful December battle.

19 February *General advance about 5 am. Troops on left moved forward to Hlangwane and Tugela, 3 of our Companies made a road up Monte Christo. Brigade stayed on hill all day. Moved about 10 to top of hill to set up signal station to try to send messages to Ladysmith. Watched battle from top, lovely views all round. Boers trekking like fun, wagons taken on by hand. Howitzers shelled small open kopjes this side of the river. Batteries on Hlangwaini fired hard. Colonel Kitchener got some Naval guns on to the front part of Monte Christo but they would not fire. Very cold, wet night. No coats.*

A GROUP OF BOERS AT TUGELA FALLS WAITING FOR THE BRITISH TO ADVANCE

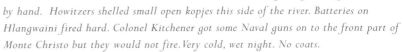

THE RAILWAY BRIDGE DESTROYED BY THE BOERS AT COLENSO WITH THE NEW BRIDGE UNDER CONSTRUCTION

20 February *Woke up very cold and wet. Rained a good deal and made us rather miserable. Brigade, all except East Surreys and machine guns, left hill at 8.30 and formed up at the bottom. Moved off round hill to 2nd Division HQ. Halted on a small kopje, had lunch off brawn etc., Moved off about 2 pm. And halted for the night under Hlangwane. A Boer gun began shelling the hill when we got there but no shells came among us.*

21 February *Woke up early after a rather miserable night to find everything very wet after rain. Went round Boer trenches on Hlangwaini with Bicknell. Trenches mostly amongst bushes and 5'6' deep, earth thrown well to front, sandbags used a good deal but very few loopholes made. Some trenches invisible and carved out of solid rock. Very little left except empty tins and empty Mauser boxes. Brigade moved about 1 pm advanced a mile or two, sat down; Canteen and waggons came up and Quaker [oat porridge] was much in demand. Moved on after about an hour rounded Hlangwaini and formed up on the plain beside the river, near Colenso, for the night. Waggons followed and we got 20 lb kit and great coats & a good night's rest. Artillery batteries over river and nearly all infantry. Boers have evacuated Colenso. Hart across. East Surreys and machine guns still on Monte Christo.*

Then at last, something of a red-letter day, the West Yorkshires followed the leading elements of Buller's army across the Tugela River. As Drummer Goodwin dryly put it,

THE STAFF SERGEANTS AT HYDE'S FARM, NEAR LADYSMITH

'…all quiet, our Generals are forming up the Idea for another battle all quick…' As indeed they were. Hart launched his battalions of Irish infantry against the Boer positions overlooking Colenso and, in scenes that recalled Hart's advance to the Tugela back in December 1899, his troops suffered dreadful casualties. Hart pushed his troops forward, massed together, and they were slaughtered in great heaps. This was not the way to wage war, it was stupidity, the more so after the battles they had fought in the past weeks to get across the Tugela. Despite the losses, Hart's men hung on to their bridgehead and, in doing so, prevented the Boers from concentrating their men against Buller's next thrust across the Tugela — this time a little way east of Colenso, and employing once again that much used and well-travelled Royal Engineers' pontoon bridge.

The West Yorkshires, along with the other battalions forming Hildyard's 2nd Brigade, followed in Hart's wake and, marching along the railway line, deployed along the north bank of the Tugela. Malcolm takes up the story once more:

22 February *Up at 2 am. Brigade moved across pontoon bridge and formed up on plain on the other side of the river* [near Fort Wylie on the north bank of the Tugela]. *Went round Colenso trenches after breakfast and picked up rounds of Boer ammunition, collected altogether 12 varieties. Boer guns sent some shells amongst our men all in column, some of our Companies bathing at the time, and we all went back helter-skelter to trees on river bank by railway bridge and formed up again there. Had a most excellent bathe in*

Tugela, current very strong. Moved 1 pm. Brigade sat on a hill a few hundred yards on; East Surreys and Queens advanced an hour or two later and we moved over to kopje where howitzers were firing. At dusk we moved along railway to next ridge of kopjes and lay on the hillside all night. Built sangars. Battalion got very mixed up with Queens in night march.

23 February *Woke up early after rather a poor night among hard rocks. Rations failed us and did not turn up until after breakfast. Colonel Kitchener taken away from us to command 11th Brigade* [Major Fry assumed command of the West Yorkshires]. *Formed a Brigade signalling station on side of hill to connect Queens and East Surreys who had gone to next ridge of kopjes. Howitzers moved up to bottom of our kopje and in conjunction with 4.7's behind Field Batteries on top of our kopje and on our right across river and also Naval guns across river, shelled a high hill to our right front. In afternoon General Hart moved his brigade along railway and river to right of our position and took a portion of big hill over Tugela Falls. Inniskillings lose heavily, only 5 officers left, a Captain in command of the regiment. At dusk the Regiment moved along railway to next ridge of kopjes and relieved South Lancashires on right of position. Half of the battalion in firing line with half in support. Built sangars.*

24 February *Boer rifle fire continues pretty hot, bullets whizz freely around the sangars. Two of our men hit by one bullet, one through the arm and the other through both cheeks of the backside. Shelling continues hot and strong. East Surreys move to right to support General Hart, Queens come over to relieve us after lunch. 5 Companies of ours under Major Fry moved to the right along railway and river to support Hart leaving B, G and H in the firing line* [Battalion War Diary: these Companies were in trenches under heavy Boer fire and could not be withdrawn] *under Major Heigham. Nicholson's pom-pom doing right good work, also maxim gun. While getting across to Hart we passed over a railway bridge under hot fire but the Royal Engineers had built up a wall of sandbags and no-one was hit. Formed up on river bank in close formation and were just going to have dinner when Boers opened a heavy fire. We moved back along river bank and Companies lined bank to protect a Boer pontoon foot-bridge. Stench of dead cattle, horses, etc. something awful.*

25 February, Sunday *Returned to place where we formed the night before, all except for one Company. We now belong to the Light Brigade under Colonel Northbrook. Armistice on to bury dead etc. One of our men found a dead Boer in the river and landed him and found £7 in gold in his belt. Beastly cold, raining off and on through the day. Had a wash in the river. Place reeks of dead cattle and dead horses... Our men talk over the situation with the Boers during armistice.*

This armistice was arranged by Buller and Botha neither of whom wished to see the agonies of the wounded men lying out on Wynne's Hill and Hart's Hill prolonged any further. It was an opportunity for fraternisation which lasted some six hours or so, and even when the allotted time of time came to an end there was, for a while, no great enthusiasm to open fire again.

Armistice up until 7 pm. 3 Companies on Outpost on left to guard iron bridge, half battalion up on crest line above Mess... Boers open a very heavy fire in the night.

26 February *Slept fairly well. Night had started very warm but morning was extremely cold. Nice cool day, no rain... Guns moved round to right and maxims put on kopjes behind us on opposite side of river. All fire away all day long but Boers hardly reply at all either with guns or rifles. Cold wet night.*

During the 25th and 26th the British forces had been extending eastwards, battalion after battalion moving up to the Tugela, crossing, and deploying on the north bank preparing to roll up the Boer left flank, looking to assault Pieter's Hill then Railway Hill and finally Hart's Hill. The attack was to be launched on the morning of 27 February – Majuba Day.

27 February *Major Heigham's 3 Companies rejoined us. Big scheme on: 3 brigades to attack simultaneously three hills in line. Barton's Fusilier Brigade on right, Colonel Kitchener's 11th Brigade (3 Lancashire Regiments plus West Yorks attached) in centre with Colonel Northcott's Light Brigade on left. Supposed to start at 9.30 am but did not get going until 12. Barton's Brigade went first along river bank, we followed at head of our brigade. Scouts under Bicknell worked well.*

TROOPS CROSSING THE TUGELA ON PONTOON BRIDGE

Nicholson took charge of Yorks and Lancs machine gun on a tripod and used it to some effect. Under a heavy fire from Boers we fire in volleys back at them. We took hill about 4 pm. General Barton having got partly up his hill and protecting us from enfilading fire. We helped Northcott to take his hill then — success all along the line. Large parties of Boers taken prisoner, any amount of loot. Few casualties except in Barton's Brigade. Relieved at dusk by one of the Lancashire regiments and went some way down the railway line and bivouacked for the night.

Malcolm did not realise at the time, perhaps he never did discover it, but the delay in getting Northcott's and Kitchener's brigades on the move nearly proved fatal for the British assault. Over on Pieter's Hill, Barton's brigade had outrun its artillery support and Botha's men were in the process of driving Barton off the hillside. As it was, Kitchener arrived in time and, with the dash he had so often displayed in the weeks before, pushed his men up the steep terraces of Railway Hill. For once, and unusually for the campaign, the Boers were driven out at the point of the bayonet. Indeed, the charge had succeeded so well that elements of the battalion out on Kitchener's left flank were also able to scramble onto part of Hart's Hill, thereby ensuring the complete overthrow of the Boer position.

28 February *Went up line about 2.30 am to Colonel Kitchener's HQ for orders. Awfully cold. Shifted bivouac a few hundred yards off line. Buller cheered by the men. Cavalry work in front by Pieter's Hill. Bought a Mauser rifle and bandolier for 30/-* [shillings]. *Diarrhoea rather prevalent, bad myself. Some fellows trousers nearly dropping off them, boots all falling to pieces. Sole off one of my boots. Cold and wet night. Built sangars on Kitchener's Hill and after put up gun pits for a battery. Quiet day. Boer doctor came in with a flag of truce to bury Boer casualties, seemed a good chap.*

In the quiet of the night, the Boers slipped away from their surviving trenches and positions along the Tugela height and, gathering up their besieging forces from around Ladysmith, they headed north into the Biggarsberg. Here, in another range of kopjes hardly different to those they had so recently vacated along the Tugela, Botha had his

men dig in and await Buller's next move. It would be a long wait. The British cavalry rode into Ladysmith later that day, and after 118 days of siege Ladysmith was relieved.

Malcolm simply noted the main events of the day in his diary. The West Yorkshires regrouped and, marching along the railway headed for the campsite at Nelthorpe. Later that day the officers gathered together and drank to the success of the campaign with some champagne they had saved for the event. Lieutenant Crossman writing in his diary soon after, had this to say:

"…A red letter day in my life and that of many others. At 7 am this morning word was passed round 'Road clear to Ladysmith'. The cheers were deafening for about ten minutes. At last we had done it. After three and three-quarter months of toil and worry. We have achieved one objective. Of course we knew we should but the relief of having done it is great."

March 3, We fell in to march at 7 am. It was steaming hot when we started, one of the hottest, and we had an awfully trying march. We crossed the Klip river by the railway bridge and marched the whole length of Ladysmith between the lines of the garrison who were drawn up lining the streets for us. Very thin and fine drawn but spotlessly clean. We were brown as berries, and thick and strong and hard but filthy was no word for us. Half the men had no seats to their trousers, none of them any elbows and the majority had the soles of their boots tied on with string. Shall have some photos worth seeing when I get back as lots of our people took shots. The town seemed wonderfully clean, but it seems lately the Boers have not pushed the siege very much. Opposite the Town hall, whose clock tower had been knocked sideways by a 6 in. shell, was Sir George White and his staff. Buller had gone through at the head of our huge long column, which took hours to go through, so there was no historical meeting in public. They had met two days before and I believe the words used were 'Glad you're here at last', 'Sorry I was so long coming'. I can't swear to this myself but I was told it by a man who says he heard them used."

2nd W. Yorks Regt
Ladysmith
1900

Coyne
Photo

As you will see that far from being 'away from all the fighting' as you rather unkindly put it, I am always well up in it, for whenever there is fighting the Brigadier must be there to conduct operations, and where he goes I go too. I have no ardent desire to be at the head of the Advance Guard every day in order to be sniped at from kopjes, and you can tell, when the time comes I am no coward, but at the same time I see no use in running unnecessary risks. If I wanted to be shot I should like to have been shot in some big engagement at the beginning of the war and not.

Nine

MARKING TIME
OUTSIDE LADYSMITH

Opposite: The West Yorkshires on parade near Hyde's Farm, near Ladysmith

For the West Yorkshires, the weeks that followed the relief of Ladysmith were a time of rest and recuperation. Many of the officers and men were ill, as Malcolm's diary entries show,

4 March, Sunday *Waggons did not turn up till about 10 am but after breakfast we soon got tents up. Lyster rather seedy with diarrhoea, others bad too. Mess very comfortable, all sorts of luxuries going. Got our valises, kits, greatcoats etc. Queen's chocolate issued out. Divisional Divine Service Parade.*

Queen Victoria took a close and particular interest in the conduct of the war, with an especial interest in the private soldiers and NCOs. One physical manifestation of this interest was her decision to make a gift of a box of chocolate to every soldier on active service in South Africa, with the intention that they should arrive in time for Christmas. The chocolate, a form of drinking chocolate made in cubes to a total weight of half a pound per tin, was shipped out in very attractive tin boxes, many of which were almost immediately sent home again by their recipients to be preserved by their families – to the soldiery, the gift was as good as a medal! Malcolm sent his home having eaten the chocolate but used the tin to enclose a collection of Boer shell fragments, bullets and cartridge cases.

QUEEN VICTORIA'S CHOCOLATE BOX.

Over 200 miles to the west, in the Cape Colony, the war was going better for the British and Lord Roberts had achieved considerable success. Roberts' army had overcome all the attempts by the Boers to resist his advance, and by early March had entered the Orange Free State, relieved Kimberley, taken Bloemfontein and, remarkably, opened peace negotiations with Presidents Kruger and Steyn. But Roberts had achieved his objectives at an appalling cost: the line of his advance was littered with the carcasses of cavalry horses and then, in Bloemfontein, the ranks of his army were swept by typhoid and dysentery which claimed more British lives than did Boer bullets.

Buller was at first given orders by Roberts to stay at Ladysmith and then, as the weeks of inactivity lengthened, Buller was asked to co-operate with Roberts by advancing into northern Natal. Buller advocated caution, and then suggested he lacked sufficient men. Roberts finally persuaded Buller to move but without engaging the Boers in battle. Buller

could not have advanced much further north into Natal for the simple reason that the Boers had ripped up the railway line and blown up more bridges and destroyed culverts and tunnels. Without the railway to haul supplies Buller could not move his army. Additionally, Buller was still seriously handicapped by a lack of cavalry and was thus unable to gather information about the disposition of the Boers.

It was not long before the 2nd Brigade was on the move, though this had more to do with camping on clean, sanitary, ground than to do with any military strategy.

8 March *4 am Marched about 8 miles NE of Ladysmith to Modder Spruit. Halted at one place for nearly two hours while the Queens had breakfast. Consequently when we arrived at our destination we found waggons etc. waiting for us. Ross sick and sent to Hospital. Daly reported very bad. Railway line and culverts wrecked all along.*

9 March *Division Marched to Sunday's River about 1 mile in front of Elandslaagte... Did a good march however getting in about 12, tents pitched by 2. Had hair cropped like a convict's. Went on Outposts with my Company by myself at 5 pm. Picquet on open veldt, Company made a long trench and we got fairly comfortable. During march we passed by Elandslaagte station - total wreck - and the battle field. Our camp is near Sunday's River.*

Here the West Yorkshires and the other battalions of the brigade remained until mid-April. It was a time to refit and repair and for new men to arrive from the regimental depots back in Britain to fill the spaces in the ranks caused by death, injury and, more particularly, disease. Malcolm's diary suggests that the days were fairly tedious and really quite boring with little to do; his main occupation seems to have been drawing up maps and making notes about the Spion Kop, Rangeworthy and Vaalkrantz actions. Apart from outpost and picquet duties, there were the normal day-to-day activities of any soldiers from time immemorial, as Malcolm observes:

...Kit inspection by the CO. Two or three rifles noticed as being rusty. Discovered that a corporal of another Company had put his fearfully rusty rifles on our piles to put the blame on us. The Scottish Rifles have got their band up which discourses sweet music from time to time.

THE MEN DISCUSSING NOTICE OF LORD ROBERTS' SUCCESSES ON 'THE OTHER SIDE'

A GROUP OF NATAL KAFFIRS IN THEIR KRAAL, NEAR ELANDSLAAGTE

CHURCH PARADE

MOVING CAMP TO A FRESH, CLEAN LOCATION AT ELANDSLAAGTE

The men of the West Yorkshires were also kept busy with inter-company football matches and later an inter-regimental competition. The officers played cricket and polo, with music provided by the regimental band who had had their instruments sent up from the base depot at Pieter-maritzburg. It was all quite reminiscent of the weeks following Colenso.

14 March *Extremely hot as usual. Grant-Dalton arrived with a draft of about 200 men, mostly reservists. He had come as far as Ladysmith by train and then walked the rest stopping one night at Modder Spruit where he was horribly bitten by mosquitoes. Nights getting colder.*

15 March *Usual programme of events till evening when heavy rain came down! Rained again after Mess when turning out the Guard etc. Ross returned from hospital.*

LIEUTENANT LYSTER INSPECTING THE RATIONS AND MEAT COVERED IN FLIES

Individual regiments were therefore required to provide details of signallers to keep the stream of messages flowing to and fro between Buller and the leading elements of his army.

23 March *Bicknell and I started at 5.30 am with our Companies to form support to Cavalry Picquets. Took snapshots of Kaffirs and bought some beads and chickens. Spatch cock and fried potato chips and fresh cow's milk helped to make a very good lunch. English Mail came out with lunch and there were four letters for me which I read in the shade of a tree by Bicknell's Picquet while watching a Kaffir making ropes out of bullock hide. My signallers kept pretty busy, Cavalry repeatedly sending messages through. 500 Boers reported near Wessels's Nek.*

Malcolm, it seems, was quite content to stand back and let his signallers get on with it. Of the Boers there is no mention at all until 10 April when,

10 April *In the middle of breakfast we were suddenly startled to hear a Boer shell*

It was not all play and no work however, as the brigade stood across the line of communication east from Ladysmith up to the front line somewhere north of Elandslaagte.

come whizzing over the Mess and land in the East Surrey's lines. More shells came in quick succession and one burst right in Crossman's tent making a great mess and filling his bed etc. with shrapnel bullets. Regiments all spread about and we took the first line and occupied a kopje in front of the camp. Boers had about 8 guns and gave us rather a peppering but only 1 killed and 5 wounded of ours. Naval detachment had 2 or 3 killed and some wounded. After strengthening entrenchments for a bit the whole force retired over the Railway and took up position on Elandslaagte Hill for the night.

Some of Malcolm's papers were damaged in this attack, including his precious map of the Colenso and Spion Kop battles. He later drew the map again but without the details of the military dispositions. The British were really quite surprised by this burst of Boer activity and their only response was to reply to the Boer artillery bombardment with long-range rifle fire and a brief burst of fire from the Naval guns.

11 April *Night march ended about 2 am and we lay down and slept till about 5 am. The Brigade was all split up along the Elandslaagte position and each Regiment made a separate camp. We are reserve regiment to the Brigade.*

LUXURIES IN THE FORM OF BEER, PACKETS OF QUAKER OATS AND BARS OF CHOCOLATE COULD BE OBTAINED AT THE CANTEEN

After sitting in the sun for a long time we eventually got camp pitched about 11 am. Men and Officers sleep in boots and puttees. Companies employed in trenching.

12 April *Relieved D & E Companies after breakfast on fatigue. Made huge epaulments for the Naval 4.7 guns. Stone walls 4' thick and sandbag revetments, also improved road. Did about 6 hours solid work. General Clery (now Divisional Commander) passed by while we were at work. Boers nowhere to be seen.*

13 April *Woken up at 3 am and got ready to move off at a moment's notice. Did not move however till after breakfast and then we and the Queens journeyed as far as the plain in front of the station and sat there for some hours. At 12 we started back for our old camp and pitched tents once more. We furnished 2 Companies for Outposts near the collieries.*

The Boers achieved little from their display of gunnery; it was all a bit like poking a stick in an ants' nest as the British rushed about with no clear aims or idea of what would happen next. It is certainly clear from the Battalion Diary, and from Malcolm's own account, that the

SOME OF THE BATTALION OX-WAGONS LOADED UP WITH THE OFFICER'S GEAR

whereabouts of the Boers was unknown; all that was known for sure was that there was a general expectation that the Boers would launch an attack on the British camps.

15 April, Easter Sunday. *Church parade 7.40. Stand to arms as usual. Large attendance at Communion Service in Soldiers' Home Tent… F Company on No 2 Picquet. Boers expected to attack but nothing comes of it. Bright moon most of the night.*

One result of the Boer bombardment was to precipitate a general movement of the British troops; the West Yorkshires moving first to Pepworth Farm and then, on the 18th, to Surprise Hill. On the 21st the Boer artillery was in action again, this time shelling Elandslaagte railway station and the collieries nearby. The 2nd Brigade, complete with artillery and cavalry, was ordered out on to the road and advanced along the Newcastle road to Intintanyone, but after a hot and dusty day out in the countryside, the movement was abandoned and the brigade ordered back to camp. Once again the infantry regiments settled down to their camp routine – more football and cricket matches, even some polo.

Then, at long last, the orders to advance north against the Boers were issued:

7 May *Reveille at 5 am, camp struck at 6 am, Parade 7.20 am to move off. Did a good march across country and halted at Modder Spruit.*

Ten

ADVANCE TO CONTACT

Opposite: The regimental doctor, Collier, just returned from De Wet's farm with two turkeys slung from his saddle bow

As you will see that far from being 'away from all the fighting' as you rather unkindly put it, I am always well up in it, for whenever there is fighting the Brigadier must be there to conduct operations, and where he goes I go too. I have no ardent desire to be at the head of the Advance Guard every day in order to be sniped at. I can tell you that when the time comes I am no coward, but at the same time I see no use in running unnecessary risks. If I wanted to be shot I should like to have been shot in some big engagement at the beginning of the war and not.

The orders for Buller's army to move north originated with Lord Roberts, who was about to start on the next leg of his invasion of the Orange Free State and wanted Buller to keep the Boers occupied in the Biggarsberg. Buller knew this country well from his service there during the Zulu war; indeed, he had raised a contingent of irregular cavalry in the district which included many young Boer farmers. He knew full well that Botha and his commandos had had ample time to dig in and create a series of entrenchments that would be every bit as difficult to overrun as the positions along the Tugela. As ever, no one really knew how many Boers remained to face Buller's forces, or how many had left this front to join the Boer commandos confronting Lord Roberts.

The problem of transporting supplies which had caused such difficulties earlier was solved by reducing the amount of gear both battalions and individuals carried (for example, company tents were to be left behind at Surprise Hill), nevertheless, a huge convoy of ox waggons was gathered together – sufficient to carry at least ten days' supplies. The main portion of Buller's force was to advance, under Buller's direct command, along the Ladysmith-Helpmakaar road with a diversionary force on the Ladysmith-Dundee road and a small force of mounted infantry with a battery of RHA (Royal Horse Artillery) out to the east of the range of hills under the command of Colonel Bethune.

The departure from Ladysmith also marked the beginning of many long marches that would last for nearly six months and take the regiments concerned many hundreds of miles from one side of the Transvaal to the other and back again. Hitherto Buller's men had not done much in the way of marching day after day. In the next five weeks they would march some 235 miles, fight several actions and endure the weather of their first South African winter. In many respects this was to be one of the triumphs for British arms – the ability to march onwards, fighting skirmishes along the way, and still remain fit at the end of it all for whatever the Boers – and the weather – found to throw at them. Officers and men alike learned to adapt to constantly living in the field, and both morale and discipline, certainly as far as the West Yorkshires were concerned, remained high. They did not indulge in such slovenly habits such as growing

beards or allowing boots to dull from lack of polish; not that this should indicate that this was a 'spit and polish' battalion – it wasn't, the West Yorkshires took simple pride in their appearance and their work habits. This is exemplified by some of Malcolm's photographs, for example one showing a kit inspection and another which offers a view of one young subaltern having his hair cut, both scenes taken deep in the veldt, South Africa's open grassland.

Malcolm recorded the events of this advance north in a new form – letters written in diary form which were intended to be circulated amongst his family and friends. Malcolm had at last realised that he simply could not communicate individually with all his relations, never mind his friends, and following the method adopted by his brother officer, George Crossman, Malcolm now wrote a general letter-diary with a covering note containing personal news to his parents. The first of these letter-diaries was written on leaves of paper torn from an-issue message book. There is one surprising omission from Malcolm's diaries and letters and that is the fact that by May, and perhaps as early as mid-April, he was in command of F Company. His company commander, Major Watts, had become so ill with dysentery that he had had to be sent down to Durban to recover. Major Watts was to return to duty on 1 June.

MAJOR FRY WHO SUCCEEDED WALTER KITCHENER AS COMMANDING OFFICER OF THE WEST YORKSHIRES

7 May *Reveille 5 am. Started (march) 7.20 am. Tents left behind at Surprise Hill under a guard. Men have two blankets each instead, and we have our valises and 20lb kits. Nice cool day, good march, went straight across country between Pepworth Hill and Intintanyone getting to Modder Spruit camp about 12 noon. Bivouacked in the same place as we halted on the way down from Elandslaagte on 17th April. Men erected shelters out of blankets and rifles…*

8 May *Outpost Companies returned at dawn. The Queens and Devons moved out a few miles to the east to support Lord Dundonald and his Cavalry Brigade. We and the East Surreys stayed in camp on our own. Waggons all packed and ready to move. Very hot day, we Officers lay under the waggons and slept and read what papers we could get.*

9 May *Up at 4.15 am. Pack waggons and the other three battalions go on, the baggage follows. We form the rear guard and are looking after the guns. We are part of a Force moving on Helpmakaar and composed of 2 Brigades of Infantry (2nd Brigade and Light Brigade) with the Cavalry Brigade under Lord Dundonald. three Field Batteries RA, one Howitzer Battery, three Pom-Poms, two 4.7-in Naval guns, four Naval 12-pounders. RE with Field Telegraph etc. and Supply Column with supplies. Moved along road for about 4 miles due East and then turned South and went another 4 miles. Halted and bivouacked for the night. Not much water to be had.*

10 May *Up at 4.15 am, marched on another 7 or 8 miles to a kopje the other side of Sunday's River, along dusty roads with bushes of mimosa thorn, and long grass either side. Plenty of kraals about and a good deal of vegetation. The crops of mealies, kaffir corn, big peas and small beans being brought in by the natives. Women go about with big baskets of corn on their heads.*

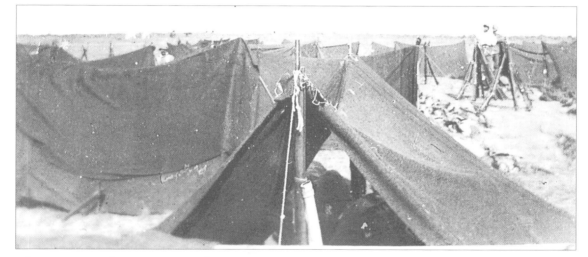

CAMPAIGNING IN THE BIGGARSBERG DURING A SOUTH AFRICAN WINTER COULD BE A WET AND COLD BUSINESS, ESPECIALLY WHEN TENTS WERE NOT AVAILABLE AND THE TROOPS HAD TO MAKE DO WITH BLANKETS. NOTE THAT THE BIVOUACS ARE SUPPORTED BY RIFLES.

Washed in Sunday's River and found my ivory soap was very useful. Discovered a big eagle-owl sitting on a nest in a cleft of the steep cliff of one of the river banks. Unfortunately no eggs.

Because the remainder of the men's kit had been left behind at Ladysmith, one of the two blankets issued to the men was used to make a bivouac (tent-like covering) while the top-coat was the greatcoat. Malcolm describes in a letter written to his mother on 11 May:

On these occasions I may tell you, as there are no tents, the men who have now two blankets apiece on account of the extreme cold at night make a 'lean-to' like this out of blankets and

rifles and then two or three of them huddle together underneath the remaining blanket. We officers have our valises and manage to keep fairly warm and comfortable. Yesterday we came on about 14 miles along a very dusty road at a good smart pace to where we are now and found that Lord Dundonald's Cavalry was here before us and had made a big camp and the RE and supplies were here also. Today we are moving on to the other side of Waschbank River another 8 or 10 miles march. All this I suppose is so that we act in conjunction with Lord Roberts and while he is busy the other side we may keep the Boers fairly busy this side. I am writing this at the chilly hour of 6 am (the weather is now delightfully mild) while we are waiting to move off but I don't know when it will be posted. I hope in time for this week's mail.

11 May *Reveille by Whistle at 4.45 am as bugles are not allowed to be blown till further orders. Wrote letter to Mother while waiting to start. We are the leading regiment and move off 6.25 am. Went on another 8 or 9 miles to the Waschbank River and bivouacked on plain near Klippoort. Found the Cavalry were already in camp when we arrived. RE mend the road where necessary and put up telegraph line as we go along. Country is now bare, open veldt with the Biggarsberg in the distance and Job's Kop to the south of us. We are in touch with the enemy. 5 Companies out on Outpost Duty, mine, F Company, is one of them. Boers snipe a little just before dark. They have set fire to the grassy veldt all in front of us which keeps burning nearly all night. Rather a cold night, brought out blanket bag and waterproof sheets but did not sleep much.*

THE WEST YORKSHIRE SIGNALLERS WORKING WITH FLAGS AND SOUNDERS

12 May *Returned from Outpost Line at 6.15 am. fatigue parties bringing out rations, rum and breakfast at 5 am and taking back greatcoats and blankets. Started marching 6.45 am. As ground is so open we move in column of Companies. Moved East towards Helpmakaar, Job's Kop still to our South. Bivouacked for the night at Vermaak's Kraal Farm, great difficulty in getting water… Each battalion finding its own Outposts, 3 Companies of ours out.*

13 May *Started 6.30 am, 2nd Brigade still in front. Queens and Devons lead, we are third. Soon after we advance the Boers open fire with 9-pounders from the Biggarsberg and shell our baggage and supply column but luckily not much damage is done. Naval guns reply. Our Naval guns are now manned by the RA, the Naval detachment having gone back to their ships. The TMI [Thorneycroft's Mounted Infantry] take a big hill near Uithoek's farm, BMI [Bethune's Mounted Infantry] are on the hills south of this and near Pomeroy and away to Greytown. 2nd Brigade advances up the hill TMI are on and push on to a hill in front, the Boers retiring before us, landing us now right on top of the Biggarsberg. Our guns soon come round and an artillery dual ensues until dusk. Our pom-poms take on their pom-poms and our Field Batteries take on their 9-pounders. Grand fun. Heard a day or two later that we wounded 2 or 3 Boers with our pom-poms and they think it unfair of us to use them ! 3 Companies on Outposts, F one of them. Bright moon all night and rather pleasant but did not sleep much.*

14 May *Rejoined battalion from Outposts at 7.30 am and formed up with Brigade in Quarter Column near the road. Two 4.7-in guns came up to crest line at dawn but did not fire. Cavalry advanced up the Helpmakaar road at dawn. Devons lead, we are*

next. Passed by Boer trenches and gun-pits, a few shells knocking about. Helpmakaar thoroughly looted by the Boers. Telegraph forms and odds and ends lying about the roads. Very unpleasant, hot, dusty march. Halted for the night at Pieter's Farm about half way to Dundee. The pursuit was checked for a bit near Helpmakaar and the RHA came into action but Boers soon retired and there was no further check. Good, level road all along the top of Biggarsberg, quite flat and covered with good grass and trees in places. Boers have set grass alight all along, making march very unpleasant. A wounded Boer, Boer prisoner and family left at Pieter's farm. Waggons arrive before dark. Very heavy dew at night. One of our Companies guarding guns.

15 May Brigade move off by bugle call, Devons still the leading Battalion. We march second. Long march of nearly twenty miles to Dundee over burnt veldt and dusty roads. We came to a steep hill half way through the march where the waggons stuck and we halted for some time. Quarter-hour halts at the end of each hour's march by Brigade bugle call. Rather done when we arrived at Dundee at about 2.30pm but there is plenty of water, taps put up at every hundred yards. We bivouac on the same ground as the Dublin Fusiliers were on when they were shelled early in the war, close to Impati Mountain. A few Europeans left in Dundee, but the place has a very deserted look, the houses all ransacked and some smashed up a bit. Waggons with great-coats, blankets, valises etc came in about 9 pm.

16 May Rested for the day at Dundee. Finished sketch of our route from Ladysmith to Dundee. Wrote home. This was a short letter to his father in which the only comment of significance was: Just think what a difference this kind of fighting is. We have come nearly 80 miles in the last week and only 15 casualties in the whole force.

Malcolm heavily underscored the address on his letter, Dundee, which says much about his delight at their success.

LIEUTENANT PENNELL'S MAXIM GUN WAS NOW MOUNTED ON WHEELS AND DRAWN BY A PAIR OF HORSES

Our drums play reveille. 10 Boer prisoners brought in and handed over to our guard. 2 German doctors are handed over to us and an Officer's Guard is put over them. Mess Sergeant brings in six chickens and a duck taken from a farm en route and we have a great feed.

They took something of a risk getting these supplies, as General Buller had absolutely prohibited any looting of abandoned farms. Buller was utterly opposed to Lord Roberts's policy of burning Boer farms, in the hope that this would force them to sue for peace. Buller reckoned that this would simply harden the Boers' attitudes and only serve to lengthen the war. It was only after Buller had left South Africa later in the year that the men in his command found themselves sacking farms, destroying crops and rounding up Boer families and their livestock.

The Mess buys some sacks of flour from the town and our Tommy cook bakes some most excellent loaves. Did I tell you that our black cook 'Sambo' or 'Mr Roper' as he liked to be called, left us when we got back to Surprise Hill. The shelling of the camp at Elandslaagte

ISSUING RUM TO CELEBRATE THE QUEEN'S BIRTHDAY, AT NEWCASTLE 24 MAY 1900

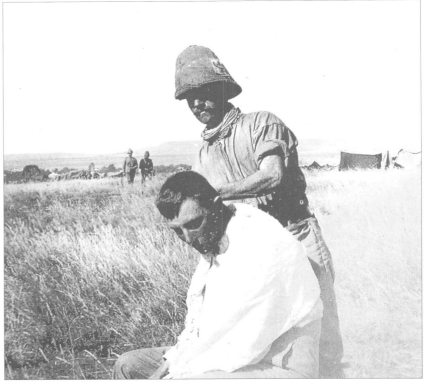

'GET YOUR HAIR CUT, SIR!' REGIMENTAL BARBER AT WORK ON THE VELDT

was too much for him - 'Me no like shells' he said and went off with his savings and now he is in rather a good berth somewhere down country I believe.

At this point, Malcolm ends the narrative in his first letter-diary and takes up the account in his second letter-diary which he compiled in Standerton, in the Transvaal, on 4 July:

17 May   Started 7 am. 4th Brigade in front. Good road along by the Railway. Reached Dannhauser about 2 pm. Waggons not in till dark. Sang songs round a fire – the Padre was in good form!

18 May   Started 4.45 am in the dark. Started late by mistake and had to go at a tremendous pace to catch up. 2nd Brigade again leading. Good hard roads and not very hilly, men marched well. My Company marched in step all the way and eventually entered Newcastle whistling and singing songs. Road bridge at Ingagane is intact but the Railway bridge smashed by the Boers. Entered Newcastle abut 5 pm. A great many Europeans left, all

cheering and waving flags etc. An enterprising photographer snaps us marching in. Very few of our men fell out, only three of my Company, two of them attending Hospital. Sang songs round a fire till the wagons turned up about 9 pm.

19 May   Reveille 6 am. 4th Brigade and Divisional Head Quarters move on at 7 am to Ingogo. Cavalry reported to be at Laing's Nek and find some Boers still on Majuba and round Charlestown. We had a quiet day in camp and cleaned up and had a good wash. Battalion bathed in Nkandu River just below Newcastle road bridge. Captain Jennings of the

GRETTON ENJOYS A BATH

DR COLLIER GETS SOME OF HIS CLOTHES DRY AFTER A DOWN-POUR

Queens came over and explained how Queens had so few men falling out on march. The Boers reported to be hard at work entrenching Laing's Nek

20 May, Sunday *Reveille 6.30 am, lovely morning. Church Parade 9.15 when Mr Drake gave us a good sermon, taking as an example of 'repentance' a mounted man riding on the windward side of troops and covering them in dust. The Queens leave for Ingogo. Made a fire by Mess and sang songs.*

21 May *Battalion parade 8.30 am. CO inspected Company's boots etc and then made a speech on marching, water, boots etc. Filled in my diary as far as possible. D E F G and H Companies on Outposts 4.30 pm. G & H Companies sent out late beyond Newcastle. Had a very intricate bit of ground to watch, all full of dongas and holes. Moon did not rise till 12.20 during latter part of my watch. Slept fairly well in spite of cold.*

22 May *At Newcastle. Returned from Outposts 6.30 am. Chilly morning, windy but sunny. Porch and Grant-Dalton go out shooting and get 7 doves and 4 pigeons. Finished my letters and diary up to Dundee. F Company played H at football but was beaten 5-0. 4 of our team were [absent] in hospital and we were rather handicapped. Report that 66 men of Bethune's Mounted Infantry were captured in Transvaal territory at Vryheid.*

23 May *Nice day. Had a ripping bathe in the NKandu River, sunned ourselves on a rock. Left my camera behind and nearly lost it. Crossman and Boyall went out shooting. Sent off my Letter-Diary and sketch to Mother and the eggs to Bertie.*

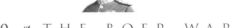

The Army Field Post Offices handled spectacular masses of mail during the war and maintained a record for delivering mail across the various theatres of operations that many modern mail-handling companies can only just emulate. In addition to the many letters and postcards that Malcolm sent back to Ireland were parcels contained such diverse items as birds' eggs, birds' nests, Zulu weapons and items of native clothing, as well as the occasional collection of dried and pressed flowers.

Malcolm had begun a letter to his brother Bertie on 7 May but did not get around to completing it until the 26th. Apart from discussing family affairs and making suggestions as to which regiment Bertie might join when he had completed his time at Sandhurst, Malcolm adds various comments of interest:

Dear Bertie,

I have owed you a letter for a long time but of course you see all home letters and don't I suppose expect very many all to yourself... I enclose a Transvaal stamp with the Dundee post-mark on it which I got in Ladysmith for 4/6d. I am not quite sure the Dundee part was not put on in Ladysmith or Durban but that is quite a trifle !

I sent home a few eggs for you the other day. Winter has set in now and I don't think I shall get any more. 4 of them are quail's eggs, 2 are pigeons or doves, one something like a sandmartin's, one is a weaver bird's and I don't know what the others are. Nearly all the small birds that build in the reeds and bushes by river-banks are weaver-birds of sorts, at least they all build that style of nest. I could have got some more but I did not think it worth while. I found a raven's nest one day, but it was in a prickly mimosa thorn tree, one mass of huge spiders' webs, on the side of a kopje and there were enormous iron-stone boulders underneath so I did not climb up nor my 'pal' either.

OFFICERS' SERVANTS AT WORK IN THE OFFICER'S MESS

Yesterday was the Queen's Birthday but nothing particular happened. The GOC suggested the best way of spending the day was to put in a record day of mending the railway line. The Boers have destroyed all the railway bridges and culverts all the way up and deviations have to be made which of course takes some time, and I suppose some unfortunates put in a little extra in honour of Her Majesty, but they did not worry us. It is very lucky this is the dry season and we shall have no more rain for months to come, or the deviations over the spruits and dongas would be useless. The men got an extra issue of rum, cheese and bacon yesterday, however, which was much more to their liking. We have been playing off the Company football matches for the Challenge Shield whenever we get more or less settled in a camp and yesterday the final tie was played and there was great excitement, the game eventually ending 2-0. The ground was fairly level but a bit rough. We got fatigue parties to work and had all the grass burnt where the ground was to be and the Pioneers put up some goal posts (made out of ration wood with a piece of wire for cross-bar) and flags (made out of Government flannelette intended for cleaning rifles). Bare patches of rock appear all over the ground which makes it rather uncomfortable to fall on. The rock is rather peculiar about here. It is still I think the same old iron-stone but instead of being in loose rocks and boulders it is in huge slabs all eaten away in kind of craters but level with the General surface of the ground.

Talking about iron-stone, I have told you before I think that all our beautiful compasses which cost such a lot are absolutely useless owing to the iron-stone and nobody ever thinks of using one. We have to go by sun, moon, and stars to find North; but we have Government maps of these parts now and it is not very difficult to find where you are. The whole place being open veldt common landmarks like hills, roads, spruits, bridges, etc., are very easily seen and besides, nearly every farmhouse is marked on the map, there being about two to every five miles or so of country. The atmosphere is as I suppose you have heard most wonderfully clear but it takes the cake just here. The Drakensburg mountains are now 10 miles away but there is nothing but an open plain between them and us and you would not think the distance was more than a mile. It is a queer country and no mistake. Thank goodness they say there are no more positions like that at Colenso, and there isn't a position we can't get round without the slightest difficulty with the force we have got now.

These Colonial Corps (BMI, TMI, SALH etc.) had rather a come-down the other day if the tale we heard be true. They are always boasting what they have done and what they could do if they got the chance and now we hear that 66 of them have been captured near Vryheid in the Transvaal. You would hardly believe how badly off we are for news. We have not seen a local newspaper since we left Surprise Hill, though they were good enough to let us have up a whacking great mail yesterday and today (two mails rolled into one) and we have had no reliable information of any sort as to what is going on the other side or indeed anywhere outside Natal. We don't know if Mafeking is relieved yet or what Roberts is doing or anything and I suppose they have it all in the newspapers at home regularly every day.

Saturday 26th. This morning the Newcastle road is black with troops and wagons and clouds of dust are flying all down the road. Hildyard's Regiments (the remains of General Warren's Division) are coming up to join us and he is bringing with him the 4 big 5in guns we had at Elandslaagte and 3 more Field Batteries and some Naval 12 pounders. They say the Railway will be repaired up to here in a day or two but until that happens and we get some more supplies up I don't suppose we shall advance. It is perfectly fiendish trying to write today – as you see I have made a most awful mess of this page already. The reason is there is a gale of a wind blowing and the Mess tent is a very airy concern, the wind getting under the waterproof sheet and swirling about all over the place and sending letters and everything else flying.

I wonder if this will be my last letter to you from South Africa or at all events Natal! There are different rumours every day about the war coming to an end and Kruger wiring home to ask for peace and all the rest of it. We live on rumours, facts and lies as if we were besieged in a town. I must stop now so goodbye and good luck,

your affectionate brother,

THE OFFICERS' MESS WITH THEIR MESS WAGGON AND BOXES OF CLOTHING

Malcolm's diary goes on:

27 May, Sunday Communion 8 am, Parade Service 9.15 am. General Buller and Staff attended the Brigade service and our Drums played. Bathed in the river before lunch, water rather nice but we had not a very good place as crowds of Tommies and Blacks were washing. Naval contingent comes into camp, also the other Brigade of Hildyard's Division. Strong wind still blowing, Sunny. CO read out an order to the whole battalion about looting after Church Parade.

28 May Started 7 am for Ingogo. Very good cool march. Road very hilly. Passed DeWet's farm, Artillery got lemons from farm. Dust very thick on roads. Waggons came in about 3 pm. Bivouacked close to Ingogo Monument put up to men of 3rd King's Royal Rifles killed in '81. Remainder of 4th Brigade and 2nd Division Head Quarters move on to Inkwelo Mountain, Lord Dundonald in a hollow by the river. [The Battalion War Diary tells us: Boers holding from Botha's Pass to Utrecht and Laing's Nek with about 5,000 men]. Pougwana 'Long Tom' fired at 4th Brigade in afternoon and wounded three men with his shrapnel. Our Naval 12-pounders replied but could not reach. D & E Companies on Outposts, B Company on Inlying Picquet goes out by guns.

29 May White frost on our clothes and water frozen after a bitterly cold night. The Boer 'Long Tom' on Pougwana is at it again. He fires shrapnel timed at 27 seconds. Shells

can be plainly seen bursting in mid-air. Naval 4.7-in guns reply and do some good shooting, silencing the Boer gun though the Boer gun is back in action later. Parties of Boers working at a gun epaulment on Inkweloane. Naval 12-pounders fire at them but cannot reach. 5-in siege gun fires and gets range in two shots, scattering the Boers left and right. Watched them through my telescope.

30 May   Night not so cold. Quiet day in camp. Flag of truce goes out to Boers. Our guns do not fire all day. Long Tom on Pougwana fires a few shots in the afternoon. My Company on Outposts. Starlight night and a very cold wind. issue of rum. Strong wind had been blowing through camp all day making a horrid dust. Mess run out of whisky and jam. Put on all available clothes for Outposts, 2 pairs socks, 2 pairs drawers etc.

31 May   Returned from Outposts 6.15 am. Awfully hot day. No firing on either side. Parties of Boers busy lighting grass fires near the Buffalo River. Some at work on epaulment on Pougwana. CO gets Defaulters to build him a circular wall enclosure to sleep in etc.

1 June   Draft of about 100 men, mostly of the 3rd Battalion, join us with Captain Smith (from the Militia 4th Battalion) in charge… My Company is Inlying Picquet. Holds trenches in front of guns.

THE REGIMENTAL POLICE

2 June   Returned to camp about 6.30 am. No firing on either side. 10.45 am Parade for fitting on serge clothing. Every man except last draft now gets a new suit of serge, the old suit of khaki drill being burnt or if good enough, washed, and sent to Base. Tents come up on a waggon but are not given out. Rumour Buller goes out to see Boer Generals offering to send all back to their farms if they will hand in arms. Armistice on till 12 pm 5th June.

3 June, Sunday   Church Parade 8.45. The Drums accompanied us.

4 June   General Hildyard called. His sister had given £50 on behalf of widows and orphans of the 2nd West York Regiment and he added £25 more. Similar amounts had been given to the other regiments of the Brigade. The money was from the proceeds of a War Hymn, the words of which were written by General Hildyard's sister. Made a sketch of the Boer position and sent it to The Graphic.

Dear Mr Editor,

I am enclosing herewith a rough sketch of the positions of the troops operating round here. As I write, the Boers hold a long position ranging from Botha's Pass (just out of the left of sketch) taking in Majuba, Laing's Nek and Pougwana Mountain, to 7 or 8 miles to the East of this Hill (just out of the right of this sketch). We have a Brigade (Light Brigade, now under General Cooper, late C.O. of the Dublin Fusiliers) and General Clery with the 2nd Division Headquarters, two 4.7-

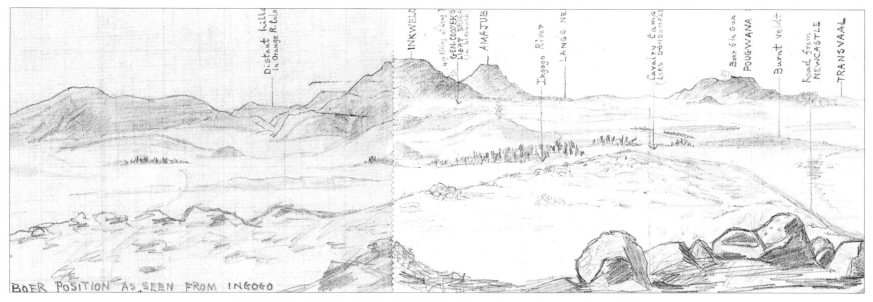

BOER POSITION AS SEEN FROM INGOGO

SKETCH OF BOER POSITIONS AS SEEN BY MALCOLM RIALL FROM THE INGOGO MONUMENT, 1 JUNE 1900.

inch guns, 12-pounders, Field Artillery etc at Mount Pleasant Farm. Lord Dundonald is encamped by the Ingogo River where I have shown in the sketch. The 2nd Brigade (late General Hildyard's) is now under Col Hamilton of the Queens and scattered about near the Ingogo Monument (put up in memory of the 200 odd men of the 3rd Battalion King's Royal Rifles who fell near this spot in 1881). We have Field and Howitzer batteries, Field Hospital etc up here too. General Hildyard's Division is at De Wet's Farm, half way between here and Newcastle, and General Lyttleton's Division is round about Newcastle itself. So you see we are pretty well scattered about the country. The weather is now getting extremely cold and we have not had our tents since we left Ladysmith. We have of course extra blankets and the men make very snug bivouacs out of them.

5 June   Cold morning. Bitterly cold wind. ASC issue bread once again. 2nd Brigade canteen comes up and we get Golden Syrup etc. Boers have decided to hold their position and fight it out. Consequently at 3.15 pm we get sudden orders for half the Battalion to move to a hill nearer Ingogo Station. General Buller moves his camp down near the Ingogo River and we are guarding his camp. My Company is on Outposts. Cuthell goes to hospital. Wrote to father.

Most of the letter is taken up with a description of Malcolm's recent experiences and is not reproduced here, however his comments on the climate are of interest:

My dear Father,
    ...The first night we got here we had a sharp frost, and we have had extremely cold nights with a cutting wind ever since. The men manage to keep very snug and warm in their bivouacs which they make out of blankets and don't feel it very much I believe, but it is different with us Officers as we have our valises only on the bare ground and they don't keep the wind out much. I have dug a hole for my valise and put a sangar round my head and it is not so bad, but on Picquet where one can't get these

THE MACHINE GUN IN ACTION

luxuries you feel the night wind a good deal...

Malcolm's father is most unlikely to have had much sympathy for Malcolm's feelings of discomfort. Arthur Riall had spent years at sea serving in the Royal Navy aboard both sailing ships and the earliest steam ships, where life would have been perpetually wet and miserable – and incredibly dirty when the time came to 'coal ship'.

Then the advance begins again and with it comes another skirmish:

8 June   *Moved off 7 am towards Botha's Pass. 10th and 11th Brigades are to take Botha's Pass, 2nd Brigade in Support. Halted near Yellowboom Farm. General Hildyard and the guns are on the hill just ahead of us, 10th and 11th Brigades further up road towards the Pass. 5-in gun back at Ingogo keeps up fire on Inkweloane. Took a snapshot of our 'Pom-Poms'. About 12 noon all guns bombard the Drakensberg Ridge and the Infantry advance. 2nd Brigade with Devons and West Yorks in firing line, East Surreys in Support, deploy and attack the steep slopes of Inkweloane. Each regiment has two companies extended to six paces in the firing line. F company is in support of the leading left company. The Regiment is on the extreme right of the line except for some Mounted Infantry and RHA who are scrambling about on their horses. Hill most frightfully steep. We have to halt every few yards near the top. Luckily the Boers are not holding the ridge and it is only when we are right on top that they commence fire. They have two or three pom-poms which give us rather a nasty time as there is no cover, the ground is quite open. We reply with rifle and maxim gun fire, the latter is the tripod pattern which is carried in pieces on a horse. Towards dusk the RHA Battery came into action on our right and fired a few shots. The Boers, about an hour before dusk, made huge grass fires which spread at a tremendous rate and by this means got their guns away behind the smoke in safety. The attack was evidently unexpected from this quarter as all the [Boer] trenches lined the ridge facing Ingogo.*

Our Casualties were: Grant-Dalton hit in two places, one man killed, and four or five others wounded. Other regiments probably nil. My company and one other on Outposts. No coats or blankets and a perishing cold night. Dug trenches to keep ourselves warm. Fog and mist most of the night.

ONE OF OUR POM-POMS ABOUT TO TAKE PART IN THE BATTLE OF BOTHA'S PASS

"It had all gone rather well and everyone felt really rather pleased. After the nightmarish campaign trying to get across the Tugela River, Buller's excellent handling of the campaign to get into the Biggarsberg, and dislodge the Boers from extremely well-prepared positions, restored both morale and the troops faith in their commanders. Success, they say, breeds success and so it was now as Buller swept all before him."

As you will see that far from being 'away from all the fighting' as you rather unkindly put it, I am always well up in it, for whenever there is fighting the Brigadier must be there to conduct operations, and where he goes I go too. I have no ardent desire to be at the head of the Advance Guard every day in order to be potted at, I can tell you, still when the time comes I am no coward, but at the same time I see no use in running unnecessary risks. If I wanted to be shot I should like to have been shot in some big engagement at the beginning of the war and not.

Eleven

SOMETHING OFF THE SLATE... UNION JACKS OVER MAJUBA

Opposite: The West Yorkshires marching through Volksrust and on to Charlestown

Buller kept Lord Roberts informed of his progress northwards, and doubtless Roberts was delighted that Buller was at last showing some energy. Roberts was probably equally delighted that Buller had been able to re-open the railway system, thus permitting the use of the tracks from Durban through Ladysmith onwards to Pretoria thereby relieving the strain on the supply lines from Cape Town. But Roberts had not forgotten Buller's hesitant handling of his troops along the Tugela and issued instructions to Buller that he was not to attempt to turn the Boers out of their trenches around Laing's Nek and Majuba. The cable with these orders from Roberts arrived soon after Buller had achieved those objectives with almost no casualties. Indeed, one of the most remarkable aspects of Buller's thrust through the Biggarsberg was the very low casualty rate. Most emotive of all, of course, was taking Majuba which, once within the British lines, became a massive 'tourist' attraction. British troops, both officers and men, scrambled up the steep slopes of the hill to view for themselves the site of a battle which had become part of the British Army's mythology. For the West Yorkshires and Malcolm Riall it was business as usual, even if taking Majuba added a touch of spice to life.

9 June *Clouds did not lift till about 10 am. Breakfast and rations are sent out to us then. Buller and staff passed by. Returned to the Battalion, which was bivouacking about 500 yards away, about 11 am. Not moving on till tomorrow. Went round Boer trenches. A good deal of loot was left in their laager. We bring across a few tents which are given to the last draft to sleep in as they'd had not had the serge clothing issued to them yet. The waggons came in before dark and we got coats, blankets etc. and a good dinner ! I dug a deep hole for myself as the ground was soft and put my valise in and had quite a good night. Some of the Mail brought along with the waggons. I got two parcels, one from Father with Chocolate Food. This last was quite the saving of me, I set to at once! A flock of sheep were driven in at dusk.*

10 June *Started 7 am. Crossed the border into Orange River Colony. 10th and 11th Brigades in front. We are Rear Guard. Halted 11.30 to 2 pm for lunch. Advance unopposed. A good deal of the grass is burnt and it is very unpleasant marching. Crossed Glans-Vlei, a tributary of the Klip River, about 5 pm and we are now in the Transvaal. Bivouacked for the night, waggons in in good time as the roads were good. Very cold night, hard frost.*

11 June *Very clear Divisional Orders issued by General Hildyard and the Programme is: 2nd and*

A BOER SEARCHLIGHT CAPTURED IN VOLKSRUST, 13 JUNE 1900

10th Brigades to attack Alleman's Nek, 10th Brigade on right and 2nd Brigade on left. 11th Brigade looking after baggage etc. 2nd Brigade moves off a short distance at 7 am and forms up in Quarter Column. Mounted Infantry and Artillery in front. Artillery fire a few shots about 8 am. Shortly afterwards the whole Column advances towards Alleman's Nek, attack commences about 2 pm. The Boers hold the kopjes on either side of the Nek and are well entrenched. You will see from my sketches that the Queens led the 2nd Brigade in the attack on the left kopje, the Dorsets led the 10th Brigade on the right kopje. The Boers brought one gun and two or three pom-pom into action against us but it was not for long. All our available guns opened fire on both kopjes: 2 pom-poms, 3 field batteries, howitzer battery, naval 12-pounders, Naval 4.7-in guns etc. the biggest and best bombardment I have witnessed since Pieter's Hill. Boers hold the right kopje in some force and are well concealed behind rocks, occupying trenches in the Nek as well. Dorsets have a pretty stiff time of it, but clear the Boers out with fixed bayonets in fine style.

Queens are awfully slow in attack on left kopje. Only about half a dozen Boers sniping from the top but we do not get up till long after the Dorsets and no Boers left then. Bivouacked for the night on the Nek. Waggons came up about 8pm. Very cold night. Grass fires look very pretty in the dark.

12 June *Started 10 am as escort to the guns and baggage. Passed by some dead Boers at*

'HAIRY MARY', A RAILWAY LOCOMOTIVE COVERED IN HEAVY ROPES TO PROTECT IT FROM BOER RIFLE FIRE; ANOTHER INNOVATION BY THE ROYAL NAVY

the side of the road who had been burnt by grass fires during the night. Mounted Infantry and RHA in front, they fire at retreating Boers beyond railway. Bivouacked 4pm near Joubert's Farm. Got some ducks and geese from a Boer farm. Passed by General Buller and staff marching in, they seemed very pleased with things generally.

13 June Started 7.30 am for Charlestown. Passed through Volksrust. Took some photos. Fairly large town, nice houses. Most of the inhabitants left behind, houses not destroyed. Good hard, wide roads. Got into Charlestown about 1pm. Nearly all houses, Railway Station etc destroyed. My Company on Outposts again. Veldt all burnt. Cold night.

With time for other activities besides marching and the occasional skirmish with the Boers, Malcolm soon took pen to paper for a longer letter to his father, the greater part of which had to do with letters and gifts sent and received. As he had already sent details of his activities home in the form of his letter-diary there was little of real news to add in the letter,

"...I started this letter at Ingogo and was unable to finish it as we 'trekked' next day and now it is the 16th and we are settled fairly comfortably at Charlestown after doing a little fighting in between times. You will see from this long list of letters, parcels, papers etc sent to me that it would take a very considerable time to answer every letter and thank every individual person for everything they send as soon as I get it,

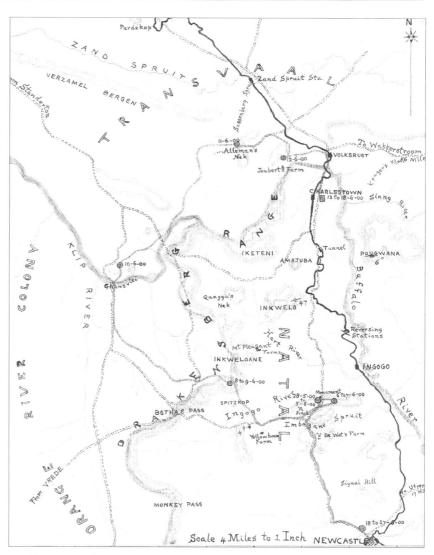

MALCOLM RIALL'S MAP OF NORTHERN NATAL SHOWING THE WEST YORKSHIRE'S LINE OF ADVANCE

especially when a good many of the things come direct from shops with no explanation whatsoever...

I can hardly realise it but I am sitting on a chair, at a table, in a HOUSE !! At long, long last we are allowed to put up tents and the Regiment is encamped in the middle of Charlestown. The little Government houses are all deserted and empty and though we officers sleep and live in tents, we use one of the houses as an Officers Mess, ante-room etc and as we have rousted out a fairly good piano out of one of the houses we have a pretty good time on the whole. I only hope they will leave us here for a week or so and give us a rest. I am sure we deserve it !

I scrambled up to the top of Majuba yesterday, saw the lovely views from the top and all the Boer trenches, and things of interest and took several snapshots. I rode my little pony about half-way up but after that it was almost a precipice and I walked the rest of the way. I shall have a lot to tell you when I get back shan't I ? I shall be able to understand the Boer War of '81 better now too. A great number of men went up the Hill today and I hear they tried to carry the top of the hill away with them ! I must confess to having taken away two bits of stone from the top myself.

I found a solitary little Iris in bloom near the top of Majuba yesterday much to my surprise. The whole hill had been burnt by the Boers and this was I suppose the only flower up there. I will enclose it in this letter if I remember. It was very pretty and bright when I found it, but is not much to look at now."

MAJUBA. BRITISH SOLDIERS VIEW THE SCENE OF THE BRITISH DEFEAT AT THE HANDS OF THE BOERS IN 1881

Drummer Goodwin noted:

"...I suppose we will stop here (Charlestown) about two or three days for a rest and we might get a bit of bread in a day or two all being well and we had a bit of a sing song at night and the Adjutant played a piano that we got out of a house close by our camp. All quiet regarding the enemy.."

15 June *Warm day. Bathed and got hair cut. Great coats have got into an awful muddle and are sorted out. Rode up Majuba with Pennell and Barlow. Took several photos. Met lots of officers and men up there and round about. Trenches on hill very fine. Got back about 5 pm. Large waggon convoys coming up over the Nek, about 200 waggons unloaded. Party detailed to pick up telegraph wire along Alleman's Nek route report Boers still about that neighbourhood.*

16 June *At Charlestown. Awfully cold night with a hard frost. Stand to arms at 5.30 am. Freezing cold. General Hildyard goes to Wakkerstroom, takes over town and Boers give themselves up. East Surreys move to Volksrust. We would have been taken but the greater part of the Battalion was on Majuba [sightseeing!]. Cold day with a biting wind.*

14 June. *At Charlestown. Returned from Outposts 8am in thick fog; leaving observation posts out. We have a small house for the Mess. Tents arrive and we pitch camp. Padre and I rig out a room in house 13 as a sitting room. Some Officers visit Majuba. 7.30m Concert outside one of houses. We raise a piano. Padre, Richards, Barlow, S/M Roberts sing songs. Drums play. Great evening. Awfully cold. Very glad of tents.* [Battalion War Diary states: 'tents pitched for the first time since May 8th'.]

17 June, Sunday *As General Hildyard has moved off, our Brigade takes over all Outposts. 6 Companies, A B C D E & F, on duty in consequence. Church Parade 9 am. Very cold and a beastly night. Picquet made a bivouac out of water-proof sheets and barbed wire. Rained first part of night, then moon came out, then thick fog towards morning. Roberts reported to be in big fight 18 miles from Pretoria.*

CROSSING THE VAAL RIVER FOR THE FIRST TIME, TOP, LEFT AND ABOVE, AND ENTERING STANDERTON 24 JUNE 1900

Twelve

STANDERTON AND QUEEN VICTORIA'S SCARF

Opposite: Outside Dundee - part of a Boer Commando awaits the British advance

Having dislodged the Boers from their various positions astride the Biggarsberg with almost contemptuous ease, but without having brought them to a decisive battle, Buller, like Lord Roberts, had no very clear idea as to what should be done next. Where were the Boers? Would they now give up the unequal contest, especially as Roberts and Buller had between them occupied all the major Boer towns and settlements? Until these problems could be resolved Buller was ordered by Roberts to suspend his advance and go on the defensive, digging in wherever his troops had arrived.

The West Yorkshires, with the remainder of the 2nd Brigade, settled down to forming a defensive perimeter around Standerton and to repairing the ever-vital railway line. For the West Yorkshires this was a period of tedium and yet hard work too. They were used as labourers, much to their disgust, to help create a railway deviation to a new bridge across the Vaal. The men were also employed in building sangars along the outpost line and in manning them. As time went on many of the units at Standerton

were moved away to new locations, and the work-load on the West Yorkshires steadily mounted until, at last, they too moved on. Although Malcolm's diaries and letters are as detailed as ever for the next few weeks, apart from one minor skirmish, the main event of interest during this period was the presentation of a scarf crocheted by Queen Victoria to one of the senior NCOs of the battalion. Thus we may quickly move on to the next phase of the war in which the West Yorkshires were involved – chasing De Wet.

However tedious life might have been in Standerton, the war was still going on as the events of 30 July showed:

30 July *Four of our Companies with four Companies from East Surrey and Queens and two 5-in guns etc. move off about 3.30 by train towards Vlaklaagte to surround and capture a small commando 300 strong located on Joubert's Kop. The Boers saw the movement and had withdrawn before our troops arrived and occupied another position. This was shelled by the artillery and the Infantry was deployed for an attack. Our men burn laagers and the Boers scoot.* [Battalion War Diary states: '300 sacks and a lot of ammunition

KIT AND AMMUNITION INSPECTION

was destroyed. Infantry returned to camp, after a march of about 25 miles, about 6pm'.] *Windy and dusty day.*

This had been a frustrating, inconclusive action and one which was very much a fore-taste of things to come. Amongst the various minor skirmishes and patrols described by Malcolm as taking place around Standerton comes the first mention of a new British tactic: farm burning. It will be recalled that General Buller was opposed to this policy, and would not permit the slightest misconduct by the troops under his command with regard to civilian property, be it British, Boer or native. In contrast Lord Roberts had from early on decided that farm burning and running off livestock were acceptable policies and, from this moment on, all troops in South Africa were to be encouraged to do all they could to dislocate the Boer agricultural economy by burning farms and crops and herding up all livestock.

'Pay Day'

Queen Victoria's interest and concern for her soldiery is legendary and is of course most readily noted by her institution of the award of the Victoria Cross. As noted earlier, the Queen took a keen interest in the progress of the war and in the care and comfort of the soldiery. Less well known is her personal involvement in crocheting eight woollen scarves which were sent out to South Africa and given to four NCOs in British infantry battalions and four private soldiers in colonial units. A recent paper on the subject provides much of the detail regarding the recipients but did not reveal why four particular regular battalions of the British Army came to be chosen to receive this unusual gift. One of the battalions selected was the 2nd Battalion, The West Yorkshire Regiment, and the scarf – or muffler as it is termed in Malcolm's diary – was given to Colour Sergeant Kingsley.

Queen Victoria received letters from one officer in whom she had a personal interest – Prince Christian Victor – her grandson. He sailed to South Africa in November 1899 hoping to join his regiment, the King's Royal Rifle Corps. They were, however, trapped in Ladysmith and, eventually, Prince Christian Victor was appointed to the staff of General Hildyard who commanded the 2nd Brigade through the early phases of the war. The prince wrote regularly to members of the Royal family, including the Queen, during this period and it is likely, though cannot be proved, that some passing reference of his to the bitterly cold nights motivated the making of the scarves. What is certain is that the scarves were sent to the prince by Queen Victoria with her instructions that they were to be given to a brave soldier from the ranks; it seems to have been left to the prince to decide which battalions should be thereby honoured. He selected the four infantry battalions of the 2nd Brigade with whom he had served through the heavy fighting to relieve Ladysmith: the Queens, West Yorkshires, East Surreys and Devons. He appears not to have been directly involved in actually presenting the scarves; in fact, at about this time, he left General Hildyard to join Lord Roberts as an ADC at Pretoria, where he died of enteric fever on 29 November 1900.

Whilst the presentation of the scarf was not recorded in the Battalion War Diary, Malcolm noted in his diary:

'7 August   *CO's parade 9 am, Queen's Muffler presented to Colour Sergeant Kingsley by the CO. Took photo of Kingsley by tin hut'.*

Later that day, after 'sudden orders' to move up the line had been cancelled, Malcolm wrote to his father:

We are off to Pretoria in the morning and have had camp struck and no end of fuss all day, so I am writing now in case I would not have time to write again before Mail day. We have had much the same routine of Outposts etc since last Mail, only the last few days have been a little stiffer than usual as some Companies of the East Surreys had to go down the line. Buller and staff and batteries, etc, and a large force left here the other day for Paardekop and thence to Middleburg I believe, and so of course we have to move from here also to take up the positions they have left and the Garrison of Standerton is reduced almost to nil. The Regiment is going to Pretoria they say, because Lord Roberts has taken so many troops away from there. I do hope we really go in the end and no counter-order comes for it would be great fun.

Some time ago Her Gracious Majesty sent out to her grandson, Prince Christian Victor, who as I think I told you, used to be on General Hildyard's staff as extra Brigade

Major when he had this Brigade, 4 woollen mufflers, knitted by herself with her initials worked small in one corner and these were to be given to 4 NCOs or men. The Prince kindly gave one to each Regiment of the 2nd Brigade. Today the CO gave away one to one of our Colour Sergeants, Colour Sergeant Kingsley by name, and a fine fellow. He is naturally very proud of himself. I took a photo of him today.

Malcolm's account is supported by another West Yorks diarist, Private W Sykes, who served with C Company:

"On the 7th we had a parade at 9 o'clock, this was in clean fatigue dress, when we got on parade the CO told us that the Queen had sent four mufflers which she had knitted [sic] herself to Prince Christian Victor and she said they was to be given to rank and file and Prince Christian elected to give them to the 2nd Brigade as the more deserving of them, one to each Regiment as he had done all his soldiering with the 2nd Brigade and in our Regiment Colour Sergeant Kingsley was presented with it. Afterwards three cheers for the Queen was given and an issue of whisky to drink the Queen's health which we did heartily."

The use of the word 'muffler' to describe the scarf seems to be peculiar to the West Yorkshires, the Devons' official records describe it as a scarf. Major Fry certainly continued to call it a muffler as can be seen from the letter he wrote on 7 August 1900 to Prince Christian Victor,

"My dear Prince,

I write in the name of the West Yorks to offer you our most grateful thanks for giving us one of the mufflers knitted [sic] by Her Majesty the Queen. I gave the muffler to Colour Sergeant Kingsley who is now one of the proudest and happiest of men in the Army. He has been in every engagement with the Regiment and at Spion Kop time he distinguished himself by the way he commanded his company when his Captain [Captain Ryall, who was not related to Malcolm Riall] was killed and the other officer of his company wounded. He is a most deserving man in every way and

a brave soldier. I have never seen such enthusiasm amongst the men as over this simple little gift. I think it brought home to them more thoroughly than they have ever realised before the real interest Her Majesty takes in Her soldiers.

We have just got orders to be in readiness to move to Heidelburg at very short notice so I must be off and issue orders. Please remember me to General Hildyard.

Yours sincerely, W. Fry."

During the Spion Kop operations the West Yorkshires had some very severe fighting on the left of Warren's force, particularly on the south-eastern slope of Tabanyama on 21 January. G Company, commanded by Captain Ryall, advanced so far in front of the general line that they had to remain isolated until nightfall and suffered heavy casualties. Captain Ryall was mortally wounded and brought under cover by Colour Sergeant Kingsley. After 2nd Lieutenant Barlow was wounded, Kingsley took command of G Company and steadily withdrew

COLOUR SERGEANT F KINGSLEY WITH HIS MUFFLER. STANDERTON, 7 AUGUST 1900.

his men to cover. These actions were cited by Colonel F W Kitchener, commanding 2nd West Yorkshires, who recommended Kingsley for the award of the Distinguished Conduct Medal.

Two of the Queen's scarves awarded to the regulars survive. One was the scarf awarded to Colour Sergeant Thomas Ferret, 2nd Battalion The Queen's Regiment, and is preserved in the collections of the Queen's Regiment in their museum at Clandon House, Guildford, Surrey. This provides us with some detail concerning the actual scarves. They were hand-crocheted in a pale khaki-coloured wool which is described as Berlin wool. Ferret's scarf is five feet long by nine inches wide and has a tassled fringe at each end of four inches. Embroidered into one end of the scarf is Queen Victoria's monogram; on Ferret's scarf this is worked in an over-hand stitch using red silk. Another scarf, that awarded to Colour Sergeant Clay of the East Surrey Regiment, is preserved in the Queen's Regimental Museum at Dover. Although Clay's scarf was crocheted in the same fashion as Ferret's, Clay's is slightly different as regards its dimensions, being four feet and ten inches long by eight inches wide, with tassles each end, similar to Ferret's, of four inches. The whereabouts of the scarves awarded to Colour Sergeant W Colclough of the Devonshire Regiment and that of Colour Sergeant Kingsley are unknown.

Thirteen
PRETORIA AND CHASING DE WET

Opposite: Marching down the road to Pretoria

The West Yorkshires would soon be on the move again, and this time their travels would take them to Pretoria – in a train, even if this meant being conveyed in open coal trucks – though they would first have to join in a hunt for the Boer leader De Wet which would involve much marching across open veldt. The Boers may have been losing some of the battles, and many men besides, but the war was far from being over; that this was the case was in no small measure due to the charismatic leadership of Christiaan De Wet, Boer farmer and politician turned soldier. Along with Smuts, Botha and De La Rey, De Wet emerged as a leading force in the Boer resistance to British arms, a fact soon recognised by Lord Roberts. Until now the British had been confronted by relatively static Boer opponents who were fighting defensive battles grouped together in large numbers. When the British either enforced a Boer withdrawal, or a rare surrender, the Boers simply fell back to new positions and the routine began again. With the capture of the major cities and the raising of sieges at Kimberley, Johannesburg and Mafeking, the Boer forces became increasingly splintered into smaller groups which, in theory, should have eased the problems confronting the British. In fact, the result was to allow the Boers greater freedom of mobility to attack the British wherever and whenever the opportunity allowed, with particular emphasis being placed on disrupting the railway and telegraph lines.

In the middle of July 1900 Christiaan De Wet provided the British with an object lesson in the new mode of warfare the Boers had adopted. Having failed to encircle and trap him within the Orange Free State, the British now pursued De Wet and his commandos into and across the Transvaal. The chase lasted for weeks and covered hundreds of miles. It was time too for Lord Herbert Kitchener to emerge from Lord Roberts' shadow by taking overall command. He now had to demonstrate his abilities in the field as an independent commander taking on a modern enemy, as opposed to the poorly equipped Sudanese at Omdurman. But cornering De Wet was not going to be easy, as Kitchener and his column commanders soon discovered for themselves.

8 August *Reveille 5am, breakfast 5.30am. Parade 6.30am. We have received orders to move by rail to Pretoria in two trains. Officers all packed in with their Companies in open coal trucks, 35 to a truck. Nice day, cold at first. A man fell off a truck going round a steep corner. Arrived Elandsfontein about 5pm, had tea… Started off again 5.30pm and arrived Krugersdorp 9pm. Men bivouacked in station yard and on trucks. Officers have dinner in luggage van and bed down in Station Master's hall. An issue of rum was given to the men who were very tired by the long journey in open trucks.*

MOVING ON – BY RAIL FOR A CHANGE

9 August *Reveille 4.30am. Had gun-fire tea* [a mug of tea laced with rum or brandy] *and started by train again 5.45am. Stop at Randfontein for breakfast and until line is clear. Detachments of 5th Fusiliers and City Imperial Volunteers* [CIV] *come along with us. Whole place is marked out into claims by white-painted posts. Start again 1.15pm. Section of 86th Howitzer Battery and Cavalry escort us on either side of the railway line. Arrive Blaubank station 3pm, other train close behind. Off loaded and pitched camp close to railway line. General Smith-Dorrien in command with Shropshire Light Infantry etc…*

One immediate effect of De Wet's cross-country dash was to completely disrupt the organisation of the various divisions and brigades. As both the Battalion War Diary and Malcolm's records show, the West Yorkshires were thrown in with troops they had never worked with before under a commander, Smith-Dorrien, who similarly had little knowledge of the men he was to command. Furthermore, the West Yorkshires would soon leave Smith-Dorrien to join yet another brigade – that commanded by Major-General Cunningham.

10 August *Remained the day at Blaubank station. Tents to be left behind when we move, kits to be reduced to 50lb and surplus kit sent back to Base. Trenches made round Outpost*

DRYING FEET AFTER CROSSING A STREAM

Line. Very windy. We Mess out in the open as we have no waggons and no shelter. Getting short of Mess provisions, especially butter and jam. KOSLI [King's Own Scottish Light Infantry] *and CIV leave in the evening for Welverdiend to try and cut off De Wet…*

11 August *4 Companies of West Yorkshires under Major Heigham left by train at 7.30. General Smith-Dorrien & Staff leave later. Major Fry in command at Blaubank. Formed a signal station on a railway truck and after breakfast got in touch with General Broadwood and Lord Kitchener, south of the railway. Kept very busy with messages between them and the CO and Lord Roberts. Wind awful, helio fell off railway truck and got smashed. Sudden order to move about 4pm. Packed all up, tents etc., G Company and sick go by train, remainder march about 17 miles to Welverdiend beside the railway line… Got into camp about 1.30am and pile arms behind the other 5 Companies who were already in. Got valises off trucks and slept well.* [Battalion War Diary: 'Lord Kitchener's column had also arrived during the day; force mainly composed of cavalry'.]

12 August, Sunday *Reveille 6am. Whole Company taken for fatigue duties; loading trucks etc… Marched about 10am in a northerly direction. Before start, Lord Kitchener came over to see us and chatted for some time. Marched about 16 miles, getting in 5pm. Had to cross a drift and took off boots, puttees and socks to wade it. Funny scene. Did not get kit* across till 9.30 but slept well then till reveille. It is reported that Lord Methuen has captured 1 gun and two ammunition waggons of De Wet's. [Battalion War Diary: 'crossing the drift caused so much delay that force bivouacked the other side for the night'.]

13 August   Rouse 2am, breakfast 2.30am, parade 3.30, but did not get well on the move till 4am. Roads not so bad, not so many stones but grass all burnt and about 10am the wind got up driving the dust etc. against us and it was most unpleasant, the men finding it very trying. The same 5 Companies of West Yorkshires follow KOSLI and Companies of CIV with Howitzers; remaining 4 Companies rearguard under Major Heigham. Marched 25 miles in a northerly direction after De Wet. No water anywhere, no regular halts, and nothing to eat till we got into camp [a bivouac rather than formal camping-ground] at Zwaartzkop at 4.30pm. Heaps of men fell out, [Battalion War Diary says: 'due to lack of food'] 23 out of 61 in F Company, over 100 of the half battalion. Lord Kitchener says he is very pleased with splendid marching of the troops — 25 miles in 12 and half hours. English farmer here says De Wet crossed drift just as our scouts appeared on the sky line. Took all his stock. De Wet's oxen and mules apparently in a wretched condition… but evidently not so wretched that he could not keep ahead of the British!

14 August   Rouse 4.30am, parade 5.50. Sick and bad marchers left behind to escort a convoy going back. Same 5 Companies lead, 2 Companies advance guard to Force, other 4 Companies, which arrived 4am to do rearguard again. Picked up some escaped prisoners from De Wet on the road who said they had been badly treated. Got to Waterval about 3pm. Nice country, passed pretty little farms in valleys. Marched 16 miles today. [Battalion War Diary: 'De Wet reported to have got through Magato's Pass, consequently chase abandoned'.]

15 August   Slept on till 7am. Some of Lord Methuen's troops, 5th Fusiliers and Northamptons, passed by early going north. Parade 9am. CIV Advance guard, Section Howitzer Battery, West Yorks and KOSLI.. Broadwood's cavalry Brigade passed by and pelted the regiments with oranges. Men rushed about and scrambled and had to be fallen in. Marched about 15 miles west to relieve Colonel Hore and 300 bushmen. Got in about 4.30pm. Other half of Regiment joined later [the battalion had been working in two halves, one in the Advance Guard, the other half with the baggage]. Other half of Battalion had almost a worse time of it than ourselves — no grub. Hart's Brigade and Ian Hamilton's troops with us now. Waggons drawn by donkeys and all sorts.

16 August   Reveille 3am, march 4.15am. Still going to relieve Colonel Hore. Lord Kitchener says in Orders he is very pleased with marching of troops and hopes they will do

A WELCOME ADDITION TO THE MESS SUPPLIES — AN ORIBEC CAUGHT BY THE REGIMENTAL DOGS

one more hard march about 16 miles, or less if Boers trek, to Colonel Hore.. Got to Brakfontein and heard the Boers had gone on our approach but the garrison had had a wretched time. Did 16 miles.

17 August   *Remained the day at Brakfontein. Great slaughtering of sheep and goats which we had driven along for rations, but they are wretchedly thin. Our Drums play in the afternoon, much to the delight of all the troops in camp who cheer and encore…*

It seems utterly incongruous that the West Yorkshires should have had their drums with them (though not the entire band and its instruments) but it should be remembered that they were supposed to have been on their way to Pretoria when they received orders to join the De Wet hunt. The drums could not be left behind so they were brought along too.

18 August   *Reveille, parade and march-off 4.30am. We are now on main road for Rustenburg. Got to camp at Twee-River after a dusty march about 4pm. Started chasing chickens and pigs and Lord Kitchener looks on amused… Up half the night getting men great-coats etc. We marched 17 miles today.* [Battalion War Diary: 'our present destination is supposed to be Pretoria which is 5 days march away'.]

BIVOUACKING ON THE RACE COURSE AT PRETORIA

19 August, Sunday   *Got tea and rum for men… Blankets etc collected about 2.30am and returned. Slept till about 3am myself. Servants find some bacon and eggs for our breakfast and made tea but we had to leave at 3.30 for the road. Arrived Rustenburg very tired and done, but without losing many men, about 1pm. Waggons in soon after. Had lunch then shaved and bathed in a little stream. Distance about 17 miles. Rustenburg a very pretty town, lots of trees and flowers.*

20 August   *Reveille 3.45… Our mule convoy went at an awful pace and our men got very done. Got into Klipfontein eventually about 2.30pm and had tea. Wore drill jackets instead of serge on march. Clothes all in holes. Did 12 miles. Promoted Lieutenant.*

Characteristically, Malcolm did not mention news of his promotion in the letter he wrote home that afternoon:

Wulhuta's Kop about 30 miles from Pretoria. 22nd Aug 1900
Dear Father,
*   another line just to let you know I am well and fit as can be. We have been marching ever since I wrote to you from Welverdiend* [a five line note that simply told that they were off on their travels by rail though without saying why], *chasing De Wet with General Smith-Dorrien's Brigade. Lord Kitchener being in chief command. We did 75 miles in 72 hours at the outset and we do about 20 miles every day and think nothing of it, though our transport does - mules and horses, dead and*

dying, litter the road all along the way wherever we go. We still have full rations, fresh meat instead of bully as it saves transport, the oxen being driven along in a herd with the column. Our clothes are all in holes but the weather is delightful and we don't feel it. The country about here is extremely pretty, wooded valleys and green corn-fields, very different to bare Standerton or hilly Natal. From Welverdiend we went pretty well due north to the Megaliesberg Mountains chasing De Wet, but he got through all right and we turned off to relieve Colonel Hore and 300 men who was surrounded by 3,000 Boers under De La Rey near Mafeking. We relieved him and then made for Rustenburg passing Lord Methuen and 5th Fusiliers on the way. I believe we are after De Wet again now.

your affectionate son,

22 August   *Reveille 4am. E & H Companies under Major Watts start off about 4.15am as escort to convoy. Battalion started about 8.15 in a westerly direction leaving Wolhuta's Kop on our left. Marched about 12 miles along a fairly good road to Wolve Kraal in native territory getting in about 1.30pm. Orderly Room — awful row about men bathing in drinking water. Very pretty camp among little craggy hills. Hundreds of kraals, with mud walls and compounds.* [This march was still part of an operation designed to block crossings of Crocodile River and hem-in De Wet.]

23 August   *Reveille 4am, Parade 5.30. A, B, E, H & K Companies left about 6am. Remaining Companies rearguard leave about 7.15 with 2 guns behind convoy. Hundreds of kaffirs come to see us off. Got into camp at Wolhuta's Kop about 1.30. B Company Outposts.* [Battalion War Diary: 'news in that De Wet definitely gone

north of Pretoria and therefore no need for a Force at Crocodile River, Battalion to return along the route it had come by'.]

24 August   *Reveille 3.30am, blankets 4.30am, and March at 5am… arrived at Rietfontein 1.30pm.*

So at last they reached Pretoria, where Malcolm soon had pen to paper for a letter home:

At the 'Grand Hotel' Pretoria, 26th August 1900
My dear Mother,
They have landed us in this much talked of spot at last as you can see, though we have been a rather round-about way to get here. We (the Regiment, Shropshire Light Infantry and a Field Battery under General Smith-Dorrien) got in yesterday after marching about 15 miles from a place called Rietfontein (half-way from here to Commando Nek) in the Megaliesberg Mountains and they planted us down on the race-course, where the Boers, as you know, kept our prisoners for some time. When we got in several Officers and men (details left at Standerton, sick etc.) rejoined us and we also got two English Mails, 20th and 27th July, which were of course most welcome. It is a fortnight since we left Standerton and as we have been marching steadily about 20 miles a day you may imagine the condition our clothes are in and what was my surprise and joy in finding the Mail had brought me just the very things I wanted: fresh supplies of underclothes, tobacco, chocolate etc and a pair of gloves. Nothing could have been nicer as we are off again tomorrow morning I believe to see some fighting at Belfast. Buller is there and of course we want to be in it. This morning we have been fitting the men and ourselves with new boots, clothes, helmets, putties, equipment etc. In the

ENVELOPES WITH VRI OVERPRINTED STAMPS

middle of it all there was an alarm and we had to get ready to move at once and when all was nearly ready a counter-order came and now they say we go tomorrow morning instead. That does not leave us much time to see Pretoria but there is not so very much to see after all so I am spending my afternoon writing letters in 'the Grand'.

I have not my Diary by me now so I can't send you a copy by this letter but I promise as soon as we get a rest to send a full account of our late doings.

Roughly, we arrived at Bank station (about half-way between Krugersdorp and Potchefstroom) on the 10th, joined General Smith-Dorrien's Brigade and marched the night of the 11th to Welverdiend (a station or two nearer Potchefstroom) then we joined Lord Kitchener and chased De Wet. We got as far as the Megaliesberg Mountains when De Wet slipped through [the net of British forces], then we turned off West in the Zeerust direction and relieved Colonel Hore and 300 men who were being besieged by 3,000 Boers. We had a day's rest there and then turned East for Pretoria via Rustenberg. Rustenberg by the way is delightful place, pretty gardens, pretty church, orange groves etc. Two days after Rustenberg we were within 5 miles of Commando Nek when De Wet was once more in the neighbourhood so off we went 12 miles to the NW to stop him but all to no purpose. He passed by quite close to our camp of the night before with 300 men that night and goodness knows where he is now. We trekked back the 12 miles and two days afterwards saw us in here.

your affectionate son,

It would not be very long before the West Yorkshires returned to Rustenburg where Malcolm would enjoy one of the more pleasant periods of his time in South Africa though, as ever, it would come to an abrupt halt in yet more alarums and excursions. Meanwhile, Lord Kitchener had launched another major sweep involving every unit he could muster. This time it was to support General Buller who was about to fight his last full-scale battle in South Africa — at Belfast — on 27 August.

26 August, Sunday *Got up about 7am, had breakfast. An alarm soon after to get ready to move at once by train to Belfast. Cancelled later and we are to move in the early morning tomorrow… Wrote letters at Grand Hotel…*

My dear Claud,

I am awfully sorry for not having written to you for such ages but you see all the letters I send home and there is nothing of any peculiar interest to you that I do not tell them. I acknowledge all your letters, parcels, etc too through them. You are awfully good sending tobacco etc and your letters always cheer me up except when you grouse, but I don't blame you for grousing for I must own your luck is a bit hard, but why you should want to come out now I can't think.

This is the rottenest part of the campaign. You might of course join in the general amusement of 'chasing De Wet'. Isn't it ridiculous making unfortunate Infantry footslog after a man on a horse, every man with De Wet by the way has a spare horse. There is a lie going that someone asked De Wet what he was running about like this for and he replied that the British had taken over his country and he wanted to let them see a little of it! Personally I have seen quite enough already. There are lots of yarns going about De Wet. Here is another. When he let the Yeomanry that he captured go he said to them 'I can get plenty of you any day, you can go.' and when he let the Derby Militia go he said 'Well, you are of no use to me and you are of less use to Lord Roberts so you can go'. We all think De Wet a thorough sportsman and treat the whole thing as a joke but all the same marching about 20 miles a day for a fortnight on end is no joke at all. We are longing to be back with Buller again, they do things so rottenly this side; No Canteens, no comforts of any kind, very little clothing even. Buller went slow but he went sure and camp life was very comfortable and nice. Everyone agrees that Buller is the best man out here to serve under.

your affectionate brother,

It is a debate that has raged ever since — was Buller's slow but sure campaign more effective than Roberts' tiger springs which left his troops in tatters, cavalry with horses that were broke down and useless, and a transport system than was totally incapable of keeping pace? Certainly, when Buller's force met with the lead elements of Roberts' outside Twyfelaar on the road to Belfast it was reported that many men under Roberts' command, officers and men both, wept bitterly to see how fit and well Buller's men looked by contrast with their own sorry, half starved, appearance. As Malcolm had already noted, under Roberts you were lucky to get your rations at all, whereas Buller had always been renowned for seeing to the well-being of his men. Nevertheless,

A 9.2-INCH GUN ON A RAILWAY WAGGON AT BELFAST STATION

Malcolm would be tightening his own belt before very long and the next day saw the West Yorkshires on the move once more, their destination Belfast where, so they hoped, they would rejoin Buller's command.

27 August *Reveille about 3am, Regiment going off by 4 trains. A and B Companies with Major Heigham left about 5am, D, K & F Companies with Major Watts got to Railway Station about 7 and returned to race-course shortly after. C & E Companies with Carey got off about 12. G and half H with Ian Hamilton left about 4pm. Pennell and I strolled into the town. Bought two sets VRI stamps at Post Office. Major Watts took us 3 Companies back to Railway Station 4pm and there we bivouacked for the night.. Slept on oat-bags on the platform.*

28 August *Breakfast on platform. Got VRI stamps stamped at Field Post Office. Going to start at 10am but had to wait for Brabant's horse. Lunched on platform. Entrained about 2pm and eventually moved off about 5pm… A huge 9.2-in gun arrived from Cape town just before we left. CO & HQ Officers in covered truck. All other Officers with their Companies in open coal trucks already filled with various stores, boxes and sacks.*

29 August *Boxes very hard. Rained during the night and I got wet to the skin through great-coat etc. Arrived Middleburg 5am. Got men out of trucks and let them bivouac under a goods shed. Remained all day in Railway Station, very dreary and desolate place. 9.2-in gun escorted by some KOSLI arrives in the afternoon. Start again 5pm.*

The delay at Middleburg was caused by an engine leaving the rails close-by and, further up the line, by a two-train collision. The West Yorkshires arrived just after the battle of Belfast, in which Buller had finally smashed through the commandos he had patiently driven from kopje to kopje all the way from Dundee northwards through Natal and into the Transvaal. There was now to be a final push into the deepest reaches of eastern Transvaal to mop up the last Boer resistance. Lord Roberts and Lord Kitchener were both convinced that with all the major towns in British hands the Boers would give up the unequal contest and surrender. It was a tremendous surprise to all concerned that the war continued on and on relentlessly with, seemingly, no prospect of an end. This was also reflected in the manner in which the campaign was conducted in the latter part of 1900 and early 1901; namely, opportunistic reactions to Boer attacks or incursions rather than an overarching strategy which would contain, and eventually defeat, the Boers.

Belfast. 2nd September 1900

My dear Mother,

We arrived here on the 30th August, that is to say the last train load of us, with self and Company on board, did. We got first orders to move last Sunday 26th and the first train load got off the next morning. We were kept fooling around in Pretoria Station, then getting off about two trains every 24 hours till the 28th and the rest of the time we spent en route, packed close in open coal trucks, which were already loaded with ration boxes, carts and other stores. There is a huge 9.2-in gun mounted on a special truck in the Railway Station here which came up from the Cape and travelled on with us from Pretoria. It is a monster and carries about 14,000 yards they say but I doubt if it will ever fire a shot at the Boers.

We are off again today, we always seem to move on a Sunday, and the popular belief is that we are going to rejoin Buller and good old Kitchener [Walter rather than Lord K] who are winning fresh laurels at the front. We are all awfully pleased at the prospect. We are going by road accompanied by Brabant's horse and will probably arrive at Machadodorp tonight. I am sitting, waiting for the waggons to be loaded, in an Officers' shelter made by our Pioneers out of corrugated iron roofing etc brought up from the deserted town of Belfast with a nice strip of coconut matting from the hotel on the floor. It is too sad leaving it all, just as we were getting comfortable and thought we were going to stay for a month or more.

You ask under whose command we are but I really do not know. We were with Smith-Dorrien till we got here, when we came under General Hutton's command. Smith-Dorrien turned up yesterday with his staff and now I don't know who we belong to. We have come across all sorts of big bugs by coming here. 'Bobs' and his huge staff, living in a Railway saloon carriage on a siding near the station, Ian Hamilton, Baden-Powell, Major Poor (Provost Marshal), Colonel O'Leary (Director of Signalling) and a lot more. The place literally teems with Generals, Staff Officers and red tabs.

The chaos in everything this side is indescribable, nobody thinks anything of Kitchener or even of 'Bobs' and everyone swears by Buller. We always had everything in apple pie order with him and things went well, but here…!!

your affectionate son,

The West Yorkshires spent most of September escorting convoys of supplies on their way to the front and General Buller. Whilst Malcolm's diary continues remorselessly day after day, his diary-narrative for this period is omitted in favour of his letters which provide a useful overview of his activities.

Waterval Boven, 8 September 1900

My dear Father,

We have got back to the Railway again as you see and I am sitting once more comfortably seated in a room while I write. We are certainly a roving Regiment and no mistake. In the last month we have journeyed from the South to the West, from the West to the Northeast and then back again to the East. We have been very fit all the time and have not had so very much to grumble at after all. We left Belfast merely to take a convoy from Machadodorp to Buller.

This letter was not in fact finished on this date but completed a month later when the battalion had arrived at Rustenburg.

Nooitgedacht, 19 September 1900

My dear Mother,

We have not been getting our Mails very regularly lately and we have not heard from home for some time now, but I got such a lot of papers and magazines by the last mail that they have kept me going with literature ever since. We had such a nice time at Waterval Boven, it is one of the prettiest spots we have been in yet and we were hoping to spend the rest of our time there but, after five short days rest, off we had to go again. We trekked back to Machadodorp where Lord Roberts, Kitchener etc. now are, crossed the Railway to the South side and moved along parallel to it on the ridge south of Waterval Boven, Onder Nooitgedacht etc. The Railway runs at the bottom of a deep valley right away down to Komati Poort from here. Now there are Companies of the regiment scattered about on all the hilltops between this and Machadodorp.

I must stop now and the Mail is off and hope you will excuse this scrappy note but you say you prefer a scrap to nothing.

your affectionate son,

Machadodorp, 22 September 1900

My dear Father,

I wrote last to Mother I think from a hill above Nooitgedacht. There was a convoy returning here that day and that is how I got that opportunity of writing. Now we have all come back here and are by degrees entraining for Pretoria and goodness knows what they will do with us when we get there. It is slow work, though, and although we got in here the evening of the day before yesterday only two train loads have left up to date. I am to go by the next train but don't expect to start till tonight or tomorrow morning, so I am spending the day putting my letters, diary etc straight. I am writing this sitting in the open as usual, a dust storm is trying to blow me and everything else along with it (I have just had to chase paper, blotting paper and all over the veldt) so excuse the blots. I must first give you my list of letters etc sent and received. [There follows a list of letters sent by Malcolm to his family, twelve in all, followed by a massive list, in excess of 60 items, of letters, newspapers, magazines and parcels he had received – these lists have been omitted here.]

I can't stand the wind any longer and have now returned to my 'mushyboo' as the men call it. This is an erection over my valise made out of four sheets of galvanised iron roofing to keep out the wind and wet and it is generally quite successful, but at present it is forming a little whirlwind of dust and flies. In case I have not time to write a good account of our wanderings when we get to Pretoria I will give you now roughly and in a few words what we have done and have been supposed to do,

2 September We are given our transport and trek 17 miles East to Machadodorp.

3 September Pick up a big convoy for Buller. Go 8 miles to Helvetia on a very hilly road.

4 September Escort convoy another 8 or 10 miles along hilly roads. A convoy of empty waggons from Buller takes on our convoy.

5 September Return with our convoy of now empty waggons to Helvetia.

6 September Trek 8 or 10 miles to Waterval Boven. Ripping place.

7–10 Sept Peaceful time at Waterval Boven.

11 September Trek back to Machadodorp.

12 September Move in an easterly direction almost parallel to railway line. Do about 7 miles.

13 September Do about 10 miles.

14 September Do about 5 miles and are now up a good height and about a mile sheer below us lies Nooitgedacht Station in a big valley. General Hutton is near Godwaan Station, French at Barberton.

15, 16 Sept Remained in camp above Nooitgedacht

17 September. Trek back about 5 miles towards Machadodorp

18 September. Waited for some Boer families with waggons and cattle to come in.

19 September. Trek back 10 miles.

20 September. Reach Machadodorp and get orders to go to Pretoria from Chief of Staff.

That is as far as I can go at present and I will fill up the remaining half sheet with a rough sketch map showing the places mentioned in case they are not marked in your map.

Love to all, your affect son,

PS You will see that ever since we left Pretoria we have been a stray Battalion wandering about at anyone's pleasure, but the Chief of Staff (Lord Kitchener) principally has been looking after us.

Machadodorp. 23rd September 1900

My dear Claud,

I scribbled you a note I think from Pretoria, which I hope you got alright... It is awfully good of you sending me tobacco so often, I have never been out yet, but then I am not a very big smoker. At Spion Kop lots of chaps were reduced to ordinary plug. Personally my pipe went wrong and I could not smoke at all. Just now, and until I can get into Pretoria, (we are sitting on our hunkers waiting for a train to take us there now) I am smoking a borrowed pipe - but then I had bad luck. Before we started chasing De Wet we had to lighten our kits and I sent all my spare pipes down, keeping two for use. When we started from this place on the 3rd of the month to take a convoy to Buller I left my haversack lying on the ground by one of the waggons and nobody noticed it. I was in an awful state when I found out. Tommy, as I daresay you know, keeps his little all in his haversack and besides both my pipes, tobacco, and matches I had all sorts of treasures in mine. Next morning, before we started off, a Tommy of another Regiment came in, to my great joy, with my haversack which he had found along with a brother Officer's 'Coat, warm, British' at the side of the road. It had evidently been brought that far by a kaffir as nothing but grub, whisky, matches, pipes, badge from Field service cap etc were taken. I was pleased to get it back but I am sorry my pipes have gone. One I had had with me through the whole campaign and the other, sent out by Father from Lalor's, through most of it... It was quite a happy thought of yours to send comic papers, they are always in great request as one so seldom gets them out here and they are a change and something novel to relieve the monotony of our daily life.

Unfortunately the remainder of this letter is missing.

Fourteen

RUSTENBURG - PATROLS AND FARM BURNING

Opposite: Another Boer farm consumed by flames

Lord Kitchener soon had the West Yorkshires on the move again. Now they were to join a newly formed brigade of infantry that was being hastily assembled and despatched under Major-General Cunningham to Rustenburg from where they were to support Broadwood's cavalry brigade. A second infantry brigade, under the command of Major-General Clements, was also assembled and worked with Broadwood along the Megaliesberg hills. It had now become clear that the Boer commandos under Smuts and De La Rey were operating from the northern side of the Megaliesberg; a virtually impenetrable, semi-mountainous range of very rocky hills thickly coated with scrub. The West Yorkshires were to guard several passes through the Megaliesberg: Oliphant's Nek, Commando Nek and Castrol Nek in particular, as well as garrison Rustenburg and provide convoy guards. With only two infantry battalions, the second being the Argyll and Sutherland Highlanders, along with detachments of Royal Artillery, it was always going to be a substantial task with a high level of risk attached to it.

Rustenburg. 1st October 1900

My dear Mother,

Here we are at this pretty place again. No sooner did we get to Pretoria than they put us into a new force under General Cunningham and sent us out here. We are supposed to be acting in co-operation with General Broadwood's cavalry Brigade but we have only come up with him today and we found him sitting very peacefully here. We have taken our time on the way,

WEST YORKSHIRES, ARGYLL AND SUTHERLAND HIGHLANDERS WITH ELSWICK BATTERY ON THE MARCH

only doing about 12 miles a day and we have taken the road following the foot of the Megaliesberg the whole way. Stray Boers are still hovering about in the hills and we have seen some quite close but they have not troubled to snipe us. A convoy is going back to Pretoria tomorrow and that is how I come to be writing, but our next move is not fixed so don't be surprised if I miss a Mail or two. It is now summer again and an exceptionally dry season they say, the rains have not come yet. The heat is tremendous during the day and we sleep with scarcely anything over us at night. Don't ask me what

we are doing or what anybody else is doing for I can't tell you. I should have thought there was very little armed resistance left in this part of the country, but they seem to be still sending various 'Commandos' large and small trekking over the Veldt dragging huge convoys along and wearing out a good deal of boot leather and horse flesh. Everybody of course grumbles and grouses and will continue to do so to the end of the war, but as a matter of fact this is the best and prettiest part of the Transvaal and I for one am quite contented to spend the rest of the campaign in this district.

The Berg is close by and the kopjes all along the foot of it are thickly wooded, the trees are in bloom and give out a delicious scent, which is very refreshing to the tired Tommies trudging along the dusty, sandy roads. Besides that the spring flowers are lovely - I found a couple of small wild orchids the other day, I wonder if it would be worth while sending any bulbs home. You asked for some I know, but surely they would be dried up to nothing before they reached you. I have got two more Weaver Birds' nests for you which I will send when we get to a Post Office or perhaps bring home myself !!

I was so pleased to get those photos from the Stores of Majuba etc but where oh! where are the missing 12 spools. I have not heard a word from Knight for ages or received a single photo from him yet. I am extremely vexed and annoyed with him and feel very deeply on the subject. The course you took with the undeveloped spools was just what I wanted you to do. If any more spools turn up let the Stores develop and print them by all means and keep the negatives until I can get satisfaction out of Knight. If Knight thinks I am going to wait for twelve months while he is making a dozen prints he is mistaken. I am enclosing one or two copies of my portrait taken in action, which you can do what you please with. I hope you will find them better than the first copy of the photo I sent to Hilda. I was waiting to have the negative touched up before I sent one to you or father. It is not anything very wonderful now but you may like to have it. There is a horrid wind blowing, my pencil wants sharpening badly and it is near Mail hour so I must stop.

Love to all,

Although written in November, Malcolm's letter to his father contained his letter-diary for October in which he provides a condensed account of his activities. These very brief entries merely tell us that the West Yorkshires, along with the other troops stationed at Rustenburg, were variously employed in burning farms and collecting up the livestock in the general area. They were also maintaining posts at the passes through the Megaliesberg in order to prevent the Boers breaking back through to the south. There was also convoy duty:

Letter-Diary with sketch map:
Rustenburg. 23rd November 1900.
My dear Father,
On the 1st October, the Regiment and most of the Argyll and Sutherland Highlanders arrived here. These with the 75th Battery RFA and a section (2 guns) of the Elswick Battery comprised General Cunningham's Force.
On arrival we found General Broadwood's Cavalry encamped and details of the North Staffords and Cheshire Regiments. 5 miles out we passed General Clements' Force moving north with the Dublin Fusiliers, 2nd/5th Fusiliers and Worcester Regiments but unfortunately we were not near enough to see any of the officers. We furnish 1 Company for Outposts holding from Brink's farm to the kaffir location.

I have drawn on a separate sheet two sketch maps so that you may follow the diary better, one of Rustenburg on a large scale and the other on a small scale showing the different treks I have been on. The duties being so varied here I will mention what each individual Company of the Regiment has been on.

2 October *G & H Companies of West Yorkshires with 2 Companies Argylls, section RFA etc under a Major of the Argylls burn a farm beyond Krondall…*

3 October *A foraging party with almost all available waggons goes out to Krondall to bring in oat hay for horses…*

4 October *A, B, D & E Companies (with F & details attached to make up 400 men) start as escort to empty convoy to Rietfontein to bring back full convoy with fresh supplies.*

9 October *2 Companies of Argylls move over to Oliphant's Nek to form garrison there. West Yorks now, and until the 30th, furnish 2 Companies day and night for outposts, our section of the line stretching from Brink's Farm to Prison.*

Drummer Goodwin had been keeping up his entries in his diary throughout 1900, even if these tended to be terse, one line a day entries. He tells us that the West Yorkshires arrived in Rustenburg complete with their drums and bugles – they had still not managed to return them to their base depot back at Pietersmaritzburg. No one was going to complain, as the drums were frequently paraded whilst the battalion was at Rustenburg. On 11 October Goodwin noted:

"Playing out in town and then we got orders to go and play at the New Zealanders camp. We got 6/- each and heard a very good concert."

Macolm's diary goes on:

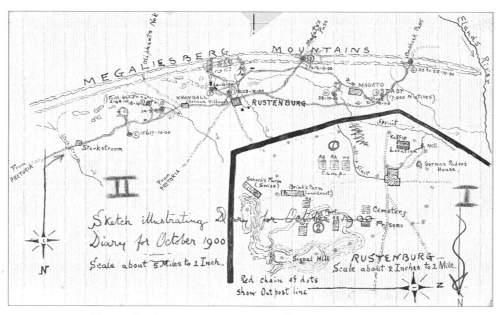

MALCOLM RIALL'S MAP OF THE DISTRICT AROUND RUSTENBURG SHOWING PRINCIPAL TERRAIN AND PLACES MENTIONED IN THE TEXT.

15 October *Three companies under Major Heigham with one of Argylls, section of Elswick's, ambulances etc, the whole under Major Young commanding RFA Battery, trek to a woody spot off the road beyond Krondall, 8 miles. We are to prevent some Boers breaking away North from the Megaliesberg Mountains along which General Broadwood's Column is moving 'clearing the country' . . .*

By the 19th this small force was back in Rustenburg and, in his next letter home, Malcolm explains what he and his regiment were. His main concern, however, is with his photographs.

Rustenburg. 19th Oct 1900

My dear Mother,

    Think of it! Tomorrow is the anniversary of the day we sailed from Portsmouth for this curious country. I have just come back from a little expedition round the district collecting stray Boers, burning wheat and waggon wheels and generally clearing up the district amid much wailing and gnashing of teeth, but such is war and we have to do these things. This district abounds in lemons at the present season and at every farm we can get lettuce, onions, sweet potatoes and sometimes beet-root and green peas. This is all of course great luxury to us and we are very thankful for it all but every place has its drawbacks and this is no exception to the rule.

    Do you know that old scoundrel Knight has not written a word to me yet or sent a single print of the photos I ordered – of Signallers etc. I shall most certainly take every film of mine away from him and transfer them to the Stores for they are wonderfully prompt and good. I am perfectly content with them. I wonder if The King has handed over my films to Knight or the Stores ? I asked them to hand the films over to one of the two but have not heard if they have done so yet and I am very anxious to see prints of all the photos I have taken. So far I have only had prints from about half a dozen spools from the Stores and have seen none of those I sent to The King, The Graphic or Knight.

    your affectionate son,

OFFICER'S MESS OUT ON THE VELDT

Malcolm's letter-diary continues with details of the troops' movements and their duties:

20 October *3 Companies Argylls and section RFA move out early to garrison Magato's Pass. C D & H Companies start 7am as escort to empty convoy to Rietfontein.*

21 October *7.30am Church Parade Service. Mr Wainman, our Wesleyan Padre, takes the service and preaches a good sermon. 1.30pm F Company and 2 Companies Argylls, ambulances etc., trek to Magato's Pass. 2 Companies Argylls leave us at the foot of the pass and relieve force already there with guns etc under a Major of the Argylls, and he takes us on to Boshoek where we arrive about 9pm having been previously drenched by a hail shower. All Infantry on Outposts. Rumour that Steyn and Botha are trying to get through the 'Berg and we are to stop them doing so.*

22 October *Broadwood, who has camped close behind us, moves on another 4 miles and blows up some ammunition. Both forces start back for Rustenburg at 9.30am which we reach about 3.30pm.*

23 October *6.30am F Company, 2 Companies of Argylls, section RFA, Squadron 19th Lancers (detached from General Broadwood's Force), ambulances etc under Major Irvine of Argylls trek to Boshoek Pass which we reach about 4pm . . . Slept in an ambulance waggon to avoid thunderstorm but never again ! The beastly mules tied to the pole kept kicking and rocking the thing about all night and of course I hardly slept a wink.*

24 October *4pm F Company takes over Outposts on steep hills round. I mount a big hill with half of Company to the east of Pass bringing with me one of our useful little water-mules.*

26 October *Clothes disreputable, boots, coat, breeches - all in pieces and tatters. 2 Companies KOYLIs (Kings Own Yorkshire Light Infantry) and section of Q Battery RHA* *(detached from General Broadwood) relieve us at 11am… Reach General Broadwood's camp at Magato Stadt at 5pm and camp for the night.*

27 October   *Reach Rustenburg via Magato Pass where we leave our section of RFA about 11am and find they have moved camp from the old spot on the grassy plain, up amongst the trees on the lower slopes of Signal Hill as they say this site is healthier now the rains have set in. Close to our camp is a work of art of General Baden-Powell's — Fort Canada — built by the Canadians when he was here. 2.30pm E & G Companies leave as escort to an empty convoy to Rietfontein. Of course guns, MI and Companies of the Argylls also take their turn in guarding the convoys, a proportion of each going with every convoy.*

28 October *Some flour has been procured and we have an issue of bread made by Boer women in the town who get wood etc provided and 3d [pence] a loaf for baking !, but it is wretched stuff, heavy as lead, and after a few days we are only too glad to return to biscuits once more. The Mess has run out of 'Quaker' so now we have as a substitute mealy meal porridge which I almost think I prefer.*

IMPROVISATION WAS ESSENTIAL FOR COMFORT OF THE OFFICERS. AN OFFICERS' QUARTERS AT RUSTENBURG

30 October *11.30am I take F Company and a brace of guides up to a high peak in the Megaliesberg because it is reported the Boers have a signal station up there. The move is kept very secret and after a great deal of panting and perspiring, in which the Colonial guide came in an easy winner, we reached the top to find…a beautiful grassy plain about a mile broad, watered by a little stream, on which are grazing 3 or 4 harmless cows and a couple of broken down horses.*

After several more days of patrolling in the general area around Rustenburg, Malcolm found himself on the march to Magato's Pass with two companies under the command of Major Heigham. Here they were to take over the blockading duties from the Argyll and Sutherland Highlanders. Somewhere to the north were the Boers but no-one knew exactly where, although there were many columns of British troops looking for them.

Magato's Pass. 8th November 1900

My dear Mother,

I arrived here yesterday and my Company and one other are to form the garrison here for a week or so. We relieved 2 Companies of the Argylls who had been holding the Pass for a similar time. We are in touch here with about 6 different forces working round Eland's River and the country south of the 'Berg; Paget, Plumer, Douglas, Broadwood, Clements, Methuen etc. It is interesting seeing all their communications to Head Quarters and hearing of all their doings. A convoy is going back to Rustenburg today so I take this opportunity to scribble a note. This is not a bad post, rather dirty!

yours

12 November *We have been in South Africa for a year to-day… Wire comes ordering us to return to Rustenburg next day.*

Malcolm's diary entries remain uninspiring, even if full of the details of the daily grind. It may be noted in passing that most of the officers and many of the men were ill with dysentery whilst the West Yorkshires were at Rustenburg. This probably had nothing whatever to do with the location but was perhaps a reaction to months of intense activity followed by a relatively slack period of garrison duty. Malcolm also makes no particular comment about the fact that they had now been in South Africa for a year and that the war is still being fought, although from the very lack of any mention of the Boers in any of the West Yorkshire chronicles, one might be forgiven for wondering where the Boers were. The short answer is that for the moment the battalion was very much on the side lines, witnessing events from afar; it was the mounted columns who were in contact — if infrequently — with the Boers. All this, however, would change soon enough.

Fifteen

NEC ASPERA TERRENT –

"Neither do difficulties deter"

DISASTER AT BUFFEL'S POORT

Opposite: 'Dug in and waiting for the Boers', the West Yorkshires holding Oliphant's Nek in an obviously posed photograph

Rustenburg was used during this period of the war as a centre for operations by the various 'roving' columns operating in the northern Transvaal. They were under the command of men such as Paget, Plumer, Broadwood, Allenby, and Clements, and they required mountains of supplies, in addition to the needs of the force garrisoning Rustenburg and the passes through the Megaliesberg. Thus, as Malcolm noted in his diary from time to time, large convoys of ox-drawn waggons made the journey from Rustenburg to Pretoria on a more-or-less weekly basis. Inevitably this regular operation would attract the attention of the Boers.

26 November *Ingles and Barlow relieve me at 5.30am and I return to camp about 6am. Collier finds that my temperature is high and I must not go with Convoy. Barlow takes over F Company. B & F Companies (with Fryer for MI) go with convoy at 3.15pm…*

27 November *Fever no better. Collier says I am for Hospital. Read papers. Ride Collier's pony down to Hospital in evening and after a long time, while a heavy thunderstorm was raging, they gave me a bed with 5 Officers in Masonic hospital House…*

30 November *Temperature normal…I am nearly all right.*

Malcolm experimented with a new form of diary for December. This was written in a notebook, sent to Malcolm by his mother for the specific purpose of making the letter diary. This notebook had perforated sheets with alternate thick and thin pages, the second intended as a carbon copy of the first. The top copy was sent home in January 1901 and the carbon copy Malcolm retained. Both copies survive. Although the letter-diary and Malcolm's personal notebook diary correspond, the notebook diary is, as before, sharper and more succinct. The letter-diary is more measured in tone though having a fuller and more rounded account.

3 December *D Company relieves C Company on Outposts at 5am. C & H Companies with CO and battalion HQ Staff with two guns leave for Elands River to help convoy which is reported to be held up by the Boers.*

4 December *Beastly day, wet and misty. Gum boots just up from the Base came in useful. About lunchtime Barlow turned up wet through with 72 men looking equally miserable - all without rifles or equipment. Of the 72 men, 40 were F Company. The Convoy had been held up by the Boers at about 6pm on the 3rd between Eland's drift and Buffel's Poort. Barlow in charge of F Company was doing rearguard. Lowe and Harrington with B Company, 2 guns of 75th Battery under Captain Farrell and a young subaltern of the RFA and Major Wolridge-Gordon of the Argyll and Sutherland Highlanders were doing Advanced Guard. When the Boers attacked, the Advanced Guard took up a position amongst kopjes near Buffel's Poort (a poort is a large water-worn gully). Barlow, 2 or 3 miles behind, had orders to hold a donga crossing the road near Eland's River. This he occupied and held till about 1pm when, ammunition having run out (the men only having the usual 150 rounds in their pouches and it was impossible to get more) and being completely surrounded, they were forced to give in to the Boers' repeated cry of 'Hands Up!'. They were taken to De La Rey who was in command and were fairly well treated. The Boers then set fire to all the Convoy waggons as they stood, after first liberating and driving off the oxen. Only a very few waggons 'for present use' were driven across to their laager. The Convoy was the first section of the whole convoy and was composed of 120 waggons of Rations, and Ordnance Stores, 6 Natal Field Force Canteens with milk, jam etc, 1 ambulance and about 6 Regimental waggons. About 9pm, and under the cover of darkness, the Boers crept up to the latter which were quite close to B Company and the guns who were still holding out and set them also on fire. Two English Mails for the battalion, rations, greatcoats, blankets, officers kits etc of both Companies were on these waggons. The prisoners [British] were now augmented by about 20 from B Company besides Conductors were allowed to take what they liked from the Canteen waggons consequently there were big brews of Quaker, coffee, tea etc going, not to mention whisky. Barlow slept with the men under a shed guarded by Boer sentries outside.*

About midnight on the 3rd the CO and his 2 Companies with the guns reached Lowe and helped to defend the position, building sangars etc. Barlow was informed by his captors that he might depart but to make for Rustenburg. He was shown the direction and off he went, the prisoners now amounting to 100, 72 being West Yorkshires, arriving in Camp about 12 noon on the 4th. Commandant Boshof, Grobelaar, Staats-Attorney Smuts and others were with De La Rey, and their force must have been 800 strong. They had no transport, no guns and every man had one or two spare ponies to carry blankets etc, all in good condition. Boers have plenty of food. Barlow being wet through and without his kit, I fitted him out as best as I could. Went down with him after dinner to report to General Cunningham.

The arrival of Broadwood's cavalry brigade and other mounted infantry units early on 4 December effectively ended the engagement. The Boers had destroyed 138 waggons and taken nearly 2,000 oxen (which we should presume they must have turned loose as there was no possibility of their having taken them away) besides stripping 75 men of their arms and equipment. Ten men from the West Yorkshires were killed. Only part of this very large convoy was attacked whilst a second, smaller, section of the convoy survived undamaged. Nevertheless, the West Yorkshires would be on short commons for some time to come.

5 December *Saw Civil Surgeon Robinson who had returned from the Convoy with most of the wounded. Wet morning, cleared at 8 and fine day. Collier returned wet through in the evening rest of wounded in ambulance…*

6 December *Collier starts 5am for Krondall to bring in sick from Convoy. Hot morning. B Company, Collier, CO and relief Companies return about lunch time. CO very pleased with the part our men played. Guns did wonders. A Company Outposts.*

7 December *Orderly Officer. 8am kit inspection and fit clothing, boots etc. Very busy all day about my Company rifles, equipment etc lost. Court of Enquiry on Barlow becoming prisoner – verdict is no fault of his own and he did very well under the circumstances. I am lent rifles and equipment of employed men of other Companies so that my men can do Guards etc. Missing men turn up at Rietfontein, all alright. D Company on Outposts.*

8 December *7.30am CO's clothes inspection. Most of Company now armed with rifles and straps. Major Watts takes A Company and 2 guns to reinforce Oliphant's Nek garrison 2pm. Write to Mother,*

Rustenburg, 8th December 1900

My dear Mother,

I have sad news for you this week but you have probably heard all about it in the papers and have at last had the satisfaction of at all events hearing the regiment mentioned. Oh! but my poor, poor Company for it was mine which suffered most. B and F Companies were acting as escort to a long line of about 120 Convoy waggons bringing in Rations and mails from Pretoria… I was not with my Company on that Convoy as the very day they started for

Rietfontein I went into Hospital with fever. I was out again in a few days but it seems almost like Fate does it not? I lost four valuable NCOs killed and one Private, five wounded and five missing out of a total strength of 64. Cruel, cruel Fate. The unfortunate men killed had all been with the Battalion since we left Aldershot. It is too sad. Young Barlow had command of my Company at the time and was taken prisoner with the men and is very sad at losing his Sam Browne Belt and all his kit – all burnt.

your affectionate son,

Malcolm had fully recovered from his short spell of illness, and was very much in the thick of events such as they were. The West Yorkshires were still engaged in much the same duties as before despite the fact that the Boers had penetrated through the Megaliesberg and were on the loose in the Transvaal.

10 December *Stand to Arms 3-3.30am, rumours of impending attack on Rustenburg. 7am finish making Range Marks in front of Fort Canada. Awfully hot…H Company on Outposts.*

11 December *Large bodies of Boers moving about and Magato's Pass now held by them.* [Battalion War Diary: 'Pass evacuated following capture of Convoy'.] *Rumour of big attack to come off on Dingaan's Day, (the 15th). Outposts trenches and other defences greatly improved. Only one post now. Cavalry details have been moved back and find the post near the town.*

12 December *7am Go with 25 men as escort to 4 waggons of supplies for Oliphant's Nek. Got back about 10.30am. One of the hottest days we have had yet. Cooler in evening owing to a thunderstorm nearby. ASC and Engineers employ gangs of natives to dig huge trenches in front of their camps.*

13 December *I am Orderly Officer. F Company Inlying Picquet. Another baking hot day. Wire to Commando Nek cut but repaired during the day. General Clements reports being attacked by Buyers. Heavy casualties on both sides.*

14 December *F Company now all supplied with rifles…General Broadwood returns*

LIFE IN THE FIELD MIGHT HAVE BEEN UNCOMFORTABLE BUT THE OFFICERS WERE WELL LOOKED AFTER

from Oorzaak bringing in 4 Companies of the KOYLIs who relieve our duties and outposts. Convoy detained at Rietfontein for safety. B Company sent out to further reinforce Oliphant's Nek.

15 December *H Company Inlying Picquet. I am Orderly Officer. Stand to Arms 3-4.15am as it is a dull morning and next to no moon. CO has an early breakfast and rides over to Oliphant's Nek to report on its defences. At lunch a wire comes in for CO to take command at Oliphant's Nek. Consequently, at 2pm, Boyall, along with the CO's servant, mess servants etc march over there with some more supplies. Crossman, Richards and I left in charge of Regiment, what there is of it left in Rustenburg. Just sitting down to dinner when 3 Officers and about a Company of 2/5th* [Northumberland] *Fusiliers turn up. They are part of the half Battalion of theirs captured by Buyers when Clements' Column was attacked at Nooitgedacht.* [The Boer attack on Clements' column at Nooitgedacht followed-on from their attack on the convoy at Buffel's Poort]. *They have absolutely no kit and are dead beat. We give them a wash, a change of clothing and some food. Altogether about 6 Officers and 300 men turn up including about 100 MI and Yeomanry. Put the Officers in to some of our Officers' 'Mushyboos' and men fit into Company shelters. Memo comes round saying we shall be attacked on all sides in the morning.*

16 December, Sunday *Stand to Arms 3am. Hold the Fort, farm and trenches but no Boers appear so dismissed at 4.30am. Crossman takes about 12 men and the Drums down to Church and I stay up here to look after our 'Visitors'. More Officers and men turn up and eventually we have 9 Officers and about 350 men (4 Companies of 2/5th Fusiliers; 80 or 90 details of Devon Yeomanry, Scotch Yeomanry, Kitchener's Horse, 2nd MI etc). Brigade Major came over and found out all he could about the action and made arrangements for feeding and sheltering the men. CO and Boyall return from Oliphant's Nek.*

17 December *Stand to Arms 2.45. I take a section of my Company and hold far corner of Brink's Farm till about 4.45am when there being no Boers around I was ordered to retire.*

18 December *Stood to Arms 3.15. I occupied trenches by barbed wire, Crossman went to corner of Brink's Farm. Dismissed about 4.45am and slept till 7am. After Orderly room I took out a party of 24 men and made two more trenches by barbed wire. Got back about*

1pm very hot and very dirty. . . . .

19 December *Stood to Arms 3.15am. Took a section as before to corner of Brink's Farm. Returned 4.45am and had 'gun-fire' coffee and lay in mushyboo till breakfast at 6.30am. 9am, I am a member of a FGCM* [a field general court martial, which would undoubtedly have been the first official enquiry into the events concerning the Boer attack on Clements at Nooitgedacht] *assembling in our Mess Tent. After this I went out to see about finishing my trenches by barbed wire and found the defaulters at work making strong sod loop-holes. At 2pm I took half my Company (15 men) and a few details as escort to three mule waggons of supplies for Oliphant's Nek garrison and was met half way by 3 empty waggons and a half Company from Oliphant's Nek. We were drenched to the skin twice before meeting them, Handed over supplies, details etc. and took over a Boer prisoner and some sacks of wheat. Rode back in the waggons and were in no time.*

20 December *Stood to Arms 3.15am and held trenches by barbed wire. Raining hard. Returned as usual at 4.45am. Boers apparently don't care to attack as there are plenty round about. 2pm took men of Company not on duty down to Mission Picquet and relieved KOYLI who then follow General Broadwood who moved today to Waterkloof, between here and Oliphant's Nek. CO comes down in the evening. There are now three extra posts, I have very few men and hardly any bayonets etc. Took a Patrol out 8pm. Very dark and very wet.*

21 December *Stood to Arms at 3.15am, reinforcing all posts from Support at the Mission. Return at 4.30am. Rather wet and cold. Improved barbed wire entanglements in front of posts, fixing on small tins to rattle. Heard heavy shelling all day in Oliphant's Nek direction. . .*

22 December *Stood to Arms as day before. . . Crossman with H Company relieved me at 4.30pm. As soon as we got into camp half the men detailed to find guards and other camp duties. Poor devils ! Shelling of the day before was General Clements, who now has 1,500 fresh troops, slightly engaged, nothing serious. About 9pm a welcome message came up to say we need no longer all stand to arms. . .*

25 Christmas Day *Stood to Arms 3.30-4.30am. At 5am the kaffirs start singing and*

THE COMFORT OF BELL TENTS WERE BY NOW A DISTANT MEMORY AS THE CAMPAIGN BECAME TOUGHER

playing a brass band in the Location. Men are on full rations today, but through some mistake there is not enough bread and they get biscuits instead. Great slaughter of chickens and turkeys which have been fattening up round camps for months past for Christmas dinners. Big service in German Mission Chapel. Shoals of kaffirs turn up. Band accompanies. Kaffirs have another service in afternoon. Sit out under gum trees and listen to it. One of the hottest days we have had. CO sent his horse down for me about 6.15pm and I rode up to camp. Francis and Lyster join us and we have a great Christmas dinner. Turkey, plum pudding etc etc. General Kitchener and Officers at Oliphant's Nek sent wires. Return to Outposts about 10pm.

26 December   A very hot day again, and I sit under the gum trees to catch the slight breeze listening to the kaffirs chanting their responses and singing hymns to good old English hymn tunes. These kaffirs sing remarkably well and it is always a pleasure to listen to them, but the whole effect is spoilt by the introduction of this silly brass band started less than a year ago and producing the most horrible discord. The men are however extremely pleased with themselves, and swagger about showing their instruments to one another. The head of the Location, who is also head of the Native Town Police, is a fine, well-built, smart-looking chap well over 6' in height. This morning he is looking particularly fine in his well-fitting black suit, slouch hat, spotlessly white collar and shirt and black shoes and, as he leads the band, his glistening brass instrument slung over his shoulder like a bandolier, he is I am sure, considered a veritable king among men by the admiring congregation collecting round. This gentleman's name is Mr Pole (I don't know how he spells it) and like all the native chiefs I have met speaks English very well, dresses like a London toff, and treats one in rather a condescending kind of manner. Mr Bodenstab, the German missionary, and I are great friends, I find him most interesting. This afternoon he came up to me under my gum tree and made me a present of some grapes and peaches. I was of course extremely thankful and told him so. Now don't imagine that these fruits are anything like the home ones of the same name, because they are almost entirely different, both in size and flavour, in fact they are almost in their wild state. At 4.30pm Crossman comes down with H Company and relieves me and I return to camp.

27 December   Spent from 7.30am to about 11.30 building a sangar to protect our camp. Broiling sun and I return limp and filthy, my arms and face caked with mud caused by dust and perspiration… Major Watts and A B E & G Companies with the Machine Gun etc, arrive looking rather done after their hot march. The Argylls relieve them… Stood to Arms 3.15-4.45am. G Company go down after breakfast to Farm and reinforces Outpost Line as there is another scare on. Boers are in the neighbourhood. Another Company of Argylls go out to Oliphant's Nek and we take over part of their Outpost Line. Drizzled rain from 5-7.30pm and stopped then. At 8pm we marched down to the Church - my first introduction to Padre Webb-Peploe. He treated us to several silly little childish stories which hardly went down with the audience. Well meaning chap no doubt - but ! Drizzling again on return from Church, but cleared up in afternoon.

This letter is mostly concerned with descriptions of the local flora and fauna and of the countryside around Rustenburg. Malcolm also has something to say about photography:

Dear Ralph

…You have asked various questions about my camera. Well it is still in working order I am glad to say and I have been taking [photos] pretty regularly up to the last month or two when I ran out of films and did not bother to order any more thinking any day we might be ordered home. Having lost 12 spools, or 144 exposures, in the Post I did not think it good enough to risk sending any more home. I still have high hopes of some of them as I expect they are in the melee at one of the big Post Offices at Durban or Maritzburg. I have taken altogether 450 odd exposures since I left England. My camera being practically no weight goes everywhere with me, in action or out of action. I had it with me all through the Botha's Pass and Alleman's Nek fighting and in that photo taken by my subaltern of me on top of Inkweloane you will see the white strap of the haversack coming over my right shoulder and underneath the water bottle and camera straps which go over the left shoulder. You asked if I carry a rifle. We were compelled to carry rifles nearly all the time in Natal but on this side it is more 'go as you please' and I carry a stick most of the time which is much nicer on a long march. I am sending you some VRI stamps which were stamped by Baden-Powell when he was here in July.

Sixteen

A NEW CENTURY –
STILL AT RUSTENBURG

Opposite: "Marching Order" or what Tommy carried on his back in addition to his rifle

Rustenburg, 7th January 1901

My dear Father,

The last Mail to leave this place was on 9th December, yesterday the Convoy we had been expecting for so long at last came in and by it we got no less than four Mails. That was at 9 o'clock last night, this morning I came on Outposts and have been very busy making sangars etc all day. The first section of the returning Convoy goes back tomorrow morning so I am busy now finishing off my letters. I am sending with this letter my Diary for December written in the book Mother sent me with black paper and agate pencil. I don't think the result is a success myself, and it is certainly hardly worth the trouble. I have written more fully than in previous Diaries and on that account you will probably find it more interesting, but I am afraid you will not understand a good deal of the military abbreviations and terms. I have sent it to you first so that you may read it thoroughly and revise it where necessary before giving it out to relations and friends. I have no doubt that Claud will be able to explain anything you do not understand. Next month I have thought of a different way of concocting the Diary and I sincerely wish I had thought of it before.

Only a few days ago I found out that a brother officer [Crossman] had been in the habit of sending home to his brother by every Mail ever since he had left England a very complete Diary written more or less in narrative form of all that had happened since the previous Mail had left. The brother used to edit this diary as it was written in rather a free and easy style, have it printed, and then send it round to all his relations. This obviated the wearisome task of writing letters to each individual separately,

which as I have often told you is a job I hate, besides which I always try to give each person I write to a different piece of news from the others and the consequence is that all my opinions, experiences, troubles etc etc are scattered amongst a quantity of letters, half of which are probably by now either lost or destroyed. This is a pity because if this war ever ends I should like to have a complete record of my own of all our troubles, and how on earth am I going to make one if all the material is destroyed and I have nothing to go on but a very small and incomplete Diary with a few exceedingly short, sketchy entries for each day? Now in the Diary narrative all this is avoided. All one's experiences, opinions etc are grouped together in a book and there is no fear of their being lost. Why, Oh! why didn't I think of this sooner. In future then you must expect a Diary of events occurring from Mail to Mail with the addition perhaps of an explanatory letter, which will also contain thanks for letters etc and any messages I want to send people. I will address the letter and Diary in the first instance to Claud at the Chantilly address and will ask him to revise and alter where necessary (mind you it is nearly 15 months since we have been in civilisation) but if he should be sent out here as I fully expect he will, I will ask you to take on the task. I am sure you can't grumble at this arrangement as it seems to me so sound, in fact I am thinking of making out back Diaries in a similar way before I have forgotten everything that occurred in those far off days.

We are told there is a possibility of our being shut up in here for 3 months on end soon so be brave. Please thank all for letters, presents etc. No time to open last letters which have just arrived this minute.

Love to all,

MANY OF THE WEST YORKSHIRE OFFICERS HAD HORSES WHICH WERE NEVER WORKED INTO THE GROUND IN THE MANNER THAT THE CAVALRY AND MOUNTED INFANTRY HORSES SUFFERED

Meantime, in Rustenburg, there was a continual anxiety that the Boers would launch an attack on the troops stationed around the town itself.

8 January   *Stand-To 3.30am. Continue building Fort York. Make a new trench in front of Mill… Hear of Lord Kitchener's latest proclamation about burning farms etc… Signal lamps reported during night.*

9 January   *Stand-to 3am. Private Plummer reports hearing a gun-shot in Oliphant's Nek direction and also seeing a rocket and lamp in Magato's Pass direction. Horrid liar ! Prove lights to have been at Schoch's Farm and kraal by Swartzkoppies. 8.30am CO inspects Company for boots, water-bottles etc. Go through accounts with Captain Bartrum.* [Although Malcolm does not state it, it becomes clear from the account below that Captain Bartrum has taken over command of F Company]. *Sleep most of afternoon in waterproof mushyboo. Lord K of K's* [Kitchener of Khartoum's] *Army Orders out. Men and Boers to be shot for anything and everything!*

10 January   *5am to 7am I am on Observation Duty on Signal Hill…*

The British evidently decided that the situation was looking bleak as they went to great lengths to ensure that the road from Pretoria to Rustenburg was adequately patrolled to prevent any possibility of a repetition of the Boer attack on the convoy at Buffel's Poort. Malcolm's diary shows an aspect of this, the creation of small, dug-in posts along the road to Pretoria.

14 January   *B & F Companies parade at 1.50am taking 4 waggons, ammunition cart and 2 water-mules. Pass a cavalry post just outside Krondall. Road very fair now that the RE have nearly*

Ox-drawn waggons on the move from Rustenburg to Pretoria

completed their work. Reached Oorzaak about 6.30am and start digging trenches… Kitchener's Horse escort to Convoy arrives about 7 and we exchange news. 2 of our waggons return to Rustenburg taking back Mails. Got more trenches dug and a little further out than Crossman's. Read the Illustrated Papers. Convoy parks and outspans about a mile off us and moves on to Rustenburg 2pm. We live practically on bully beef and biscuits as Mess has hardly sent us out anything. Half F Company on Outposts finding 7 or 8 posts. Poured rain in the night. Indian mules and 2 African mules stray in the night but all turn up next day. Marched 9 miles today.

15 January   *Remain Oorzaak. Have breakfast early and then Bartrum and I go out with a half Company and a waggon for wood and supplies to clear farms up the valley. There are several families still left. We find any amount of fruit, chickens, ducks, pigs etc in deserted farms which Tommy is very pleased to bring back to camp. Major Irvine with 2 Companies of Argylls and 2 guns, who had been with General Clements, pass by after the convoy en route for Rustenburg. This helps us to believe a rumour that we are going to Pretoria by return convoy.*

And at last comes the welcome news that the West Yorkshires are to load-up and march to Pretoria, but there is still time for individual companies to clear and burn a few more farms.

16 January   *Remain Oorzaak. 3.30am gun-fire coffee. About 4am Captain Bartrum and self with half Companies of B & F start off for Modderfontein straight across country sending waggons by road to bring in families. Our orders are to bring in all families and destroy all foodstuffs and ovens. We get off two houses-full in two journeys by 11.30am. Find signalling rather difficult at first. There are several more families in front. The fruit at this season is mainly pomegranates, peaches and apples with a few lemons here and there. We get some kidney beans and cabbages. We burn all wheat, oats and hay and then return to camp driving 4 wee pigs in front of us getting in about*

12.30. Put Boer families in 3 tents. About 5pm all Battalion except Lyster and a few servants trek past and bivouac at the next spruit. Empty Convoy follows. We are to be rear-guard to Convoy and scheduled to reach Pretoria on the 19th. Half F Company on Outposts...

18 January *Up at 3.30am and I start off as Advance guard travelling on waggons as before. Pass remains of burnt convoy in half-light before sunrise and can't see much...*

19 January *Rouse 2.30am and leave about 3am... walk the rest of the way into Pretoria, part of the way beside the waggons of the Boer families. Halt 12 to 1.30 for lunch opposite Western Fort. Move on again and about 4pm are literally swept of the road by a hail storm... Marched 18 miles today.*

Any thoughts that the West Yorkshires entertained about lingering in Pretoria for any length were quickly dashed as the battalion was soon on the move once again.

Transvaal Hotel, Pretoria. 20th Jan 1901
My dearest Mother,

We are on the move once again as you will see from this address. We got in here from Rustenburg last night and are entraining today for Belfast where we will be once more under General Smith-Dorrien, whom we liked very much when we were with him before. Excuse this awful writing but the hotel pen is not a success.

We are now by way of joining a Brigade at Belfast under Colonel Spens of the KOYLIs (Kings Own Yorkshire Light Infantry) composed of the Suffolks, the Camerons, the Essex and ourselves in General Smith-Dorrien's Division. We shall probably see some fun, hope we come out well.

your very affectionate son,

CHASING DE WET WITH SMITH-DORRIEN AND LORD KITCHENER

The Boers had achieved a great success at Buffel's Poort and had gone on to achieve an even more spectacular victory when they caught, and comprehensively defeated, Major-General Clements and his column at Nooitgedacht. Unlike the British, with their absolute command of the railway network and almost instant communications in the form of the telegraph, the Boers could not mount a combined and sustained offensive which might drive the British back out of the republics. All that the Boers could hope to achieve was to prolong the war and hope to win their case at the conference table. There was also a general election looming in Britain which might bring the Liberals back to power and, as Smuts thought, create the political will to achieve peace with the Boers without actually defeating them in the field. For the moment, the most visible result from the Boer victories in December was the virtual dislocation of most of the British military dispositions across the Transvaal and Orange Free State together with an upsurge in Boer activities in all areas. One particular aspect of this renewed Boer activity was a co-ordinated attack by Botha and Viljoen against the British-held railway stations along the Delagoa railway line on the night of 7 January. The Boer attack was vigorously pushed home but the British were able to hold their ground; although driven off, the Boers did break up the railway line and destroyed a number of locomotives and much rolling stock.

The British, or rather Kitchener's, response was to take a sledge-hammer to strike at a will-o'-the-wisp, with inevitable results. First, however, the widely scattered British forces which had been expected to contain the Boers north of the Megaliesberg hills had to be re-grouped – leaving some in Rustenburg but creating a new force in and around Pretoria to be used in forthcoming operations elsewhere. The West Yorkshires were to be part of this new force. To begin with they were to assist in clearing the country of Boer families in the areas close to the railway line around Wonderfontein, and to help in the gathering up of foodstuffs and livestock. This formed part of Kitchener's policy of driving the Boers out into the open where superior British forces could confidently be expected to overwhelm resistance. Neither Malcolm nor his brother officers left any critical comment on this policy in their private papers; they had been given a job to do and do it they did without comment.

Any hopes that Malcolm might have had of spending any time in Pretoria, were soon dashed as orders came through for the West Yorkshires to entrain for Middleburg where they were to join a new formation under Colonel Spens, their objective was to provide part of a particularly large escort for a convoy of supplies which were to be distributed along the troops along the railway line towards Wonderfontein. Malcolm's account for the operation has been omitted here as in many respects this convoy duty was almost a rehearsal for the next phase of operations – an advance to Piet Retief in southern Transvaal.

On trek. The officers' mess somewhere in the field

Wonderfontein, 28th January 1901

My dear Father,

We have now joined Smith-Dorrien's Force and are what is called Colonel Spens' Brigade (Colonel Spens commanded the Shropshire LI when we were with them in the XIX Brigade on the De Wet chase). Spens' Brigade then is the Infantry portion of a Column under General Smith-Dorrien moving about in the district between Belfast and Standerton. The other Regiments are 1st Camerons, 1st Essex, and Suffolks. The artillery consists of 3 heavy guns (a 5' drawn by 12 horses and two 'cow guns' i.e. 4.7's or 5' drawn by oxen), a Field Battery and a half (part of this is 4 guns of the 66th battery of Colenso fame) and 3 pom-poms. Then there are 18th and 19th Hussars, 5th Lancers, ILH [Imperial Light Horse], and a lot of MI Companies under Colonel Henry. This is quite different fighting to any we have had before as the county is so different. Not a tree to be seen anywhere, nor a hill, only flat undulating 'rolling veldt', the rolls taking place every mile or so and the ground is now covered with long wiry grass with a few flowers scattered here

and there. I am now just outside Wonderfontein.

your affect son,

THE MULES WHICH CARRIED THE WEST YORKSHIRES' MACHINE GUN AND THEIR BARRELS OF WATER WERE LOOKED AFTER BY INDIAN TROOPS. THE SAME MEN ALSO ACTED AS STRETCHER BEARERS – THEY WERE NOT ALLOWED TO CARRY ARMS

Seventeen

INTO THE EASTERN TRANSVAAL... LAKE CHRISSIE AND PIET RETIEF

Opposite: 'The regiment was turned loose with bayonets to destroy green mealies and to starve the Boers.'

The advance into eastern Transvaal utilised seven columns, commanded by men who would become illustrious enough in time, including French, Allenby, Smith-Dorrien, with Paget and Plumer not so far behind. The columns themselves involved thousands of men – both infantry, cavalry and artillery – and massive numbers of ox-drawn waggons which, effectively, would determine the pace of the advance. The start line was the Delagoa railway and the columns were supposed to march out with intervals of about eight miles or so between each column. Naturally enough, this spacing was soon lost as the various columns, individually, encountered either the Boers or natural obstacles such as rivers. Out on the eastern flank was Smith-Dorrien, with, amongst his command, the West Yorkshires. With them was a huge convoy of ammunition and supplies. The nearest British column, Campbell's, was by mischance 12 miles away, thus leaving a huge gap to be exploited by the Boers.

With the British now re-deployed and replenished all along the Delagoa railway line, it was time for a new advance against the Boers and, in the following week, column after column of British troops, mostly mixed brigades of infantry, cavalry and artillery, wheeled off the railway line and moved south and east like a huge beating line to try and bring the Boers to battle or, failing that, pin them against the borders of Swaziland and force them to surrender. It looked simple enough on paper, but Boer opposition and dreadful weather conspired to make this an appalling episode for the British.

What of the Boers? It seems there were few enough of them, perhaps 4,000 in all, of which probably half were commandos drawn from the south and east Transvaal. Many of these men were released to return to their homes and families to do what they could to save families and livestock. The remainder, under the overall leadership of Botha, moved off to the north and east of the Transvaal into the path of the most eastern of the British columns – Campbell's and Smith-Dorrien's.

Although Malcolm's diary provides a continuous narrative, his letter-diary, which he sent home to his parents soon after the events described took place, offers a more interesting account. This covers the period 1-6 February 1901, and includes two maps of the position at Lake Chrissie one of which was drawn by Lieutenant Crossman who also wrote an interesting account of this action. Malcolm's account takes up the story:

1 February 1901, *The West Yorkshires are with Colonel Spens' Brigade encamped round*

IN THE TRANSVAAL - MARCHING ONWARDS

Wonderfontein Station. We have taken over the Essex Regiment's lines, tents and all, and now we have the proper number of tents per Company and Officers are two to a tent. 3.45 am my servant wakes me up and after a short struggle with sleep I am on my way round to visit the two Inlying Picquet. These posts found by F & G Companies. It is bright moonlight and I have no difficulty, though the Posts are rather far apart, one being just below the Station and the other at a farm-house some way in the opposite direction. On my way back I examine the trenches and barbed wire entanglements made by the Berkshire Regiment. Each trench is a fort in itself and has a sleeping compartment at either end. The sleeping place is merely an enlarged section of the trench, roofed over with corrugated iron sheeting [covered presumably with earth], and constructed above the level of the bottom of the trench so that it does not fill with water.

11 am, we have a Company Parade to inspect rifles, check ammunition, etc. Our Drums play in the afternoon, and Corporal Sherry, the big drummer, draws a big crowd as usual but the wind swings him round and round and he has rather a job with it. A supply of putties comes up for the Battalion and, besides fitting out the Company, the War news is rather tame. General Smith-Dorrien also publishes a summary of our late 5 days Carolina trek. Our casualties had only amounted to about 30 in all. He praises us, the Suffolks and MI.

2 February *CO has a Parade at 8.30am when he inspects the Companies, looks at boots etc. Dr. Collier holds a battalion medical inspection at 10am when he picks out the crocks who can't march.*

Awfully hot day but cool afternoon. The men's' spare blankets are returned to Store in the afternoon leaving them with one blanket per man. Our Drums play again in the afternoon. Lovely, moonlight night, a little chilly. …

3 February, Sunday *Rouse at 3.30am. Waggons are packed by 4am, we parade 5.30am and march off* [heading for the Swaziland border and Piet Retief]. *General Smith-Dorrien's Column is composed of: Colonel Spens' Infantry Brigade (Suffolks, West Yorkshires and Camerons), Colonel Henry's Mounted Infantry (3rd and 4th MI and Imperial Light Horse), three 5-inch guns one of which is drawn by horses, the other two by oxen; about 8 Field guns and 3 pom-poms. We march about 18 miles to Twyfelaar on the Komati river. The Suffolks are awfully bad at falling out and some of their men fall out in the first half-hour and get right back to Wonderfontein — Lucky devils!*

Awfully hot day and a most trying march, at one time we do 2 hours on end, but hardly a man of ours falls out and General Smith-Dorrien compliments us on this afterwards. Water too was a difficulty today as, although this part of the country is full of 'pans' (natural, circular depressions full of stagnant water), there was no running water till we reached Twyfelaar.

Last time we came here we left the high ground and keeping round to the right entered the hollow of Twyfelaar and were promptly attacked by the Boers, but this time, knowing the ground better, we stick to the high ground and circle round to the left. A mile or two outside camp we pass a big farm surrounded by a cluster of trees. This is the first we have passed today, since leaving Wonderfontein, to break the monotony of the open, rolling and undulating veldt we have here. There is not a hill to be seen on the whole horizon, nothing but the top of the next long 'roll' in front of

WAITING FOR TRANSPORT. THE WEST YORKSHIRES PREPARE TO MOVE OUT INTO THE FIELD ONCE AGAIN

you. This operation is commonly known as 'chasing the sky-line'. The expression originated in the Orange Free State. I believe, where it is even flatter than it is about here. Just beyond the farm we have a longish halt and the four rear Companies, E F G & H, are allowed to fill water-bottles from the Regimental water-cart. Personally I can go through the longest march on one filling of my water-bottle (I have the same kind as the men now, I lost my Officers' Pattern the very first day we got to Ladysmith) and Porch, I know, never carries one at all. But the men are terrors for water. Before we have gone 5 miles, and oftener before that, you can bet your bottom dollar there won't be a man in our Company who hasn't his water-bottle drained to the very last drop. Of course the more he drinks the more he wants to drink and the more he sweats. At the end of a long march without water en route he is almost beyond control and without reason. He will then, if allowed, drink the filthiest bog-water at the side of the road, quite regardless of enteric and after effects. We have all tried to break him of this habit but no one has yet succeeded. Kipling was right, never was Tommy given a better name than an 'Absent-minded Beggar'. He is and always will be!

On reaching camp we leave the greater part of the Force on the high ground this side of the Komati River, cross over and camp on the far side on flat ground close to where we were last time we were here. This is about 3.30pm and as we have had nothing to eat since breakfast at 4.30am (bar an 'emergency' biscuit carried in the haversack) we set to with a will when at last they get some food off the waggons for us. Soon after our meal General Smith-Dorrien, with his ADC, comes over to call. The General congratulates us on our marching powers and explains the present situation and tells us all about these parallel Columns, where they are going to and what they are for. We are to reach Lake Chrissie by the 6th, General Alderson to get to Ermelo etc., etc. He also explains this to clusters of men outside [the Mess]. In the evening the waggons of the convoy come across the river and park up close to us. At Dinner we have a luxury in the shape of fresh pine-apples, which must have arrived by train at Wonderfontein just before we left. Lovely moonlight night.

4 February Parade at 5.45am. Force moves on in the direction of Carolina. Suffolks are the advance guard, we are in the main body and Camerons have the rear guard. The ground is very boggy about here and the waggons stick a good deal. We have orders that on this trek we are to bring in all families from the farms, collect all livestock, destroy all foodstuffs and ovens, and when possible, to destroy all crops. The consequence is that after going a few miles and a large field of mealies is spotted close by, the whole Battalion is turned on 'caedare' - cut, burn or slay. Rifles are slung and bayonets brought out and then the slashing commences. Mealies at this season are big, green and juicy and the cattle love them. An ox in a mealy field is the equivalent of 'pigs in clover' out here - or it should be if it isn't ! One slash with the bayonet cuts down the big stalks but the little ones of the second crop have to be pulled up. Tommy rather likes this new form of work, but the next job F Company is turned onto immediately after this, namely - pulling waggons out of the soft ground - is an ordinary, every day job and requires a lot of exertion and he is not nearly so well pleased. One mule waggon has its rear wheels buried 2 feet deep and looks hopeless, however by double-spanning (hitching on the span from another waggon) and getting half the Company to shove we succeed in getting it out and onto firmer ground. General Smith-Dorrien insists on keeping his Column well closed up and that accounts for the long and frequent halts we have on every march now [which earned the columns the sobriquet of 'caterpillar columns' from the Boers].

At 11.15am we start off moving again, very slowly and keeping south of Carolina, not following a road, but trekking straight across the veldt for our destination, Lake Chrissie, picking out of course the best ground for the transport.

About 1.30pm we have another longish halt and eat a light luncheon of bully and biscuit and jam, but don't take our straps off as we don't know how long the halt is for. About 2pm we are on the move once more and soon after 3pm we halt for the night on a

ANY PAUSE FOR A BREAK WOULD HAVE BEEN WELCOME

farm location called Onbeken. Most of the West Yorks are employed through the night on Outposts and Picquets. The ground is open and there is a good moon but unfortunately the grass is long and the dew heavy so we get sopping wet.

5 February 2am, I send round to my four posts to roll up their blankets, great coats and oil sheets and send them into camp. Parade at 4am joining the remainder of the Battalion on the march. Today we are the advance guard with the Camerons following. On these occasions the mounted troops are well in front and only the first company move in extended order, the remainder follow in Column formation as the ground is so open. Before we have been many hours on the march some Boers are seen moving about on the high ground on our left and one of the 5-in guns poops off once or twice at them. One shot is a beauty and gets right into a party of a dozen or so first go. The ground is still rather soft and we move very slowly to let the Column close up. Now and then a hare or some quail cause a slight diversion, especially if they come close to or right into the ranks as they sometimes do, for Tommy is very keen on making any additions he can to his rations. While walking along I notice some pretty blue flowers of the crocus species, and, at one of the halts, I dig some bulbs up with my long knife. At this same halt Cantor and I take refuge from the merciless sun in the shade of a waggon, halted close by, and find two Sergeants of the 5th Lancers have also taken refuge there. The 5th Lancers were besieged at Ladysmith, then with us after that in Natal, and then went to Lydenburg and of course we had a long 'bukh' over our different experiences.

2.30pm we reach the village of Bothwell on the side of Lake Chrissie, feeling rather fatigued from our ten mile march in the hot sun, especially as we have had nothing to eat since breakfast at 3am. We make up for lost time now, though, and enjoy a hearty cold lunch. Tonight the West Yorkshires are holding rather a long Outpost Line and it takes 4 1/2 Companies to hold it: G H A B & 1/2 of F Company are told off for this job. My skipper takes out half of F

Company that he had in Support the previous night and I remain in camp with the other half. It is a good bright moonlight night with a heavy dew. I sleep outside the Mess Shelter tonight with Porch and some others, which is wrong of us as we should be sleeping alongside our Companies !

6th February Woken up at 3am by hearing bullets singing over our heads and dropping all around us. Thought at first it was only a sentry firing at horses, or something of that sort, and prepared to go to sleep again, but was very soon startled out of this illusion as the noise did not stop and the bullets were coming over thicker and I saw Porch getting up. It was not many seconds then before I had helmet and straps on.

By this time the men too were all up and finding their present position too hot for them (one poor chap, Corporal Taylor, was shot dead in his Company lines and another man was hit shortly after while unlacing the cover of the machine gun at the head of the Battalion). One party under the Sergeant-Major I see streaming down from the lines towards me. I ask what their orders are and what Company they belong to and soon discover they are a mixture of all Companies, some of my own men amongst them, with no particular orders. I take command without further orders and get the men to line along the edge of the farm garden and road facing Lake Chrissie, then to lie down and fix bayonets. The Sergeant-Major is a bit nervous I fancy for whenever the bullets come singing overhead a little thicker than usual he fancies the men in front of him are firing and shouts out in an agonised voice 'Don't fire, Don't fire !'. I go over and reassure him and presently when things have settled down a bit I send him across to the lines to report what I am doing to the CO. As I have already said it was a fine moonlight night but now there is a slight mist and one can only see two or three hundred yards. All this time a perfect shower of bullets has been passing over our heads from the right and now (3.10am) we hear firing in the thick wood on our left with an occasional report louder than the rest like a revolver shot.

SLASHING DOWN FIELDS OF MEALIES WITH BAYONETS - 4 FEBRUARY 1901

(This turned out to be the MI having a battle of their own amongst themselves and I am afraid in rather a state of panic refusing to recognise even Colonel Spens' himself who tried to stop the commotion. The occasional loud report was I believe an old burgher with an elephant gun having pot shots at the camp !). A minute or two after this a mob of stampeded horses rushes across my front, coming from the direction of the MI lines to my left rear, and passing along in front of the Battalion lines, they circle eventually around the camp. Many of these get shot en route and one lot branched off from the rest and made straight out of camp, never returning. The remainder went on as I said round the camp and at one time got between the attacking Boers and our Outposts. The wily Burghers took advantage of this, some of them getting in amongst the horses and so getting closer to our Posts. And now one of our Pom-Poms comes into action, fires a few shots on my left, but why I have never yet discovered except possibly that it might have been to reassure the MI who were playing at hide-and-seek round that quarter and did not quite know where they were. (Some of them I was told afterwards were actually crying with funk in the wood !). When I say MI I mean practically all the mounted troops for I believe the 5th Lancers and even the Gunners too lost their heads and fired at random anywhere and at anything. One of the 5th Lancers I heard went clean off his chump, got under a waggon and blazed off the contents of his magazine at his own Officers' Mess! To this day the MI firmly believe the Boers got right into camp and hid under waggons. Certainly one hoary-headed old Burgher seems to have got into the Camerons lines and was chased all round the shop there, even going through their Officers' Mess, but eventually got safely away. Then, they say, bits of another Boer were found in the ILH lines and that, if true, is I fancy the sum total of all that got into camp that night.

About 3.30am some MI come across from the left and line along the road between my chaps and the wood, but fortunately our services are not required as the Boer attack is only against one point and that, as you will see from the map, is against G H & A Company lines.

We heard afterwards that two or three other Commandos were to have attacked our camp simultaneously at other points, but, perhaps fortunately for us and certainly most unfortunately for the present attack, they failed to turn up.

Well, there we lay on the wet grass praying for the daylight to come for we felt instinctively that when dawn came, and provided all went well with us, the Boers would draw off. Shivering with cold I bitterly regretted not having slipped on my great coat, which would of course have been wrong of me had I done so, for a black coat in that light would give anyone away and here is where the 'coat, warm, British' comes in for it is khaki coloured. I might have got it even now for it was only a few yards off but I could not leave my charge, and apart from this the bullets were flying beastly low just then ! The rattle of volleys about this time, away over on the right, was a cheering sound and we felt that it was all right in that quarter anyway. Shortly after 4am the day began to break, the firing grew less and finally stopped altogether. Then all stretchers were requisitioned and the dead and wounded brought into camp. I stroll over to C Company on my right to hear what has been happening over there and find Harrington gloating over a Mauser rifle, but they have sad news for me. Poor Cantor has been shot in the head with an explosive bullet and is dead. In front of the Outposts' line is the grim result of the stampede; half a dozen dead horses lying in all sorts of positions, some with their feet stuck straight in the air. I forgot to mention that shortly after 4am a strange figure came past me from the right. He was a robust, elderly man with a dark moustache and a jolly, red face (something like Uncle Willie), a Boer hat on his head, a shawl or rug thrown over his shoulders and pyjamas and gum boots on as far as I can remember. The men said he was a Major in the ASC. I could not make him out for a long time. He turned out in the end to be our jolly, good-natured, Brigadier - Colonel Spens ! I stared at him very hard at the time and in the end took no notice of him, thinking he might be a conductor or doctor or something of that description.

Finally, about 4.30am, the MI who have horses left go out in pursuit and we Infantry return to camp. You may wonder why no guns were fired from camp at the retreating Boers but as I have already said there was a thick mist on and this had not quite cleared when the MI went out but they took with them a big gun, field guns and all sorts. It was too late, however, as by this time the Boers had got well away, waggons and all.

The next surviving piece of letter-diary starts of 10 May 1901, and whilst Malcolm's letters and daily entries in his diaries offer vivid impressions of his daily life, they are as nothing when compared to the descriptive narrative he provides in his letter diaries. Drummer Goodwin's diary has, by this stage of the war, become very perfunctory and is has to be said that it reflects his general disillusionment with the progress of the war. Lieutenant Crossman, as ever, wrote a heroic comment on Lake Chrissie:

"Personally, I was woken up at five minutes to 3 by hearing Ping--Ping--Phit--Phutt--Phutt and all at once hopped into the trench and got the men in too. The trench was

MALCOLM RIALL'S MAP OF LAKE CHRISSIE, POSITION OF INDIVIDUAL COMPANIES OF WEST YORKSHIRES ON NIGHT 5/6 FEBRUARY 1901

only a foot and a half high as the ground was rock, except for about three inches of soil on top, so I could not make more. Then two of my men came running back wounded. They were part of what remained of my sentry line. I had only visited them an hour before. Then we saw the dim figures of the Boers coming on literally in swarms. There must have been 300 or 400 coming straight for my picquet. I would sooner not talk of what happened after that. It is too ghastly. I know that my revolver spat out viciously till the ammunition was gone and then I yelled and shouted at the men and thank God we kept 'em out of the camp. One bullet went between my lips and was turned sideways and I got splinters of bullet all over me. When I come home I will tell you more. At present the mere remembrance of it makes me feel sick. The CO was kind enough to say we had done magnificently in the morning but my poor Company is a wreck now. Out of 48 men of my Company on Outpost with me 5 were killed and 12 wounded - or more than one man in 4 was hit. This does not include men with scratches. Four of my rifles and 3 bayonets were smashed to atoms by bullets. God preserve me from this sort of thing again. It was awful - awful. Time is gradually getting us over it now but it will be a long time before I forget it. The noise was awful. I captured two Boers but if I had known at the time that all their bullets were soft-nosed I would… well, they would not have been captured. Poor Cantor was an awful sight. Half his head was gone. When daylight came it was an awful place. 40 bodies scattered across a space as big as the lower field and about 40 more wounded things groaning and crying. How any of us came out alive I do not know. Now let me forget it once more till I am home."

Sergeant Traynor was awarded the VC for his part in this action. The skirmish at Lake Chrissie created such an impression on the officers and men of the West Yorkshires that in later years their annual remembrance dinner to honour the Boer War veterans, and their fallen comrades, was named after Lake Chrissie rather than one of the greater actions that they had participated in during the relief of Ladysmith. Malcolm's diary continues:

7 February *Remain Lake Chrissie. Stood to arms at 2.30am. Still moonlight then and mosquitoes and gnats very bad. MI go out along road at 4.30am and their Post retires from valley below. At 4.30am sent in blankets etc in case we move suddenly. 5.30am return to camp. Pours rain all afternoon. Soon after lunch Colonel Campbell's Column comes in and camps on opposite side of valley – this column consists of the Leicesters, 18th Hussars, and a few guns. E,*

F, G & H Companies on Outposts 5.30pm. Connect up with Leicesters' line. E Company on left of line. I have three section trenches for Outposts with one in Support. Dig good trenches and cut mealies. Rain stops about 5pm and there is a fairly clear night. Moon out a bit.

8 February *Remain Lake Chrissie. Got all posts awake and men lining trenches at 2.30am. Misty moon. 4.45am put men on from each post to cut mealies and improve trenches. Men work well. We return to camp 5.45am. Starts raining at 6am and continues steadily till 9am. Write to Father. [Letter/45 which provides a very short description of the Lake Chrissie action and has been omitted.] Letters taken by Hospital people who are taking the sick to Ermelo and thence to Standerton. Biscuit ration is 5 biscuits per man. Rains hard all afternoon till 4.30pm when it clears. A Field general court martial is held in the Mess. G, H, A & B Companies on Outposts, trenches full of water. Mosquitoes very bad and I am bitten all over wrists.*

9 February *Rouse 4am. Column moves off 5.30am in a NW direction following telegraph wires. Outpost Companies go on first as escort to Field Hospital etc. E Company leads remaining half Battalion. Colonel Campbell's Force moves over to Bothwell as we move out and we leave him a 5-in gun. He is moving parallel to us and in echelon. He captured a letter from one of the Johannesburg commando saying Boers had 28 killed in night attack. About 2 miles out waggons stick in mud very badly and I am kept till 11.30 getting them out. Took several photos. Cross a spruit about half way running very strong. Reach Lillieburn 2.30pm and find a Boer convoy streaming into camp – Colonel Henry had captured about 50 waggons, 13,000 head of sheep and cattle, and 8 Boers etc etc. 5.20pm E & F Companies go out and cut mealies. Men on 3/4 rations. B, C & D Companies on Outposts. Remainder of Battalion in line behind instead of Quarter Column. Very dark night. Spots or bites on hand getting worse and bigger. Several snakes killed on march.*

10 February, Sunday *Rouse 4am, Breakfast 4.30am. Sheep strewn all over plain make a curious spectacle [the Battalion War Diary explains, volunteers were called to kill sheep, the men being allowed a penny a head for each sheep killed. A good many volunteered.] We have kidney, liver and mutton chops for breakfast. Men on full rations and 3lb mutton. Fatigue parties sent off to build bridge over drift and make road. Parade ordered for 11am but we parade eventually 2pm. Bridge over spruit, the Umpulusi River, is very good with old waggons etc used as supports. Made by Thompson, RE [Royal*

CROSSING RIVERS PRESENTED THE BRITISH WITH THE CHALLENGE OF GETTING ACROSS QUICKLY. THIS WAS NO EASY TASK WITH SO MANY OX-DRAWN WAGGONS, AND THERE WAS AN EVER-PRESENT WORRY THAT THE BOERS WOULD ATTACK WHILST THE CROSSING WAS TAKING PLACE. MALCOLM'S DETAILED ENTRIES OFFER AN INSIGHT INTO THE TROUBLE THE BRITISH TOOK TO ENSURE THESE MANOEUVRES TOOK PLACE WITHOUT MISHAP

Engineers]. *Move onto top of high ground above drift and halt for night at 4pm… D, E & F Companies on Outposts. E Company on left. Make section posts and good trenches. Cover front of trenches with sheep skins. Good night, slightly misty and chilly. We are at Warburton.*

11 February *Stand to 3am. Parade ordered for 6.10am but cancelled and delayed till sheep are all slain. Parade eventually at 8.30am. Good road with level slopes. Cattle driven along in a huge herd and we keep with them nearly the whole way. 12.30 we reach very rocky ground and the whole column gets very jumbled up. Umpulusi River not far in front… and camp on high ground this side of drift about 3.15pm. Place called Craigie Lea. In helio communication with Colonel Campbell and Generals French and Alderson. 3.45pm Porch takes 50 men down to the drift. I take another 50 men down at 6.15 but return as we are not wanted. Most of the Camerons across with a 5-in gun. Stream very strong and 4 feet deep, some mounted men fall off and have narrow shaves. F, G, H, A & B Companies on Outposts, remaining Companies in line round camp. Go to bed early. Bright moon then. Marched 10 miles.*

12 February *Remain at Craigie Lea. Rouse 4.30am, Breakfast 5am. No hour set for parade owing to drift. Woke up feeling very refreshed and enjoyed a good breakfast. 6.45am take original fatigue party down to drift and put men to work collecting stones to make bridge and improve the road. Both Generals down and all staff etc. Harrington relieves me at 9am. Bridge is soon completed and mule waggons get across fairly rapidly. F Company on drift fatigue 2.30pm. Camerons, Suffolks, most of mounted troops and convoy across by 3pm. West Yorks cross at 4pm leaving B, C, D & E Companies to take up Outpost positions 5pm. E Company spread out in a single line behind and supporting B Company who hold a long line of rocks. All Mess together – chickens, apricots etc. Good night, sleep well, heavy dew.*

13 February *Rouse 3.30am, moonlight and heavy dew. Breakfast 4am and parade 4.30, General muddle. Get across drift on a rickety plank and go straight up to Battalion HQ where CO meets us and sends us out to a kopje on left of camp where we find Bartrum with F Company and some of the ILH. Wait there till 7am and then move on as Rear Guard. Some sniping on left flank and left rear and 5-in gun replies with a few rounds. We march to Woodstock getting in about 6.15pm and find half the camp is the other side of the next drift. G & H Companies on Outposts and we get some grub. Dig a long Company trench in a mist and get settled down about 10pm. Marched 15 miles today.*

14 February *Stand to 4am, greatcoats sent in and breakfast for men brought out 4.30am. Parade 6.15am and cross Umpulusi river which is nearly 2 feet deep and continue along this curious winding road in a SE direction. After going 4 or 5 miles the column splits up and Colonel Spens takes about half the force. MI, Suffolks and West Yorkshires with a 5-in and a few other guns move on south, the baggage and remainder branching off for Amsterdam. We go on to the Swazi border and at Litchfield's Store. 7 or 8 Boers snipe us. We fire guns and thousands (2,000 odd) of rounds at them. Halt 11.30 till 2.15 while this is going on having a hasty lunch at 2pm. Then, Suffolks and MI with 2 guns are left at Litchfield's Store and we trek back in WSW direction. About 4pm we reach Tweepoort and here West Yorkshires, MI and 2 more guns stay. Remainder go on to Amsterdam. Position is mainly composed of rocky kopjes. We find about 8 posts and build sangars.*

15 February *Remained at Tweepoort. Fine morning and I sleep a long while after daybreak regardless of my Outposts. Get men to work on entrenchments after breakfast. About 1.30pm CO takes out the 2 field guns, some MI and three Companies. He goes out about 4 miles in an SE direction to capture a party of Boers with an ox gun. Sees a few Boers (who get away) and rounds up 100 sheep. Awfully hot day and very close. Watch CO's operations from the top of Signal Hill. Can see Amsterdam from here, also General French's and General Alderson's columns to the south of us.*

16 February *Remain at Tweepoort. Misty morning and a wet misty day. Put up barbed wire in front of the two left posts and improve the sangars in morning and afternoon. About 5pm Colonel Mackenzie and ILH come in bringing a 5-in cow gun, also more sheep and cattle etc. There is to be a biggish move from here soon but in which direction we do not know. C & D Companies ordered to parade at 5am to go out with Colonel Mackenzie, also B Company at 5.30 to collect Boer families. E Company finds Outposts.*

17 February, Sunday *Remain at Tweepoort. 6am go up to the Mess and find nearly everybody has already had breakfast at 4.30am owing to expected move. Lowe starts at 6.30 with some empty waggons to take Boer families into Amsterdam. 9am E Company builds and improves sangars. Move does not come off owing to heavy mist. 12 noon Collier and Francis return from packing away the 40 odd Boer women and children into waggons. Scotch cart sent down later for more barbed wire and wood. 2pm build more sangars though still very wet and beastly. 5.30pm. Two new alarm posts are put on.*

18 February   *Remain at Tweepoort. Breakfast at 4.30am and C & E Companies stand by to move at 5am (and afterwards at half-hour's notice) as escort to 5-in gun with Colonel Mackenzie's Force. Thick mist and rain all morning. Sit in mushyboo most of day and complete Defaulters Book with addresses etc and write up Diary. 1pm Provost Marshal (Daniels) comes up from Amsterdam to see farms etc, tells us French has captured Mrs Smuts. Hear also that convoy under Burn-Murdoch has only 10 days' supplies and will not arrive till the 22nd [this being the main supply column for the British forces in the eastern Transvaal – like the West Yorkshires, he has been slowed down by the weather]. Consequently rations are cut down a bit. Mess has run out of butter, whisky etc. 1.30pm Carey with C Company goes out with ILH to farms to the south-east to collect food etc but does not get much. Rain stops 1.30 till 2.30 and I get some of my clothes dry. D Company goes on with building sangars. Awfully dark night. Wrote to Father.*

Tweepoort, Nr Amsterdam, Transvaal. 18th Feb 1901

My dear Father,

Once more a hasty note and I hope it may catch some outgoing Mail soon. We have been marching ever since I last wrote and are now hovering about the Swaziland border, hunting stray Boers and collecting cattle, sheep, etc. It is not a bad job but the weather just now is horrid, the sun has just put in an appearance a few minutes ago for the first time for four consecutive days. In the meantime we have been soaked and as we have no tents or cover of any kind Outposts and making entrenchments have been a most unpleasant experience. All the same the weather makes no difference to our health which is the main thing. The Queen of the Swazis came through our lines the other day on her way to see General Smith-Dorrien. I did not see her myself but I hear she was very strong in wind and body, more especially the latter and strutted away at the head of her escort like a champion walker on a running track ! We expect more supplies in a day or two and then we shall probably go off again in some new direction. We arrived here on the 14th and leave I don't know when.

your affectionate son,

19 February   *Mist has lifted slightly and we have heavy rain instead. Breakfast 4.30am and we wait once more to move. This time A, D, E & F Companies under Major Watts are to go to Litchfield's Store and B & G Companies escort a 5-in gun with ILH. Clears up about 8 and we eventually start about 8.30am. Reach Suffolk's camp at 10.30. Colonel Mackenzie's Column, ILH, 5-in etc move out eastwards and some troops from Amsterdam co-operate; Colonel Campbell and 2 Companies of Camerons come up to hold Tweepoort. H Company goes out to bring in more families etc. C Company is only Company left in. Soon after we arrive at Litchfield's Store (whole Battalion of Suffolks gone out) a Swazi flag of truce comes in and Chief Gondo holds a palaver with Major Watts who hands over to him General Smith-Dorrien's present of 50 cattle and 1,000 sheep for the Swazi Queen. Keeps fine all day. Start back at 6pm and get in at 8. D Company relieves Camerons Outposts, E Company in Support. Return from dinner at 9.15 and hear B & G Companies coming in with cattle etc; the 5-in gun gets stuck in mud. Rains again. The two Columns today captured: 1 Boer, 2,200 cattle, 15 mules, 3 waggons with oxen, 1,000 sheep, 30 horses with saddles and 30 horses without saddles. 1 Boer killed, 2 Boers wounded, 28 waggons destroyed (13 of these by the Swazis), also 27 Boers surrendered bringing in 500 cattle, 4,000 sheep and a Cape Cart.*

20 February   *Supports retire at 5.15am. Not raining now and we get blankets, greatcoats tools etc on waggons by 6am. Heavy rain comes on at 7am and parade is altered from 7.30 to 8.20am. D & E Companies then move out to head of baggage on road, 2 Companies of Camerons behind. Remainder of Battalion goes by Joubert's Farm road, ILH come on later. Move off down road at 9.30am. E Company advance guard, halt 10 till 11. Catch up with Battalion and move behind. Two bad drifts in pass. Harrington has an awful job driving sheep along. Rejoin Battalion and we pass through Amsterdam 1pm, cross a spruit and camp about a mile beyond on a plain. Colonel Campbell's Column left this morning heading south. Fine morning with only occasional showers, wet afternoon and drenching rain. Lunch about 2pm in open off cold pork and mutton and biscuits. Suffolks arrive later, also ILH. Tired and sleep under a waggon for a bit. At 5.45pm E & G Companies go out on Outposts, B & F Companies in Support. I find two half Company posts and keep in touch with Camerons on right. Poured rain all night but I sleep all the same, lying in a pool of water.*

21 February   *Remain Amsterdam. Wake up soaked to the skin. Visiting patrol returns about 4am after getting itself lost twice. Light just coming. Visit Sergeant Kenyon soon afterwards and find the Camerons have evacuated post on right. Put a section in it and see Cameron officer. Retire 5am leaving an observation post out. Get into dry clothes and have* breakfast. No move today. River too high to cross. Heavy rain stops with daylight and it drizzles on and off all day. Rations are getting worse and worse, 1/4 of biscuit now, no jam, and butter at one meal only. Tommy willing to pay 2/- for a biscuit. Evening clear, no rain. B, F & C Companies on Outposts. Rains nearly all night but not nearly so bad as night before. Mushyboo very successful and I sleep without getting wet. 22 February   Remain at Amsterdam. Sky clouded over and raining slightly. Rained nearly all night long but not so bad as night before. Can't move today. River 5 miles on is 300 yards wide and Colonel Campbell is stuck there. Besides this there is another river 30 yards wide between us and the convoy. General French wires total of bag of all Columns on this trek already exceeds: 600 Boers killed, wounded or taken prisoner. Captured 119 horses used as remounts, 433 others, 32 mules, 50 waggons and 24 other vehicles in use, 55 waggons and 22 other vehicles destroyed, 733 sacks of mealies taken and 341 destroyed, 2 tons of oat hay destroyed. Included in above General Smith-Dorrien's Column accounted for: 37 Boers killed, 107 wounded, 18 prisoner and 28 surrendered to Major Lancing of ILH at Wolvenkop.

23 February   Remain Amsterdam. Still biscuits for breakfast in the Mess. Plenty of kidneys. Men's rations today, besides meat, 8 oz mealy meal and a little bacon to make mealy cakes. A clear morning and no rain but still cloudy. Have a bath and dry most of my clothes.

'MAJOR WATTS INTERVIEWING SWAZIS AT LITCHFIELD'S STORE WHO WANT TO KNOW HOW TO TREAT DUTCHMEN IN THEIR TERRITORY.'

Rifle and ammunition inspection 8.30am. Rains again 10 till 11 but clear after that and a nice afternoon. Ingles takes out G Company and part of F Company to farms on other side of stream in morning and returns soon after lunch with 5 loads of dried and green mealy heads. D, E & H Companies on Outposts, E Company in Support in two half Company trenches behind H Company. Fine night till moon down about 10pm then a thick misty rain.

24 February, Sunday
Remain at Amsterdam. Misty morning. Return to camp about 5am. Church parade Service ordered for 8.45 but this is put off owing to misty rain coming which however clears soon after 9am. Voluntary Service held at 11am. Turns out a fine day and a lovely afternoon. Men's rations today, besides 2 and half lbs. of fresh meat and a 1/4lb of maconochie, 8 oz mealy meal, 2 fresh mealy cobs, and 2 peaches. Mess give us out today 2 biscuits each, the very last of our reserve supply. 5am A & C Companies go out to farms south of here on other side of stream. Returned at 5pm rather done with some cattle. Cows distributed to units and we get between 20 and 30. Everyone has tremendous appetites and demands second helpings of everything. Fill up gaps between meals with hard, almost tasteless, peaches. 5.30pm E, F & G Companies on Outposts; E Company in 3 trenches, 2 Outposts and 1 Support. I stay with No 2 Post and put up mushyboo. Heavy dew but no rain.

The next day the West Yorkshires loaded up their equipment and set out to march to Swaby's

Store at Derby which was no great distance away but, owing to the recent rains and the depth of water in all the drifts, it was to prove an arduous march.

25 February   *Stand to 3am but it is not light till 4.30am, return to camp about 5, breakfast 5.30 and parade 7am. March 5 miles to Compies River but find it will take some time to cross and main column marches back about a mile and camps on high ground above river. Get in here, Sterkfontein, about 10.30am. MI collect more big flocks of sheep on opposite side of river. Men's rations today: 2 and half pounds fresh meat, quarter pound bully beef, 8 oz mealy meal, 3 fresh mealy cobs, small amount of pumpkin and wheat to mix with dinners, besides coffee for breakfast and cocoa for tea. 3pm take E Company out to a big mealy field just out of camp to cut mealies for mounted troops. Cut away till 5.30pm and then return with a waggon load of cobs and stalks. Awfully tired and go to bed early. G, B & A Companies on Outposts.*

THE WEST YORKSHIRES USED BUNDLES OF STRAW FROM A HAYSTACK TO BURN THIS FARM DOWN HAVING FIRST REMOVED THE TIN ROOFING

Result of operations since 27th January: Boers killed, wounded and captured 392, Boers surrendered 353, Canon taken 4, Rifles 606, ammunition 161,630, Horses and mules 6,504, trek oxen 4,362, Cattle 20,986, Sheep 158,130, waggons and carts 1,604, mealies and oat hay over 4 million, Knox dug up a 12 wheeled limber containing 21 5-in howitzer shells. Boers trekking east to Gnomi Forest and the Swazi Queen says the Boers are stealing her corn and shooting natives.

26 February   *Breakfast at 5.30. Very heavy dew on long grass. Waggons are getting slowly across the drift. 7.30am big veldt fires started around Amsterdam. MI go out reconnoitring in this direction and a pom-pom fires a few shots… 11.45am F, B & E Companies move down to the drift behind G & D Companies; Cavalry holding on till we cross the drift. Cross over on a rather rickety RE swing bridge in single file and join rest of Battalion, formed up about 1pm and eat lunch. Move on again at 2pm. Reach Wolvenkop about 6pm. Very wet from crossing small drifts. Dirty camp. Half a dozen sheep skins and entrails in my Company lines smelling abominably. Outpost line extraordinarily close to camp. H & A Companies on Outposts, B and half C Companies in Support.*

27 February   *Parade ordered for 6am but put back a bit owing to mist and we move off eventually at 6.40am. Reach the Shela River about 9.30. Waggons get across drift all right and we have a strong footbridge. Force halts on the far side and we manage to secure a small avenue of trees which is very welcome as the sun is well out today. Mealies and sugar cane in fields alongside. Move on again at 1pm. Go for half a mile and then sit down again for an hour or so in baking sun. Meanwhile cattle and sheep go along a road to the left and the waggons and remainder of Force go right along for General Alderson and Campbell's camps a few miles ahead, pass them by and follow high ground curving round to the left. When most of the Force has passed we form line to the left and cut down a huge field of mealies in the dip below. Move on again at 3.30pm and after an hour's marching strike into* remainder of Column. Camp down about 5pm at Swaby's Store, at Derby. Men rather done, green mealies do not agree with them. We Officers are given a very good wheat ration now and Mess gives us brown bread at all three meals. C, D, E & F Companies on Outposts in section trenches. Heavy. dew. Men have maconochies and bully beef boiled together at 9pm. Marched 10 miles today.

28 February   Remain Swaby's Store Colonel Henry and nearly all mounted troops are out in Swaziland after a Boer convoy. General Alderson has left his last camp. Dig trenches again 3.30 to 4.30pm. Go on Outposts 5.30pm and keep men digging till about 9pm to complete the trenches. Lovely night. E, F, G & H Companies on Outposts. Lord Kitchener wires he is very pleased with excellent work done by troops out here. De Wet defeated in Orange River Colony, his guns and pom-poms captured.

SEE OPPOSITE

1 March   Remain at Swaby's Store. Moonlight night till 1.15am when thick mist comes in and I get Supports to put a sentry on. Fog lifts about 5.15am and I am just starting for camp when it comes on again. CO and Major Watts come out about 5.30am as MI patrols have just been sniped by a few Boers. Return 6am. We have started mealy coffee at breakfast. Snipers turn out to be 30 Boers waiting to catch our convoy. Convoy which comes in morning has only 15 men of the 12th Lancers as escort but luckily 2 Companies of Camerons and guns go out to meet it and drive off Boers. Convoy consists of 7 waggons with biscuits, cheese, coffee, oats etc. Fine day. Sleep most of morning. 2pm E & F Companies go down to valley about a mile out and cut down mealies returning 5pm. At 3pm Harrington and 30 men from C Company escort some Boer families into Piet Retief. Starts raining fairly heavily about 7pm and goes on for most of the night. Force now has 7 mealy grinders and 1 coffee mill, all kept in work day and night. G, H, A & B Companies on Outposts. The Swazi Queen has ordered scouts all over her country to locate Boers, waggons etc and to convey information to nearest British post. General Botha to meet Lord Kitchener at Middleburg today and discuss peace proposals.

2 March   Remain at Swaby's Stores. About 6am two Boer snipers fire at the Outposts on left of Camerons line. MI go out but the Boers get away. 1.30pm, I take Pioneers and Defaulters and a waggon to Swaby's Store to get some zinc sheeting but find most of it gone when I arrive. Load up with wood instead. Very heavy hail shower comes on about 3pm and we shelter at Store. Return about 4pm. 2pm A, B, E & F Companies improve entrenchment of Outpost line as we shall probably stay here some time. 5.30pm A, B, E & F Companies on Outposts, D Company also Outpost on a hill in front of Camerons line. Put up my mushyboo behind Support trench. We had cheese at lunch and dinner, and brown bread. Heavy shower comes on while at dinner and it is a cloudy wet night though fairly bright. Colonel Henry's captures of families, cattle etc come in about dusk.

3 March, Sunday   Remain Swaby's Store. Put sentries on Support trenches at 2.30am and keep them on till 6am. Mist does not lift till 6.30am when we are allowed to retire. Church parade ordered 9.10am but nearly all Companies are employed and I don't think we send any representatives. 8am E & F Companies under Major Watts go out with 2 guns and 2 troops of 5th Lancers, all under Colonel King of 5th Lancers, to Swaziland to bring in Boer families, mealies etc. Farm is about 7 miles out at the bottom of a valley. We rode on waggons for 5 miles. Guns, part of F Company and part of 5th Lancers stay on high ground while we go down below. Ground is awfully wet and swampy and we reach farm about 11am. There is a mill there full of oats and mealies and 3 farms in all. Get about 40 bags of mealies, 20 bags of oats and 2 families. Destroy the mill by breaking up and burning. While this is going on I have been busy with 2 or 3 helpers filling a sack with vegetables and fruit, get a few of the following: pomegranates, green figs, cape gooseberries, rhubarb, cucumber, vegetable marrow, pumpkins, cabbage, onions, carrot, turnips, and beetroot. Also two geese. On the way back a post of the 5th Lancers is surprised by a few Boers; 4 men wounded, 1 taken prisoner but released. Return 2.30pm and get in about 5.30. Lots of loose horses driven in. C, G & H Companies on Outposts. Marched 14 miles today.

4 March   Remain at Swaby's Stores. Mist clears off fairly early and it is a nice morning. Jam and half a pound of biscuits today for rations but no mealy meal. Butter and Quaker have run out in the Mess and we have mealy porridge instead. 8.30am A & B Companies out cutting mealies. More tin got from Swaby's Store and some shelters are put up by the Pioneers. Roll Boer tobacco is issued, 7 oz. free and plenty more on payment. I get some and it nearly makes me ill, but I damp the twist and make twists of my leaf tobacco and cut them both up fine and then dry again and the result is not bad. Rains at 12 and on and off all afternoon and is a cloudy evening. 12 more waggons on the Convoy came in from Piet Retief in evening. E, F, H & A Companies on Outposts. Cloudy night. Light but moon does not appear.

5 March   Remain at Swaby's Store. Thick mist comes in 2am and continues more or less as heavy rain all day. Supports retire 6am and I go back too by mistake but come out again. Get breakfasts brought out (mealy porridge and fresh milk, rather nice) and put men on to improve trenches and make footpaths through long grass afterwards. Mist and rain all day and all night. Rum issued in the night. Consequently I stay on Outposts all day and am

relieved by H Company at 5.30pm when I go on Support. CO and Major Watts come round in the afternoon. H, A, E & B Companies on Outposts with barely half on the hill and half in Support. Wrote to Mother.

Swaby's Stores, 12 miles N of Piet Retief 5th March 1901

My dear Mother,

  This is an interminable trek! It is certainly novel and interesting but parts of it are most unpleasant. We have been nearly a fortnight now practically without Government rations and have been living on the country. Luckily this part of the country simply teems with sheep and oxen and so long as we stay here we shall not be without meat anyway. The principal foodstuff in the way of corn is mealy plant of which there is an inexhaustible supply all over the Transvaal and it thrives particularly well about this district. In the green state it forms a great delicacy for all animals, and the mealy cobs, raw or cooked, we find not half bad eating, though most indigestible! Then the dried grain is the regular corn food for horses, mules etc but just now we keep all we can get to replace our biscuits. The Force has collected about nine grinding machines and day and night fatigue parties are kept at work grinding mealies down to meal which is issued to the men at the rate of 8oz per diem per man and makes first rate cakes and chupatties. A very small quantity of wheat has been collected and this is also ground down to meal but issued to Officers only and we make ripping brown bread out of it. Mealy corn has several other uses yet though! Fine mealy meal as I think I told you makes capital porridge, rather like hominy. Besides this, mealy meal makes a very good thickener for soup. Last but not least we make coffee out of it!! This is done by roasting the meal in a camp kettle (dixie) lid over hot embers. There are probably more uses still but I think that is all we know of at present. General French is sending us on a few waggon loads of food every day but I expect it will be a long time before we are on full rations again. However we are not doing too badly and if only the weather were a little more genial I might call it enjoyable.

    I am writing this scrawl seated in a mackintosh on the stone loop-hole of an Outpost trench at 9.30am. There is a thick Scotch mist on as you will see from the paper [much splattered and water-marked] and my boots, puttees and socks are wringing wet with water collected from the long grass. my quarter-inch of pencil is nearly exhausted and I shall soon have to stop as the last Mail bag closes at 10. While I think of it, my supply of indelible pencils has run out and ink is too dangerous (even if I had any) to carry about loose in one's kit on the trek so you might send me a few pencils next time you write and mind the leads are strong. I have some long leads but no holder for them. The little flat pencil you sent in a case was awfully nice - what a pity it was not indelible !

The Diary is getting on slow but sure. I keep three Diaries now with this new arrangement. The first is just rough notes of each day's doings, the second a fair copy into the pocket Diary and the third an enlargement of this for you. The latter of course takes the longest as I write a young letter for each day. Next time I write I will send as far as I have completed if I have it by me. At present I have nothing by me but my wet self and I only got this by getting my servant to go back to camp as I heard a Convoy was going into Piet Retief today and would take letters.

Love to all,

Malcolm's entries in his diaries continue daily in a similar vein with their detailed entries concerning the weather and the work that the West Yorkshires were doing. The following extracts provide the highlights of their existence in difficult circumstances for the next fortnight until, on 15 March, the battalion was again on the move.

6 March   *2am put on sentries in Support trenches as mist thickens. Mist and rain continues all night and all today without the slightest break. Every place and everything covered with mire. Keep my posts out in Support line as we are for Outposts tonight and there is no good in moving back into camp now that we have all mushyboos up here and the ground beneath them is more or less dry… 8am C & D Companies escort all the Boer families, and surplus cattle collected here, down to Piet Retief.*

8 March   *Stops raining 5am and clouds break…*

9 March   *Remain at Swaby's Store. Wind has done a complete change. Fine morning and a glorious day. Get into helio contact with Spitz Kop* [the Battalion War Diary identifies this as a transmitting station from which messages to Volksrust and Wakkerstroom were sent]. *Can see the mountains all around. Corporal Cordey finds 350 rounds of Martini ammunition in a spruit whilst washing… Meat ration reduced to 1 and 1/4 lb. meat.*

10 March, Sunday   *Remain at Swaby's Store. Cold wet morning. Church parade off.*

Rains hard all day. Hear that the Swazis have risen against the Boers. Battalion not moving tomorrow. Cheese and jam issued. Write up more Diary. Summary: Swazis have slain 20 odd Boers. Write note to Father.

Swaby's Stores. March 10th 1901

My dear Father,

Here we are still and here we are likely to stay for another few days yet I believe before moving down to Piet Retief. A mounted orderly is going down there today and will take some letters, so I am scribbling another note to let you know that all is well. It was only a few days ago that I wrote my last note from here but the time they take to reach the line is so uncertain that I think it highly probable these two notes will go by different Mails. When oh! when shall I get a Home Mail I wonder? It is horrid being cut off like this and I want so badly to know how poor Mother and Grannie are. I promised to send a piece of that new Diary when I next wrote but I have added so few lines since my last note that it really is not worth while.

The weather has been almost as bad here as at Tweepoort and at this very moment it is pouring cats and dogs and I am on Outposts tonight! The war news these last few days has been very cheering, all these guns, ammunition, waggons etc - not to mention Burghers themselves - being captured. Today we hear that the Swazis have risen, killing 8 Boers, wounding more and several have fled into Piet Retief to give themselves up ! That is good but pray heaven ! they won't mistake us for Burghers too and start wiping out the white man generally ! That would be most unpleasant especially as we are practically on the border here.

The Convoys have come up all right in the last few days and yesterday there was great rejoicing as we were put on full rations once more. However the mealy grinding fatigues continue and I suppose we are laying in a store of meal for emergencies. Jam and cheese are a great treat after being without them for so long.

Yesterday some 350 rounds of Martini ammunition were found by some of the men down near a spruit here and I expect there will be great excavations in the hope of unearthing a gun. Yesterday too the sun came out for the first time in four days and it was a lovely day. We could see the distant hills all round and got signal communications with a hill somewhere near Wakkerstroom and so got a summary of news in, which was of course very welcome.

I am finding that pipe lighter you sent me very useful these times as of course matches like everything else have run out. I am now reduced to smoking coarse Boer tobacco but the other day on a farm destroying expedition I came across a sack of dried tobacco leaves. This was a great find and I took a handful away with me and have been employed ever since making them into rolls and then cutting the latter across with an old razor! I did not think I would be reduced to making my own tobacco but so it is! Did I tell you that we now have a Dairy of our own, that is to say before we left Amsterdam the milk cows were taken out of the rest of the captured cattle and distributed to Regiments and units. We got about 20 odd cows and calves at first. Some of these of course had very little milk and now we have 8 or 9 left but it is very nice to have fresh milk for our coffee and mealy porridge at breakfast, and again for tea in the afternoon, especially as we have run out of condensed milk entirely.

your very affectionate son,

15 March *Misty but not foggy. Parade 6.35. March to Piet Retief, good roads, very hot, and get very done. Take a snapshot of the Boer guns dug up here [one of which is now in the Royal Armouries collection and on display at Fort Nelson, Hampshire]. Big camp in sight 10 miles out. Force occupies hills around in half Battalion Posts. Get in about 1pm having marched 14 miles. Storm comes on before kits arrive. A, B, C & E Companies under Major Watts on our hill. Rig up shelter of sorts. B & C Companies on Outposts. Harrington is Adjutant. Sleep in Mess tent.* [Battalion War Diary adds: 'Camping grounds very dirty and smelly, General French's troops having left the same ground in the morning'.]

16 March *Major Watts and Harrington explore farms nearby but find little. Shave and wash. Rig up a Mess. Make an oven of stones and tin but it is too damp to roast meat tonight. Try to sleep but too windy. A & E Companies on Outposts at 5pm. Finish trenches for kneeling. Lovely night. Come in for dinner. Chilly and don't sleep much. Moon not up till 2.30am, sun rises 5.15am.*

17th March, Sunday *Fine morning. Glorious sunrise, heavy dew. Return to camp at 6am. Some shots heard near ILH, this turns out to be some of them going out to a wood to catch some Boers; they failed. No porridge or kidneys for breakfast. 7.30am drizzled rain slightly. Took out 3 sections E Company and a waggon down to a farm and brought back zinc roofing, barbed wire etc. 8.15am Major Watts took B & C Companies down to a Church Parade, returning at 10. Go down to farm again at 11 and bring back more roofing and wood. Also got a few onions and beans. Then comes an Order to stop work on trenches. Sleep most of the afternoon. Built myself a tin shelter. General Smith-Dorrien comes up, also the CO. New scheme for Outposts devised.*

'SNAPSHOTS OF DAILY LIFE WITH THE WEST YORKSHIRES. BEER COULD BE HAD, OCCASIONALLY, BUT AT A PRICE!

By now it had become clear to Kitchener and his senior column commanders, especially French, Smith-Dorrien, Hildyard and Dartnell, that the original concept of the drive – to pin the Boer commandos against the Swazi and Zulu borders – had failed. The various columns had certainly achieved much in dislocating the local economy, indeed the Boer farms had been turned into virtual deserts, with their livestock run-off and their crops largely destroyed, but the Boer fighting men themselves, had, as ever, eluded capture. The decision was taken therefore to renew the British efforts in the southern Transvaal once again using Piet Retief as a general operating base and a collection point for the vital food convoys. Out went the orders, 'Dig in and fortify Piet Retief'.

Accordingly, two lines of defence were constructed around the town: a ring of forts on the high ground supported by an inner line of trenches. Each fort to be held by a company or half company according to its size. Malcolm's diary records the West Yorkshires' endeavours to make the best of their situation whilst digging trenches and creating forts. This was a full-scale defensive position which harked back to the warfare of half a century earlier – to the Crimea and scenes that Malcolm's father, as a midshipman, would have witnessed.

The weather continued to be miserable and the availability of food fluctuated from a state of semi-starvation to one of bonanza whenever a convoy made it through the waterlogged countryside from Natal. Malcolm's very full diary entries have been edited to provide a general impression of what occurred in the following weeks, with the fine detail of each company's activities omitted.

PRIVACY WAS ALMOST NONEXISTENT BUT A WASH IN THE FIELD WOULD HAVE BEEN WELCOME

18 March *Start to work on new forts. We are to make two half Company forts…Thunderstorm passes over while at dinner and nearly floods Mess.*

19 March *Misty morning. Come back too soon. Lowe and I look after the right fort, Carey the left. Scheme altered slightly. Drizzly day and beastly cold…… My blankets are still wet but I pile them over me and sleep fairly well. I have to get up twice in the night, owing, I think to the issue of rum.*

20 March *The mist lifts about 10 and the sun comes out a bit and it remains fairly fine for remainder of day. Harrington on fatigue again, Lemon gets more stakes. Major Watts puts up stakes around Carey's Fort for barbed wire. Lowe and I take right Fort. …..bread issued still to Officers. Fair night.*

21 March *Lovely morning, return early. Carry on with construction of Forts. Lowe and I take right Fort. Slow work, we have not got a wall all around it yet.* [Battalion War Diary notes: 'a convoy of rations arrived from Volksrust but no stores and no Mail'.]

22 March *Still working at forts…*

23 March *7.30am Major Watts takes B & G Companies with 50 MI and 2 field guns and treks of to Normandie* [Battalion War Diary reveals that they were there to form and entrench a camp for the purpose of guarding the telegraph wires]. *A Company working to improve town defences. D & E Companies start fort in front of ILH. ……*

24 March, Sunday   *Church parade 10.15. Local padre attends. H Company work on defences all morning. A & E Companies work on defences in the afternoon.*

At this point Malcolm's formal diary is, for the moment, abandoned and his only record of events are terse entries in his notebook diary which, at this point, is composed of scraps of paper torn from a Dutch child's lettering schoolbook. The battalion digest is similarly uninformative with single, or occasionally double, line entries telling us that little of note took place.

31 March, Sunday   *Still at Piet Retief*

3 April   *Major Yale arrived [from UK] with a convoy carrying mostly oats bringing with him whisky, butter and soup etc.*

5 April, Good Friday   *D & half F Companies on Outposts. Take photos of tin-shelters, cookhouse and church. 10.15 Church Parade with two padres. 2.30pm take Colour Sergeant and 30 men to Redhill Fort and 11 men to York Fort. Relieve Harrington. Make a scheme for sentries — 5 men on day and night. Lovely night, slay flies by the score. Bed at 10.30pm.*

6 April   *A good breakfast — porridge, liver and toast, scone and jam and coffee. Move cookhouse to rear of fort. Dig water holes. Put up men's shelters. Took a bath. I have a touch of diarrhoea. Flies awful. . . .*

COLLIER CHANGING INTO DRY CLOTHES

10 April   *Feeling a bit cheap. Continue writing letters and making map. CO comes up about 11am and tells me I am to take over Fort York. Convoy comes in bringing Daly, Boyall and Welchman and mail of 22nd Feb. Boyall relieves me in the afternoon and I hand over E Company, Fort York etc. I am now to command F Company as Bartrum has put out his knee. High wind blows all morning. Colonel Campbell's Force comes in and occupies ground between Forts.*

12 April.   *CO and Major Watts come round in the afternoon. Write letters all morning. Clothing and Canteen stuff is distributed. Get shirt, socks and drawers. Meet Collier 2pm and give him a letter for Mother and say good-bye to him.* [Battalion War Diary relates: 'Nothing to record. Empty convoy started to return to Volksrust taking the following officers: Captain Bartrum; 2/Lt Porch, sick list; 2/Lt Barlow, transferred to 1st Battalion; Civil Surgeon Collier left for England his place being taken by Civil Surgeon Dyer'.]

Piet Retief, Transvaal. 12th April 1901

My dearest Mother,

Since I wrote last I have been feasting on an accumulation of Mails bringing letters, tobacco, chocolate and all sorts of good things. We had six Mails in all at once. You remember the state of mind you left me in when I started from Wonderfontein on this trek - yourself and Grannie both ill - well, the first Mails I receive after two months of anxiety and the very first letter that is handed to me is black-edged letter from Father. Imagine my feelings. Well, I suppose I must give you the usual list of letters and parcels received. it is a fine fat one too, which is more than I can say for the thin list of things I have sent home !

First of all I want all my films [i.e. negatives] collected and kept by the Stores so that I can constitute them at my Agents and send them orders for any Photos I may want at any time. To do this I have written two notes to Knight and 'the King' and I leave it to you to send them on or not as you think fit, for I am rather doubtful as to whether these two have returned all the films they have received from me. You said nothing about the 103 prints I was so overjoyed to receive. Do you know there were 72 Photos in that lot I had never seen before, representing 6 spools I had almost given up as lost, and can you imagine my relief from the consequent state of anxiety I was in over them ? I have not yet ceased to gloat over them ! I have still hopes of recovering the remainder of the absentees now but I fear the chance is very remote. I have now opened a Deposit Account with the Stores and hope that they will bother you no more with Bills and films and worrying questions.

I told you I think how useful the tinder pipe-lights have been on this trek. We have been of course without matches nearly the whole time. Your soap and matches too came at a fortunate time, but most welcome of all were Father's and your parcels of chocolate and tobacco.

Now for news. Since I last wrote, on the 15th March, we came in here from Swaby's Stores and found General French's Columns had just left to go South to round up the South Eastern corner of this country; which they have now completed. In the meantime we, General Smith-Dorrien's Force, have been holding this place as a sort of Base and as the town is in a hollow surrounded by hills we have forts on the hills all round, about a mile or so apart and then

a strong Outpost Line inside this ring down below round the town itself. The West Yorkshires are holding 3 of these forts with half Companies, the remainder of the Battalion being down in the town. I am at present in the central fort of our three - Fort York - but I have also been in the town and at one of the other forts as well.

Each Corps has commandeered a house in the town for an Officers' Mess and we have been fairly comfortable, though till the last Convoy came in the day before yesterday with some Stores we had been living and thriving on our bare rations. In a day or two we expect to leave for the Railway line - Wonderfontein or Pan I believe - via Ermelo. That is the bare outline and the detail I will leave for the Diary which I hope to bring up to date soon.

Please send out note-paper and envelopes and occasionally blotting paper. They keep the rottenest trash in this line at the Canteens. Woollen gloves will be useful for a birthday present!

Your affectionate son,

Sure enough, the next day the West Yorkshires abandoned their newly constructed forts, one imagines quite thankfully, and set out to march back to the Delagoa railway. It is curious to note though that a truly massive convoy, some 500 waggons, had arrived on the 10th from Volksrust bringing with it vast quantities of supplies; but the Boers were on the loose and the presence of thousands of British troops (in excess of 14,000) in southern Transvaal was pointless. For Smith-Dorrien and his column, another long, tough march lay ahead of them, their destination was to be Wonderfontein from where they would move on to Pretoria. The Transvaal, however, was not about to let the West Yorkshires march away quietly.

Eighteen

WITHDRAWAL FROM PIET RETIEF

Opposite: A mid-day break on the march somewhere in the Transvaal

13 April   *Fine morning though cloudy at times. Got football ground ready after breakfast and cleaned up Forts. At 10am a message came up that we are to leave Piet Retief at 2pm. Washed in big bath in stream and changed into new clothes. Topping fine lunch: chops and welsh rarebit, sardines, plum pudding, bread and butter and marmalade. Leave Fort at 1.30… 150 Supply waggons follow… Sleep the night in Edgeworth's tent who has a Pontoon section behind my Company. Drizzles slightly, warm night. C & D Companies on Picquet, remainder of Battalion spread out in a circle around the camp. The remainder of General Smith-Dorrien's Column remaining for the night in Piet Retief. Marched 4 miles.*

14 April, Sunday   *Misty morning. Edgeworth goes off at 6.30 and builds a pontoon bridge across Shela River. Parade at 7.30am, move along at a good rate. West Yorkshires are advance guard, Suffolks rear guard. More goats and cattle taken. Reach Shela river 12 noon and sit down for a long while. H Company go off to burn and destroy a farm close by as a Carabinier [6th Dragoon Guards] has been shot by a Boer sniping from there. House is destroyed using gun-cotton. E & D Companies help at drift. 2pm the Mess boxes are opened and we have lunch. C & F Companies relieve E & D Companies at the drift. I succeed in ruining a rope. At 3.30 B Company relieves F and E & F Companies trek into camp a mile or so on as we are for Outposts. All three Columns are together in one huge camp… Marched 13 miles.*

15 April   *Fine morning… West Yorkshires have Rear Guard… start off at 10.45 and go along at a good pace. About 2pm we catch up with the Mess mule and eat cold mutton and some bake as we go along. About 4pm we come up with the Convoy which is parked, name of the place is Panbult. Colonel Spens, the GOC and Advance Guard have gone on but we are stuck as there is a bog in front. Colonel Campbell in sight on our left. 2 or 3 Boers seen in rear. Heavy dew but sleep well. Marched 10 miles, moving in a north-westerly direction.*

16 April   *Did not continue the march till 2pm owing to the difficulty in getting the Convoy across the bog. A better road is then found to the right. Transport crosses bog but bog gets worse and worse. All four Companies work at getting waggons through but only a few get across. HQ with four Companies are four miles ahead, H & D Companies form Outposts around Convoy with E & F Companies in Support… Only moved 2 miles today.*

17 April   *Night awfully hot but slept fair. Ground easy to dig. From 5.30 till 7.30 help to get waggons across bog. A good road is found to the right again and we trek on again at 11.15am… Trek about 7 miles to Compies River which we reach in the dark. E Company on Outposts; F Company split into halves, half in a long trench on road to river and other half protecting bridge. Midges bad. Cold with a heavy dew. Marched 8 miles.*

A FIELD BATTERY OF THE ROYAL HORSE ARTILLERY GOES INTO ACTION

Despite their progress, the Boers were not about to let the British columns emerge from the bogs of central Transvaal unopposed:

18 April   *Send in blankets of half Company at 4.15 and start off at 6.15, West Yorkshires are*

Advance Guard… Cross Umpulusi River in bare legs. F Company then help waggons across a small spruit from 10.15 till 12.45 and then join A & H Companies. Lunch and move on at 1.45pm. Boers reported to be out in our front. Join Crossman with F & H Companies as escort to the 5-in gun. Watch our Companies taking a position in front covered by artillery fire. [Battalion War Diary: 'the enemy offered a certain amount of opposition from about 1.30pm taking up a position on a formidable hill, Bank Kop, directly on our front'.] *B, C & D Companies in firing line in centre with E & G Companies on left and mounted troops, and pom-poms, under Colonel Henry on right.* [The Boers retreated under this attack.] *We capture some 500 or so sheep and some hens. Trek on and camp on top of nek at 4.30pm at Grobelaar Farm. Marched 17 miles.*

19 April   *Start off at 6.30am after 2 Companies of Suffolks have relieved us. Pass two or three farms and climb to top of a hill along a good road reaching Roodeval about 10.30. Some Boers were seen on hills around and were shelled by the 5-in gun and pom-poms. Good view over a very flat country from here. All farms in district nowadays are thoroughly cleared, furniture burnt, windows and doors smashed. Marched 8 miles.*

Then, the next morning, the West Yorkshires are once again in close contact with the Boers:

20 April   *C & E Companies take on Allenby's waggons about 6am. Suffolks are Advance Guard today with West Yorkshires as Rear Guard. There is some rifle fire in rear and a gun in front.*

[Battalion War Diary shows this is a quite complicated withdrawal: 'ILH with HQ and 4 Companies West Yorkshires covering movement of convoy across drift and being harassed by Boer attacks. B & D Companies and RHA come into action and eventually Boers draw off'.] *A & F Companies trek on at head of ox Convoy. I stop at first drift till 12, pulling down houses and cut mealies to make road. Lemon goes onto the next drift and I pass him about 1pm and find mule and ox Convoys parked up by his drift. Trek on soon and get into Smithfield about 4.30pm. Pass a lot of farms today and more horses and cattle are captured. Boers close in on Rear Guard on hill behind and the big guns fire. Two men of ILH wounded, we account for one or two Boers. Put my Company on Outposts at dusk and put Ingles out at 11pm. Suffolks lend us 10 sets of tools and the men set to work making trenches 11.30pm. Drizzles slightly but a warm night. New moon. Marched 8 miles.*

21 April   *Remain at Smithfield to allow the ox teams go out to graze and rest. Remainder of Convoy comes in. Fine day. Had a bath, clean up and a hair cut. Sounds of guns in action heard.*

22 April   *Parade 6.10am and move on shortly afterwards. Trek along for about 12 miles passing innumerable pans and finally cross the Ermelo Road with Lake Chrissie on our right, 2 or 3 miles off. Reach Lillieput at 12. A great deal of gunning is heard on our left [west] and our 5-in gun fires a round or two.* [Battalion war diary shows: 'Colonel Campbell's Column apparently engaged in a rear guard action throughout most of the day'.] *Transport keeps up well. Our pom-pom fires in front and a Boer pom-pom fires a few rounds back…Marched 16 miles. We move again on 24th.*

"OPEN FIRE!"

24 April *Thick fog in early morning. Up at 4.30am. Move eventually at 8.45 as Rear Guard trek 3 miles to high ground and then put out Observation posts and big guns shell Boer snipers all round. Move on south and west to more high ground. Convoy goes on well. Get into Klipfontein about 5pm. B & H Companies on Outposts. Have lunch and tea, then dinner at 7.30pm. Hear that we are to go to Pretoria !! Marched 12 miles.*

25 April *See a comet. A & F Companies parade 5.15am under Major Watts. Remainder at 7.30. We occupy high ground about 3 miles out of camp and co-operate with MI but can't get a round off. Awfully hot day, march in new serge coat, feel beastly sore. Boers on sky line in small parties and they snipe an ox waggon coming into camp. C & D Companies on Outposts. Marched 10 miles.* [Battalion War Diary shows the force halted to allow the rear to close up and, because the next water supply was too far on down the road, the force halted for the night.] *Marched 10 miles*

26 April *Start off 7.25am with mule Convoy. Rear Guard sniped a bit and pom-pom plays. Hot day though a cool breeze, good road and regular halts…Men get lots of water. Supposed to be going 20 miles but we halt at some pans called Vlakfontein with Strathrae in sight on ahead. Get in 4pm and go straight out on Outposts, C & F Companies. Gets posts settled down and trenches made in the long grass… Marched 16 miles.*

But the end was in sight and the next day the column entered Wonderfontein and reached the end of their march out of Transvaal. Here they are given orders to move on:

30 April *Move by train to Pretoria.* Having arrived at Pretoria, the West Yorkshires were deployed in company strength units to various forts and strongpoints around the town and the railway. Before long these men would be manning the corrugated iron and earth blockhouse strung along endless lines of barbed wire running alongside the railway lines on a duty that was exceptional for its boredom coupled with appalling living conditions and irregular rations.

Malcolm was fortunate to be able to escape this duty, for on 21 May he was posted off to join one of the mounted columns in Major-General Elliot's division operating in the Orange River Colony – Britain's name for the newly-annexed Orange Free State.

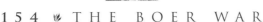

THERE WERE NO TENTS ON THIS MARCH – SLEEPING ARRANGEMENTS WERE PRIMITIVE WITH OFFICERS AND MEN ALIKE TAKING COVER FOR THE NIGHT IN BIVOUACS LIKE THIS ONE

Grand Hotel, Pretoria. 3rd May 1901.

My dear Mother,

Here we are in Pretoria again.

On the 26th April Smith-Dorrien landed us, the West Yorkshires and Suffolks of Colonel Spens' Brigade (the Camerons left us at Piet Retief and took back empty waggons to Volksrust and then came on here and are, like us, forming part of the garrison of this place) and the ILH, 5th Lancers and 3rd MI under Colonel Henry, here. We had 'lovely' weather the whole time but part of the journey back was slow owing to difficulties of the ground; for two days we were stuck in a bog and it took all the energies our tired animals and worn-out selves could muster to get out of it. I don't think I told you that I met one of the Grimshaws two or three times on this trek. He is in the Dublin Fusiliers MI Company and I think his name is Cyril and was with Claud and me at Crawleys at one time [Crawleys was probably a crammer that prepared both boys for their Army entrance examinations]. *The first time I saw him he was guarding 3 dug-up Boer guns at Piet Retief and recognised him instantly as a Grimshaw, though he did not at first know me. Another Bray 'soldier' I met was Jack Darley. The first time I was able to get a chance to speak to him was one day when we were stuck in the bog and he came down with some of his men to relieve my Company pulling the waggons out. After that I did not meet him till the day before yesterday when he and I travelled in the same train together. I was coming up with my Company and two others (we got in here at 7pm last night) and he was coming up by himself to get some Mess Stores for his Regiment who are now stationed at Belfast.*

I arrived here as I said with 2 other Companies late last night and the rest of the Regiment got in the day before. We and the Camerons are here for a rest which indeed we need very badly as we are reduced to about 400 men all told ! This probably means we will stop here for at least 3 months, if not more. This is written, as you will see, in great haste so I have no time for answering questions etc. Love to all, your affectionate son,

Malcolm's next letter home tells us little aside from mentioning that he is busy training signallers and that his younger brother, Bertie, has arrived in South Africa with the Leinster Regiment. The next letter after that is rather more interesting:

Transvaal Hotel, Pretoria. 13th May 1901

My dear Claud,

I am just off to a Garrison Board which has been condemning a lot of ASC Stores and have dropped in here for a drink before starting back again to Camp, so I take this opportunity to drop you a line.

This place is most peaceful, the shops are all open again and everything is resuming a normal aspect. The weather is fairly pleasant, hot and dusty days and cold clear nights. I had awfully bad luck the other day. General Kitchener wired to know if I could be spared to go out with him as his Signalling Officer and our CO, because he has some big grievance at present against him would not let me go, though we are simply full of Officers. The next day a message came from the Staff Officer in Pretoria to know if an Officer could be spared to go out on some Column as Signalling Officer and again he said no. I think it is awfully rough on me as it is probably the chance of a lifetime.

Looking back on that last three months' trek of ours down by Piet Retief and the Swazi border I think it is one of the rottenest times we have had since we have been out here. I should

like a Column now, though, this is just the right time of year and anyway trekking is always better than sitting still. Here I am supposed to be struck off all duties to put through a batch of 20 Signallers, which in itself is no sinecure, but I am taken for Orderly Officer every second or third day which means visiting posts on rocky kopjes in the middle of the night etc and am also taken for Boards. Besides this I am of course losing the extra 6d a day which I used to get for Commanding a Company. The Company commander has absolutely nothing to do but sit in a Fort or Blockhouse and gets shooting, some even a horse and can visit the town when he pleases. I am as you can see tremendously on the grouse but I think I have reason to be.

your affectionate brother,

Then Malcolm's hopes are finally satisfied:

Pretoria 21st May 1901

My dear Father,

My chance has come at last. The CO has at last allowed me to go out as a Signalling Officer on one of these Columns and tomorrow I am off to Standerton to report myself to one General Elliot. This to me is doubly pleasing because I shall in all probability come across 'Brer B' at Standerton and oh! how I crave to see a relation again. I don't of course know what Column I am likely to go with yet or where I am likely to go once I leave Standerton but I hope I will have a chance of doing some good. The longer the war lasts now of course the better for me! This will anyway be a long way better than sitting down here doing nothing, I was beginning to get tired of it. The weather now is lovely, it is a ripping time of year out here.

your affectionate son,

This marked the end of Malcolm's service with the West Yorkshires in South Africa. For the rest of the campaign he would be seconded from his regiment. His first posting was to Colonel Bethune's mounted column (later to be commanded by Colonel Lowe) before joining, in January 1902, the divisional signals staff as the signals training officer. Eventually, in the spring of 1902, Malcolm fell ill with enteric and was put on the sick list. After a spell in hospital, first at Harrismith and then close to Cape Town, he was put on extended sick leave and sent home to his family in Ireland. Before that though Malcolm would have to do a great deal more marching and, unlike his days as an infantry officer, much riding.

Nineteen

SIGNALS OFFICER
WITH BETHUNE

Opposite: Little wonder that the British hardly ever caught the Boers when they rode horses like these

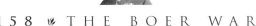

By the middle of 1901 it had become reasonably clear to Lord Kitchener and most of the other senior British commanders that the war was becoming bogged-down and that, unsurprisingly, the Boers were not at all willing to stand and fight. Kitchener's earlier attempts, described in part above, to drive the Boers to the peace conferences by using a massive number of troops sweeping across the Transvaal had met with very limited success. It was felt that part of the failure of the strategy lay in the substantial use of infantry with only limited cavalry or mounted infantry support. The new strategy had two main elements: the use of almost entirely mounted columns to sweep across the areas of Boer opposition, and the construction of strings of blockhouses connected by barbed wire – like so many bead necklaces – strung along the line of the railways and across strategic sections of the country.

The overriding impression that is given by almost all of those who witnessed and wrote about this phase of the war in their letters and diaries is that the British were chasing a phantom who had no intention of being caught, and who could anyway outride the poorly mounted British troops. For the British officers, from the most senior down to the subalterns it was a desperately difficult time as they sought to satisfy Kitchener's endless demands to perform well, to provide the intelligence that would pin the Boer commandos down and, when it came to the actual fighting, to win against all odds. Success was measured in the numbers of Boers killed or taken, livestock rounded up and farms burnt during each sweep – the bag – in a manner more reminiscent of a pheasant shoot than

conducting a campaign of war. The beaters were of course the columns operating in the field, and their very success depended upon their mutual co-operation – which seems at times to have been singularly lacking – and their ability to communicate with one another.

In the northern areas of the Orange River Colony it fell to the division commanded by Major-General E Locke Elliot to sweep the veldt. Malcolm's next letter home clarifies his situation which, at this juncture was still quite uncertain as he had not yet been appointed to a specific column commander:

MALCOLM, BOOTED AND SPURRED, ALTHOUGH HE IS ACTUALLY WEARING MARCHING BOOTS AND PUTTEES, AWAITS THE ORDER TO MOVE OFF. NOTE HIS GLOVES – IT COULD BE BITTERLY COLD ON THE VELDT.

Standerton, 30th May 1901
My dear Father,
I have had quite a new experience since I last wrote, that is to say being 'on my own' for a bit. I left Pretoria Station at 6am on the 22nd landing up here about 4pm but alas no Leinsters and no Bertie and you may imagine I was greatly disappointed. The worst of it is nobody seems to know where the Leinsters are at all. I was told they might possibly be at Harrismith. Probably you will know before I do ! Well, to continue - I arrived here and went up to General Clements' Headquarters and reported myself and was told to go over to the Garrison Adjutant (the other side of town and Railway Line) and he would tell me where to go and told me besides I should probably stay here five or six days. This I was rather expecting in spite of the fact that I had been bundled out of Pretoria at express speed. The Garrison Adjutant told me I would find a tent and accommodation in the Rest Camp, close to the Railway Station, so off I went to the Railway Station to tell my servant to take my valise up there. By this time it was dark, but there was a misty moon out and in the half light I slipped off my straps

and things inside my tent in the Rest Camp never noticing the horrid state it was in. This was left as a treat for me when I woke up in the morning and discovered the floor was littered with old bully-beef, jam and other tins, bits of bread etc etc. I forgot to mention that one of the first persons I met when I got off the train was our old Padre, the Wesleyan minister – Wainman – and of course we had a lot to say to one another. Well, next day I thought I had had enough of the rest Camp so I journeyed over to the Padre's house and discovered the poor old man cooking his own breakfast in the back kitchen. He had no servant and was sleeping in the same room with a Railway Official, two Tommy train guards occupying another room and the third room was occupied by another Official who was just then away. This latter room full of dirt and rubbish, I moved into, as I thought it was at all events better than a filthy tent in a Rest Camp full of 'scallywags'. The Padre and I used then to have our meals together, my servant doing the cooking. On Saturday morning however the Padre went off to Heidelberg as he was going to hold a service there on Sunday. In the meantime I had been getting my things in order for the trek, for I discovered when my total baggage was weighed at the Railway Station it came to 300 lb odd and we are supposed only to have about 60 lb! I had also got hold of a pony with saddle, bridle etc and was generally getting all I wanted together.

Shortly after I arrived another Signalling Officer for General Elliot's Columns turned up and he too started getting his kit together. Yesterday morning we got orders at last to trek and we started off with a Convoy for De Lange's Drift but we did not get more than a mile or two before we got the order to turn back. Then Colonel Bethune's Column came in saying that General Elliot was at Harrismith. So now we are attached to his Column, myself to the KDGs [King's Dragoon Guards] and the other officer to the 3rd Dragoon Guards. I shall probably eventually be with either Lowe's or De Lisle's Columns. Love to all.

your affectionate son,

1 June *Start 9am for De Lange's Drift on the Klip River… 7DG and IY [7th Dragoon Guards and Imperial Light Horse] of Lowe's Column trek with Colonel Bethune. Camp down on far side of drift. Wear 'British Warm' and gloves all day. Get into camp about 3pm…*

And so Malcolm's diaries continue their daily tale of his life in South Africa. But, as we have seen, he occasionally reworked his diary into a letter-diary which he sent home to his family and this provides an altogether more readable account. Letter-diary number 9 was the last Malcolm wrote, and his letters, which are even more infrequent during this the last phase of his war, are not particularly enlightening, and we shall have to resort once more to the personal diaries. These too are very sparse and Malcolm's entries for the year from 1 May 1901 to 1 May 1902 are just half the length of those for the preceding year. That said, Malcolm's diaries still contain details that are missing or censored from either his letters or his letter-diary and, where sufficiently interesting, these details are inserted into letter-diary number 9. The significantly reduced volume of Malcolm's personal record can in part be explained by the increased workload that was placed on his shoulders, as a column signals officer he was constantly at the beck and call of his column commander for pieces of signalling or transmitting messages, which might mean simply taking a note by hand on horseback (e.g. Malcolm noted under 5 June that his colonel used him as a galloper), whereas as a commander of a company of infantry there were many occasions when Malcolm had been able to devolve responsibility for his men and the work to his company NCOs. There is also a case to be made which suggests that after his initial enthusiasm for the new job, Malcolm soon enough recognised that the war was not going well and that, even though mounted, the British were still not able to match the mobility of the Boers. After his recent experiences in the Transvaal, marching to Piet Retief and back again, this must have been singularly depressing, not that Malcolm ever really stands back to take stock of the long-term situation. Like most of his brother officers his primary concern was to do his duty. Thereafter, his concerns were far more matter-of-fact and mundane, with food and warmth taking a high priority.

In today's world of virtually instant communication it is hard to imagine a time when communicating was extremely difficult and subject to the vagaries of the weather. Overall control of the war in South Africa was managed through the medium of telegraphic signals sent down the network of telegraph lines which mostly lay along the line of railways. This network of telegraph lines was at the mercy of Boer sabotage and, until the deployment of British troops in blockhouses along the railway lines, the telegraph was often cut. Occasionally a telegraph line was laid out behind an army as it advanced, as was the case in Natal, for when Buller's army advanced a company of Royal Engineers erected telegraph posts with a line connecting Buller with the main line back at the railway. The mobile columns working on the high veldt of the Orange River Colony could only make use of, or be contacted by, the telegraph when they were on or close to the railway: at Harrismith, Kroonstad, or Wynburg for example. Thereafter any signals that were directed to any individual columns from Lord Kitchener, or communication between columns, relied upon various simple if short-distance methods of communication, the principal being the heliograph.

The heliograph was quite simply a steel silvered mirror mounted on gimbals and supported on a tripod which relied upon reflecting flashes of sunlight to create the long and short bursts of light necessary to send signals in Morse code. At night, when a heliograph could obviously not be used, the signallers in South Africa used a lantern called the Begbie lamp, a noisome thing which burnt oil through a wick, illuminating a shutter system behind a lens. This transmitted the messages in Morse code, in a manner similar to the Royal Navy's Aldis lanterns. These two methods of signalling tended to be used for communicating between larger formations, while semaphore flags were utilised for sending messages between small units, e.g. between companies of Infantry. It seems fairly clear from Malcolm's signals logs that within a mounted column signalling was conducted either by sending a galloper (a man with a written note on a horse, or occasionally a bicycle,) but, more frequently, by using the heliograph or lamp. Lastly, many messages were sent between columns by runner, usually referred to in heliographed or lamped messages as a 'boy' and this would have been a young black native who ran the risk, allegedly, of being shot out of hand by the Boers if caught.

It is readily apparent that these methods of signalling, and thus Kitchener's control over his widely dispersed military formations, depended on fair weather and good sunlight. Given that the weather was frequently quite useless to the signallers and that some of the column commanders loathed each other so much that they refused to communicate with one another – and bearing in mind the huge area of the country - we can begin to understand why this phase of the war dragged on for so long and why the Boers were able almost effortlessly to evade the British.

In early June 1901 Malcolm was quite content with his lot, he was off on a big adventure, or so it seemed to him then, and he was going to be something that he cared passionately about doing well – signalling. Let us return to his story as he himself wrote it. Letter-diary number 9 was a multi-edition [3 copies] covering the 1 - 5 June and includes 22 - 30 May. It also includes an unusually long entry for the 1 June.

1 June 1901 *Leave Standerton at 9am with Colonel Bethune's Column. Pick up Tindell, Signalling Officer to one of the other Columns of General Elliot's Division, by the 3rd DG lines. This is a perfectly beastly day. It is blowing hard right across our line of march and as all the veldt is burnt for miles around we look rather like niggers before we have gone very far. This reminds me of our fine marches along the Biggarsberg when the Boers took to burning the veldt to cover their line of retreat and we poor devils had to march through the ashes after them. I was foot slogging then, and now I am mounted which makes a great difference. The wind today is*

biting cold and I am not a bit too warm with my 'British Warm' over my ordinary clothes and gloves on my hands. Not being on any job in particular I am an 'independent trekker' so Tindell and I just go along as we please, finding ourselves at one time with some advanced squadrons or guns at another with the baggage, at times cantering along for a bit to get our ponies warm and at times getting off and walking to get ourselves warm. We cross the Klip River at de Lange's Drift and camp on the other side about 3pm. The baggage comes in a bit later and I get my mushyboo put up. It gets colder still in the evening and I get nearly frozen at dinner as I have no rug to put round my legs and the wind comes swirling through the draughty little Mess shelter. Consequently I am only too glad to go to bed early and get under the blankets, but I am in for a bad night, I am not the only one who is cold and restless. My mushyboo is just behind the other two Head Quarter tents, and close to them is the Veterinary Officer's charge – the sick horse lines. These brutes manage to pull up the pegs holding down the rope they are tied to and every now and then they get tangled up round my mushyboo and in spite of my loud and angry remonstrances refuse to take themselves away. This is serious for after a lengthy deliberation, dozing off and having to wake up again, I have to crawl out of my nice warm kennel and hunt them away, only to be woken up a bit later by the brutes stamping and munching the grass close round my head again. I hit at them with my stick but it is no good, up I have to get again, and how I bless those horses.

2 June *March to Vlakplaats, a mile or two outside Vrede. General Elliot is outside Vrede. Report myself to him and I am informed I have been appointed Signalling Officer to Colonel De Lisle's Column which I will join in a day or two when we reach him. I am feeling very sore from all the riding and go to bed early not feeling very well.*

Contact is soon made with the Boers but with inconclusive results:

3 June *General Elliot and his staff march on with Colonel Bethune's Column, to which I also am temporarily attached. Colonel Lowe moves off to the right. Fairly cold. Veldt burnt. Go on about 12 miles to David's Vlei. Horses increasingly dusty. Ride with Crawford [the veterinary surgeon to the column] and Jagger [the column doctor]. Rear Guard comes into action and the 3DGs make fools of themselves and have about 7 casualties, 1 killed and 18 taken prisoner but are released having first been stripped of weapons, clothes and horse. Sandell and Denny, both Signals Officers to Bethune's Column, get captured! The DG's Outposts are a bit sketchy.*

RIDING WITH BETHUNE STILL MEANT THAT DRIFTS HAD TO BE CROSSED — WITH THE INEVITABLE DELAYS THAT SEEM ALWAYS TO HAVE ACCOMPANIED THESE MOVEMENTS. HERE, G BATTERY RHA ARE MAKING A DIFFICULT CROSSING FOLLOWED BY THE COLUMN'S WATER CART

4 June *General Elliot and his staff, and myself, leave Colonel Bethune's Column early and join Colonel De Lisle's Column at Woodside. Colonel Lowe is at Tafelkop, Bethune is at Leeuwkop and the whole of Elliot's division is moving west. I report myself to Colonel De Lisle and find out all I can about his Signallers and their equipment. There are 8 Signallers in all, 4 of whom are Corps Signallers, the remainder belonging to the 6th MI. Their equipment is: 4 good heliographs, 1 broken helio, flags, lamps, etc.; sufficient but no glasses or telescopes. I get a cavalry mare from the Div remount Officer.*

5 June *Move to Schurwapoort, 20 miles. Start 8am, devilish cold. My new mount is a bit rough and awkward. Keep close to Colonel De Lisle. Lots of buck and hares about. Boers in front and the pom-pom is brought into action to clear them. Colonel De Lisle keeps well up on the advance guard. Lots of stock about. Cross the Noll spruit and halt for three hours from 12-3pm. Lovely day, grass is burnt in all directions. Sniping in front, flanks and rear, though the Boers are very chary of their ammunition. Colonel De Lisle uses me as a galloper. Move on to Wilge river after halt. 6th MI capture 8 wagons, and a Cape cart across river. We move on again to the right and shell a little and capture another wagon, a tremendous amount of cattle, oxen, sheep, and horses etc. Steep sides to river. Cross over and drive some stock back over river into camp. Schmidt goes out after some cattle.*

Occasionally the contrast between the entries in Malcolm's personal diary and the letter-diary written for his family are quite startling as the next day's entries show. The letter-diary gives:

6 June *Column marches to Graspan, about 15 miles. I remain as before with Colonel De Lisle. About 2pm an Orderly comes in from the front reporting that 200 men sent on at 5am have captured a Boer laager but are now hard pressed and want reinforcements badly. There is no helio with this party but as it so happens it would have been useless owing to the nature of the ground. Colonel De Lisle goes on at once with about 200 men and 2 guns leaving me behind to come on with his CSO, Colonel Fanshawe. No messages were exchanged anywhere in the Column to my knowledge.*

But in his diary Malcolm recorded:

6 June *200 of 6th MI go out 5am. We start about 10am owing to wagons etc and stuff taking so long to cross drift. Captain Legge blows up a mill on the left. Halt about 2pm. I am out sending messages. Having great difficulties with my mare. When I return a group of Australians from the 200 come in. Colonel De Lisle goes on at once with the guns and 200 MI and leaves me with Colonel Fanshawe. We trek along and find Colonel De Lisle shelling a position in front and wagons trekking all over the shop. After sending a message or two we go in support with IY and guns on the right. Boer women*

COLONEL BETHUNE (CENTRE WITH PIPE) AND SOME OF HIS OFFICERS

ride back on guns to the camp. Been a hell of a fight. 3 officers and 21 men killed and 20 wounded. 20 Boers killed and wounded, 44 captured along with 12 wagons, 43 carts, and 500 people. Also 500 cattle, 2,000 sheep, 60,000 lbs of mealies, 15,000 lbs. wheat. Officers killed were Cameron, Strong and Meyer of 6th MI who had caught convoy at 9am. There were two laagers by kraals of 70 wagons each. Cape carts got away. 50 prisoners or so charged by MI. Outposts put out but withdrawn later as our Colonel is expected. Men appear on the sky line and go back, appear again and go back. Crawford and White go out but are taken prisoner. Then firing commences on all sides. Lower laager had to be abandoned. Men shot with their hands up. Boers jump on wounded men and break their ribs. Sladen retires into kraals and men make loopholes in the sides. De La Rey and De Wet present. Boers try white flag and call our men beggars etc but to no purpose. Camped at Graspan, marched 5 miles.

The letter diary continues Malcolm's description of the work of Major General Elliot's columns as they work their way westwards, pushing the Boer commandos into either fighting or flight and, at the same time, wrecking Boer farms and driving off the livestock.

7 June *No night work. Column marches to Reitz, about 6 miles. Soon after starting we get into communications with Colonel Bethune and two of my men receive part of a long*

message from him, the station then being taken over by the Divisional Signals Officer. Colonel Bethune camps about a mile from Reitz. In the afternoon I am ordered to join Colonel Bethune's Column, exchanging with his Signals Officer, Lieutenant Tindell. Owing to delay of transport I do not proceed till the morning.

SKETCH MAP SHOWING TREKS WITH MOBILE COLUMN, JUNE 1901

8 June *Ride over to Colonel Bethune's Camp and report myself to Colonel Bethune. Get in touch with Colonel Lowe's Rear Guard on our right soon after 11am and send an important message to Colonel Lowe from Colonel Bethune who gives me a free hand – ripping ! Grass fires tremendous in afternoon. Do not get in touch with Colonel Lowe again nor with Colonel De Lisle. No night work. Camp at Kroon Spruit. Marched about 12 miles.*

And that first message that Malcolm sent for Bethune to Colonel Lowe? This was the first message that survives of the 747 signals that Malcolm and his signallers recorded in two volumes.

Signal/1

Prefix	Time	Location	No Words	Time	Date	Mss No
SB	n/a	n/a		12.20pm	8.6.01	1

To: Col Lowe From: Col Bethune

Repetition of message sent to you by runner last night. You are to march today to Riet Valley tomorrow Quaggafontein - I am at Kroon Spruit tonight we can communicate further from there.

9 June *Marched about 20 miles to Quaggafontein. All three Columns converge today on Lindley to get supplies from a Convoy expected there. One or two short messages exchanged between Units in the Column. No inter-Column communications by day.* [*Malcolm's diary gives us a rather more 'human' version of the scramble to get into Lindley. 'Awful mess up of Columns, Lowe cuts in in front of us onto road. Get into Lindley at dusk and find De Lisle and GOC in the town, and Lowe in front of us. Get settled down after a lot of swearing and bother. Rig up lamp and get DHQ and Orders. Have a lot of bother with Lowe's lamp. Freezing cold'.*] *Pick up General Elliot's HQ in Lindley soon after dusk and get orders for Colonel Bethune and Colonel Lowe, my station transmitting Orders to Colonel Lowe.*

Signal/2

Prefix	Time	Location	No Words	Time	Date	Mss No
XB	6.30pm	Lindley	101	6.35pm	9.6.01	4 & 5

To: Col Bethune & Col Lowe   From: General Elliot

The convoy of supplies is on Stinkfontein if Col Lowe will pick up rations there at 9am afterwards marching towards Waterval. Col Flint and Details from Kroonstad will be attached to Col Bethune's Bde for the return march and will join him en route. All Col De Lisle's captured wagons and cattle will join Col Bethune who will march at 10am. The Divisional camp at Kroonstad will be on the Kromspruit about 5 miles south of the town. The OC wishes to see Col Bethune at 8am tomorrow morning.

Colonel Bethune's Column is fairly well off for signallers and equipment. The KDGs and 3DGs each have enough men and heliographs for their own units, and I have a Brigade establishment of a Sergeant and Trooper of 3rd DG and a Lance Corporal of the King's Dragoon Guards with 3 heliographs and lamps etc.

10 June *Move off at 10am, take over all stock, refugees, etc of the other columns and pick up convoy, under Colonel Flint, at Stinkfontein. Then moved a few miles to Kleinfontein; about 12 miles. This Column is now going straight on to Kroonstad taking all stock, Boer prisoners, families etc of all the Columns, the other two Columns keeping behind us. About 12pm a night expedition of about 150 men and a pom-pom under Colonel Owen go out to try to capture some waggons, a Begbie B lamp being used to indicate the rendezvous. I ascertain that they have a helio, flags etc before they start.* [*The diary adds: 'Refugee wagons have extraordinary wooden bathing machine like coverings. Prisoners mostly old and*

LIEUTENANT PATTON-BETHUNE

CORPORAL HUDSON (COLONEL BETHUNE'S ADC AND HIS ORDERLY). NOTE THAT THEIR HORSES ARE IN REASONABLY GOOD CONDITION AT THIS STAGE OF THEIR TREKS.

infirm and have to walk and object to crossing drifts. Beastly cold and uncomfortable night'.]

11 June *Column moves in 3 Sections owing to the amount of baggage. I arrange for inter-section communication being kept up. After going a few miles Colonel Owen can be seen plainly on a hill ahead of us but owing to the clouds I cannot get a light on them for more than a minute at a time and it is the same with them. This continues till we get up quite close and then we discover they are all right and have no messages of importance for us. Camp just the other side of Kaalfontein bridge. Cannot get in touch with the other Columns. No night work.*

12 June *Column moves on as before in three sections. Try again to get in touch with the other Columns but meet with no success. Colonel Bethune gives me an* *absolutely free hand. If I want to get another Column I take the Sergeant and a helio with me to the most likely place, leaving the Lance Corporal and Private with a helio with Colonel Bethune. March about 13 miles to Wonderkop. Country is all open and undulating about here, and has been nearly all the march; Lindley being about the only place where the ground was at all broken and even there are no very high or distinctive hills. [The diary adds: 'The Boers are very cheeky and give rear and left flank a hot time. 5 farms burnt, a lot of meallies etc destroyed and some refugees brought in. Mr Wilson comes over and chats about burghers and their ways etc. Get into camp about 1pm. Good march. Another night expedition. Thompson and Denny-Smith with a troop of KDG go out to some kraals. Get nothing and find no burghers'.]*

13 June *I go on with Advance Guard to try and get Kroonstad as early as possible to send in some important messages, but owing to the nature of the ground I do not get Gun Hill till reaching our camping ground at Kransspruit Noorg. Nearly every day during this march there has been plenty of sun and the weather has been excellent.*

14 June *Remain at Kransspruit Noorg. All messages for this Column from Kroonstad come through my Signal Station direct from Gun Hill. General Elliot and the other Columns come in in the afternoon. General Elliot and staff go into the town, the Columns all camping at Kransspruit. I have no communication with the other Columns. I interview the Ordnance Officer, Kroonstad, about heliographs etc and get the units of my brigade to indent for what they require. Write to Director of Signals asking for some signallers for the PWLH [Prince of Wales's Light Horse] as they have none.*

The day also brought the first communication Malcolm received from Lord Kitchener's staff. Note that Kitchener was usually referred to in messages as the 'Chief'

Signal/9

Prefix	Time	Location	Words	Time	Date	Mss No
000	9am	PR	56	10.15am	14.6.01	18

To: Col Bethune Kroonstad   From: Chief

15th June K5411. Have you no idea of direction taken by Elliott did he follow up enemy on 9th have you been in touch with him since then. Are prisoners taken by Broadwood and De Lisle included in number y

The British, having completed another sweep through the grasslands of the Orange River Colony, were soon preparing the columns at Kroonstad for another sweep. The next signal gives some idea of the level of intelligence information that Kitchener and his staff had to work with:

Signal/13

Prefix	Time	Location	No Words	Time	Date	Mss No
000		Bloemfontein	203	9am	15.6.01	22

To: Col Bethune, Kroonstad From: Intelligence, O.R.C.

14th June S29: Holtfontein reports a laager at Klipfontein 12 miles east thereof moved on 13th to Modderbult 6 miles further east. These would be some of P. Devos men. Centre. One report says a Boer meeting is soon to be held at Kwaggashoek 21 miles SW of Boltfontein. on 12th Boshoff reports a Boer laager at Laddil 12 miles to NW and on a date received here as 9th but possibly later. Pilcher engaged Jacobs at Jagtbam his HQ 10 miles S of Boshoff capturing 6 prisoners, 5 wagons, 22 carts, 500 cattle, 200 horses. Pretorius with Jacobsdal men said to have been at Doordje S of Jacobsdal on 11th. South. Two small parties reported moving N from Riet and Kaffir confluence on 23rd probably from party reported there yesterday and said to be under Brand. Another small party reported on Doomplaats 15 miles W by S of Edenburg today a few 5 miles E of Kruger Siding moving NE. Bethulie natives report finding traces of a body of men moving N from Katfontein 9 miles E of Bethulie on 12th. Repeat as usual.

It was a busy day for Malcolm as some twenty messages were received, many of which were simple administrative messages dealing with requisitions, courts martial and promotions – the long arm of Army bureaucracy could indeed reach far:

Signal/15

Prefix	Time	Location	No Words	Time	Date	Mss No
SB		Buluwayo	28	9.55am		24

To: O.C. of P.W.L.H.   From: Registrar High Court Buluwayo

Law required for some days yet kindly grant him extended leave as his future evidence important.

Signal/16

Prefix	Time	Location	No Words	Time	Date	Mss No
SM	9.30am	HQ	24	10am	15.5.01	25

To: C.S.O. Elliot's Force   From: C.S.O. Kroonstadt

Captured horses in here tomorrow instead of today all kraals at present full.

15 – 19 June   Colonel Bethune's Column moves across to Kroonspruit, camping close to Colonel Lowe's Column. Communications with Kroonstad now obtained by means of a Cyclist Orderly taking the messages to and from a telegraph operator at Colonel Lowe's HQ. Brigades are reformed. The KDGs and PWLH are taken away from Colonel Bethune and he is given the 4th IY instead.

20 June   Remain at Kroonspruit. 4IY arrive in the afternoon. Wire at once to Director of Signals asking for signallers and equipment for them, as they only have 3 signallers who are any good and no equipment.

21 June   Get reply from Director of Signals about 12 noon. Go into Kroonstad to get equipment for IY but find no heliographs left. Get them lamps, flags etc however.

22 June   March to Meercatfontein. 8 miles. Cannot get in touch with General Elliot still in Kroonstad nor with Colonel De Lisle on our right and south of us. No night work. Wrote to Mother…

Column and was appointed Colonel De Lisle's Signalling Officer. Here I got another horse, this time a big cavalry mare. I had luckily brought some Mess Stores (food plates, knives, forks etc with me) for I was put in a Mess with the Intelligence Officer and Chief Commandeering Officer, both of them Colonials and roughing it a bit. I could not raise a servant but they were good enough to let me put my horses with theirs and we had a black boy to look after them, another cape boy doing the cooking and all the rest we did ourselves. It was a nice change and I was getting quite to like the life when on the 8th, at Reitz, I was ordered to exchange into Colonel Bethune's Column, as Colonel Bethune's Signalling officer, Tindell, belonged to Colonel De Lisle's regiment and he wanted to have the chap with him. This suited me all right as I wanted to be with Colonel Bethune and besides my former groom belonged to the KDGs of his Column. On rejoining Colonel Bethune then I got my KDG groom back again, had a tent all to myself, and was put in a Mess with three other members of the Brigade Staff – two of them Australians (Provost Marshal and Remount Officer) – and the other an RE Officer doing Intelligence. The only drawback to the exchange was I lost half my kit bringing it across. This was a most

A BOER PRISONER CAUGHT WITH EXPANDING BULLETS IN HIS POCKETS IS BROUGHT BEFORE COLONEL BETHUNE

Kroonstad 22nd June 1901

Dear Mother

On the 13th June I got I here with Colonel Bethune's Column too late unfortunately to send off a letter to catch the Mail - at least so they said that week, for this week the time has been extended unusually long. Now for the account of my travels.

On the 29th May as I think I have already told you I was attached to the KDGs in Colonel Bethune's Column. On the 1st June we started off for De Lange's Drift and the next day we joined General Elliot just outside Vrede. On the 4th I moved over with General Elliot to Colonel De Lisle's

serious loss to me for all my Diaries, my camera and various other treasures were in the missing box. The very next time the Columns came close together (at Lindley) I went over to De Lisle's Column and made every possible enquiry about my things but nothing could be traced. However I offered a reward for the Diaries and rejoined my Column. As luck would have it when next the Columns met again in here [Kroonstad] I went over to De Lisle's Column and sure enough there were the Diaries and camera and the best part of the lost kit. You may imagine my joy. If I were to lose those Diaries I should regret it all my life, I feel certain. Nothing absolutely could replace them.

We had a most enjoyable trek and the weather was delightful. I told you there was a

Commandeering Officer in one of the Columns I was with. This is a new institution now that the country has to be devastated, all stock collected and families brought in, and he has a busy time of it too on the march. Another new idea is burning all the veldt grass so that the Burghers shall have no grazing for any cattle and stock they may still have. We are off again today on another long trek of a month or two somewhere round about in the Northern ORC [Orange River Colony] so if you don't hear from me for a month or so you will know where I am. Please tell Edith the gloves are in daily use, at least, one is for I unfortunately lost the other, and it is a fine fit.

your affectionate son,

23 June *March to Klompte Doorn. About 8 miles. Good day but some passing clouds. Get in touch with Colonel De Lisle's Column but cannot find Colonel Lowe who is supposed to be between us and Colonel De Lisle. A few messages exchanged in the Column. One lamp out with a Picquet at night.*

24 June *March to Modderfontein. Good day. A few passing clouds. Get in touch with Colonel De Lisle about 9am but he has no message for us. Shortly after Colonel Lowe's Column answers our light and sends a message for the Brigade Major. I then give them KQ [?] to a message from Colonel Bethune, which they answer and then close their Station. Get them again later on, however, send my messages and receive one from them. No night work.*

25 June *March to Driespruit, about 12 miles. Find Colonel Lowe's Column just in front of us soon after starting. Get into communication with his Rear Guard and send a message for the CSO. The two Columns keep parallel to one another 3 or 4 miles apart. Country as before, open and undulating with no kopjes or sudden rises. Get in touch again at 11.30am and exchange some messages:*

Signal/50

Prefix	Time	Location	No Words	Time	Date	Mss No
XM	0 am		10	11.45 am	25.6.01	62a

To: C.S.O.   From: Bde Major Bethune's

Fighting strength today 964

Signal/51

Prefix	Time	Location	No Words	Time	Date	Mss No
SM			41	11.40am	25.6.01	63

To: Bde Major   From: C.S.O.

Kaffirs here say tail end of large convoy crossed Bloem Spruit last night at Makkuwansbank going East. They saw last wagons crossing East ridge about 2 hours ago very few men number of wagons not known.

Occasionally there surfaces in these messages very real evidence of the difficulties some of the column commanders had working with each other, as the next message shows:

Signal/52

Prefix	Time	Location	No Words	Time	Date	Mss No
XM			17	1.20pm	25.6.01	64

To: Col Lowe   From: Col Bethune

My compliments and thank you for burning veldt in front of me all morning.

Signal/53

Prefix	Time	Location	No Words	Time	Date	Mss No
SM	4pm		67	4.30pm	25.6.01	65

To: Col Bethune   from: C.S.O.

Please wire Regimental number and next of kin of Pte Harry Ward and O. Selliears 4th IY wounded also nature of Lt Bennet's wound 4th IY wounded June 4th. You killed two Boers and wounded two more yesterday. Think you should get some more wagons tomorrow. G.O.C. directs no more veldt to be fired. What have you done today.

Signal/54

Prefix	Time	Location	No Words	Time	Date	Mss No
SB	5.45pm		90	6pm	25.6.01	66

To: C.S.O.   From: Bde Major, Bethune

In reply to your last message Pte Ward no regimental number next of kin Mrs Ward The Grove Isleworth Middlesex Pte Selliears not known in 4th IY Lt Bennet wounded thigh severe. We today saw spoor of wagons and followed it for five miles but saw nothing. They were reported as having left Rietfontein at 8am this morning. Destroyed a mill yesterday and two ovens and chimney today. There was sniping all day on our left flank. Orders re Veldt fires noted.

Signal/56

Prefix	Time	Location	No Words	Time	Date	Mss No
SM	6.55pm		40	7pm	25.6.01	68

To: C.S.O. Gen Elliott From: Col Bethune

Your kaffir arrived here.....

Signal/57

Prefix	Time	Location	No Words	Time	Date	Mss No
SM			16	11am	25.6.01	69

To: OC IY From: Captain Armstrong

Send a gun to shell left ridge held by Boers.

But, like so many of the signal sequences, this last message is only a tantalising glimpse of operations taking place on the veldt. The signals records for the 25 June end with Signal 60 and we are given no clues as to what happened next, but must assume that the Boers either drifted away or were driven off.

Diary entry 25 June, continues:

…General Elliot's camp is about 2 miles from ours and communications are easy. Good day, plenty of sun. A little lamp work. I get IY to take lamps out on Picquet so as to give their signallers some practice.

26 June *Misty till 9am. When the mist lifts Colonel Lowe's camp has been vacated and communications are impossible. March about 12 miles to Grootspruit. The road we take is in a valley, and owing to the lie of the country we can see no distance on right or left and communications are not maintained till we get right into camp when the Senekal Hills come into view. Receive a short message from Colonel Lowe's Rear Guard but receive no further messages.*

27 June *At 2am Colonel Harrison and two squadrons of IY go out to surround a farm a few miles on. 6am, two guns and 100 men go out in support. There is a good deal of firing but no Boers are captured. The Column starts moving again, goes a few miles and then waits for Colonel Harrison's party to join us. While the Column waits I succeed in getting in touch*

with Colonel Lowe's Column and some messages are exchanged [which perhaps should be read as transmitted, through Lowe's column onwards to General Elliot's staff, as the only messages recorded make no reference to Colonel Lowe]. *High ground on my right all the way after this and beyond the flankers so I do not get in touch again. Good day, plenty of sun. Skeet Kopje has a good command and might be useful for a future station. Camp at Zuurfontein. Moved about 11 miles.*

Signal/60

Prefix	Time	Location	No Words	Time	Date	Mss No
XM			101	10.30am	27.6.01	72

To: S.O.T Gen Elliott From: Tpt Off Bethune

Your wire 24. Grease five hundred lbs wheels E.P. front twelve hind twelve bolts 3/8 inch by six inch three dozen fish plates six pair wheels scotch cart four belly bugles six mule mangers thirty brake screw L.P. complete dusselbooms six. Pads and straps and tugs two mule reims or chains fifty ox reims 150 ten span mule harness ten sets swingle trees twelve lifting jacks sixteen. Mules 100 natives eighty mule wagons broken down to exchange five. All urgently needed. IY are quite unequipped.

Signal/61

Prefix	Time	Location	No Words	Time	Date	Mss No
XB		10am	77	27.6.01		73

To: C.S.O. From: Col Bethune

Two hundred IY under Col[onel] Harrison made night march last night to surround Boers reported in farms. These were supported at daybreak by a hundred men and two guns. Boers were either warned or heard us coming as the two farms were empty and Boers were on hills around. One man IY wounded. Boer casualties unknown. Some stock rounded up and forage destroyed. Fighting strength today same as yesterday.

This was the last letter-diary Malcolm sent home. There are no references in his later letters to letter-diaries and the presumption must be that he wrote no more of them. There is also a large gap in the entries in Malcolm's diaries with the next sequence beginning on 18 August. It is clear however from the entries in the signals volume that Malcolm was engaged during this time in one or more sweeps across the veldt with the occasional skirmish against small parties of Boers. At the same time the destruction of Boer farms and collecting of Boer livestock continued apace.

Signal/65

Prefix	Time	Location	No Words	Time	Date	Mss No
SB			65	Recd 2.45	28.6.01	78

To: Col Bethune   From: C.S.O.

If you have news of wagons in front of you General suggests your pushing forward a party by night to Mallans Drift on Sterkfontein there is a Boer Hospital there and also a store kept by a German. The Boers seldom sleep on farms within ten miles of a column but turn out after dinner and sleep in the hills.

Signal/66

Prefix	Tim	Location	No Words	Time	Date	Mss No
XB	Recd 2.15pm		112	Sent 3pm	28.6.01	79

To: C.S.O. Gen Elliott   From: Col Bethune

Laager of many wagons and cape carts left Kaffir Kop early yesterday and reached Lindley yesterday escorted by Princeloo [sic Prinsloo] and Haasebrook commandos. They collected at Kaffir Kop on 26th and waited to see our direction. They were 24 hours ahead of me and I had parties twelve hours ahead of me so they got too much start. I would have made a dash on Lindley this morning but that place is too strong. Five Boers killed yesterday Mr Malan's farm here it is a hospital but no Boers at present in it. Dr says he expects one or two from Heilbron. No further news.

The difficulties of communicating and the anxiety this could generate are exemplified by the following exchange:

Signal/68

Prefix	Time	Location	No Words	Time	Date	Mss No
XB	8.45am		40		29.6.01	81

To: C.S.O.   From: Col Bethune

Am sending you a note by runner today too long for message. Am bringing along Mr Malan as his son in law has gone away with all his stock and his son is on commando.

Signal/71

Prefix	Time	Location	No Words	Time	Date	Mss No
SM	1.40pm		32	1.40pm	29.6.01	84

To: Itl Elliott   From: Itl Bethune

All wagons which were on our front and left flank have now trekked to Reitz and Lindley. Total of 250 wagons under Commandants Haasbrook M Prinsloo and Cooper.

Signal/73

Prefix	Time	Location	No Words	Time	Date	Mss No
SM			24		29.6.01	86

To: Col Bethune   From: C.S.O. Elliott

Message too long to signal referred to in this mornings message has not arrived was it despatched and how.

Signal/74

Prefix	Time	Location	No Words	Time	Date	Mss No
XM			9		29.6.01	87

To: C.S.O.   From: Col Bethune

I sent a runner to you at 6pm should reach you shortly.

Signal/75

Prefix	Time	Location	No Words	Time	Date	Mss No
SM			7		29.6.01	88

To: Col Bethune   From: C.S.O.

Runner arrived

Sometimes messages would be sent simultaneously by several methods:

Signal/81

Prefix	Time	Location	No Words	Time	Date	Mss No
SB			94	12.20pm	30.6.01	93

To: Gen Elliott via Kroonstad   From: Gen Rundle via Harrismith

544 24th June. Your FA 122 received today. Without preserved meat your requirements will take nearly two hundred wagons at five thousand pounds each. I will arrange on these lines with meat on the hoof but shall have to use all my wagons and remain immobile until I get them back from drift. Shall be glad to know your proposed movements and dates after third to enable me to make my own arrangements and complete with you as directed by Chief.(Given to Lt Inglis P.W.L.H. for Gen Elliott and sent also by runner).

Kalkoen Krans, outside Harrismith. 3rd July 1901

My dear Father,

We got in here last night and we are off again, I don't know where, tomorrow I believe. We have had a rather interesting trek and the weather has been delightful. We saw a few Boers every day and indulged in the usual amount of sniping. We have collected a large amount of stock again and brought along a lot more refugees, both Dutch and kaffir, and after a few more treks of this description the country will really begin to look a bit empty and bare, but so long as there is the smallest scrap of food and ammunition left I suppose these silly Boers will keep the field.

your affectionate son,

The signalling continued unabated, with requests for materials and food and news of incidents:

Signal/105

To: Supply Officer Gen Broadwood   From: Sig Off Bethune

Law tells me you have a spare drum of oil mineral colza please let me have it first opportunity.

Signal/106

To: Dir of Sig AHQ   From: OC 4th IY Bethune's Clm

Shall require six signallers four helios and telescopes for my battalion. Have only lamps and flags at present and no signallers.

Signal/107

Prefix	Time	Location	No Words	Time	Date	Mss No
SM			40	11.45am	6.7.01	13
To: C.S.O. Gen Elliott		From: Col Lowe				

Pte Collins Pagets Horse taken prisoner by Boers yesterday returned and is now in my camp. No 4247 Pte S Crowther KDGs slightly wounded yesterday. Fighting strength today 774.

And an occasional glimpse of the Boers even if they are away off on the skyline:

Signal/112

Prefix	Time	Location	No Words	Time	Date	Mss No
SM			10	9.50am	9.7.01	18
To: Col Bethune		From: Col Aspinall				

Forty Boers reported on my right

Signal/113

Prefix	Time	Location	No Words	Time	Date	Mss No
SM			23	9.55am	9.7.01	19
To: Col Aspinall		From: Col Bethune				

Make the camp where we halt today. Catch the Boers if you can. Whose guns are firing in front.

Signal/114

Prefix	Time	Location	No Words	Time	Date	Mss No
SM			9	0 am	9.7.01	20
To: Col Bethune		From: Col Aspinall				

The guns are Col De Lisle's

Heilbron 15th July 1901

My dear Father,

We got in here on the evening of the 13th; the other Brigades of the Division turning up about the same time. We had rather a nice trek on the whole, though it was not until the last two or three days that we made any captures and they were only small ones. Still a capture of any sort cheers one up these days when the Boers, ammunition, wagons, stock etc are all very scarce. I got a Mail of the 14th June in yesterday and I at last got a letter from Bertie and find if I had only known I was very near him when we were camped at Harrismith. I don't know that I could have gone so far as he is but still there was a chance. It is sad, as I don't know when another chance like that will turn up and Harrismith is so far by rail.

your affectionate son

Despite the pessimism that he expressed in his letter to his father, Malcolm was able to get his leave and find his brother, Bertie. Malcolm probably arrived at Bloemfield Bridge, where the Leinsters had left two companies, around the 20 July having spent several days travelling down to Pietersmaritzburg to go to the West Yorkshire's Depot. Letter/59 appears to have been written several days after leaving Bertie.

In train near Heidelberg, Transvaal. 30th July 1901

My dearest Mother,

I left Bertie to do the home writing as I was feeling uncommonly slack, but I hope to make up for that by this Mail. I had a very pleasant little week's holiday with 'Brer B' but it was too expensive to be frequently indulged in, as, of course, I was 'on leave' and had to pay for Railway fares etc. However, if it had cost £100 I believe I would have gone ! I was simply dying to see a relation once again and hear verbally all the news from home. It turned out to be a birthday outing as well, though we quite forgot about that at the time. I found him in a nice snug little Mess living a most luxurious and happy life – for South Africa – and I rather envied him, though as I have always said I prefer trekking to anything else. We did not do very much in the shooting line but we played golf and had plenty of riding and polo and had I only been staying a little longer I could have indulged in my old love, rifle shooting, for they have quite a good range at Harrismith where the Yeomanry etc practice.

I have not yet told you how I got away from my Column in the first instance. When the Columns got to Heilbron I got a few letters by the Mail and amongst others one from Bertie saying he was at Bloemfield Bridge, that 2 Companies of his regiment had been left there and the remainder were on trek with General Rundle. I knew that General Rundle had been on the right of our Columns keeping up the right bank of the Wilge River, so I said to myself Bertie must still be at Bloemfield Bridge as he would not be likely to leave it till his Regiment returned, and as luck would have it I was right.

MALCOLM AND BERTIE AT BLOEMFIELD BRIDGE, NEAR HARRISMITH, 23 JULY 1901

As soon as we touched the main line (at Grootvlei just above Vrede Fort Road) I got leave from Colonel Bethune to go down and see General Elliot and get my leave if I could. Colonel Bethune himself by the way had already got his leave and was off to Durban by the first train for a change of air, leaving Colonel Lowe to take over his Brigade. I boarded the very first train down to Vrede Fort Road, saw General Elliot, Colonel Lowe and Divisional Signals Officer etc etc and eventually succeeded in getting a few days' leave. Off I rushed again to the station only to find there were no more trains going up that day. I slept in the station for the night, borrowing blankets from our Supply Officer who had just brought in his train of supplies for the Column from Kroonstad. He happened to be an O.C. (Claud may possibly remember him - Law of Gownboys, in the VIth when I joined) so of course we got on well together. We went on to Grootvlei first thing next morning where I had some breakfast, packed what kit I wanted and caught the Mail up to Elandsfontein. Slept the night there and caught the Durban Mail next morning, saw our old padre, Wainman, at Standerton, and so on to Newcastle sleeping in the train. On again the next morning to Ladysmith, from there to Maritzburg passing all our old battle-fields on the way, looking now quite peaceful and ordinary, stopped a few hours at Maritzburg to have a look at my kit in the Baggage Room and arrange things with Ross at the depot Mess, and then caught the 'up' Mail at 10pm sleeping in the train and getting into Ladysmith early next morning in time for breakfast and to catch the Harrismith train. At about 3pm I got to Bloemfield Bridge and there, to my great joy, found Brer B looking as fit as a fiddle and very surprised at my turning up so unexpectedly.

I am now on my way to Klerksdorp where I hope to join my Column once more. I hear the Mail leaves tomorrow so I must send this off now.

your affect son,

In fact Malcolm missed rejoining his column and was left to kick his heels at Bloemfontein, having moved on from Klerksdorp to Kroonstad.

Bloemfontein Club, 9th August 1901

My dear Father,

I got here about two days ago. They cleared me out of Kroonstad with the rest of the details of General Elliot's Division, as they heard the Division would probably turn up somewhere here, and tonight some of the Officers from the Columns have come in here as they reached Brandfort a day or two ago and the Division is now trekking down here along the railway.

This is not a bad place but very similar to every other South African town of any size and one's money goes just as quickly! The place seems to be in thorough working order, the shops are all open and pretty well stocked, there is electric light in all the streets, hotels and shops, a theatre with a very fair Company playing 'His Excellency the Governor' which I saw last night, and tomorrow night 'The Second Mrs Tanqueray' which I shall probably see too. Altogether I am having a fairly pleasant time for my first 'leave' in South Africa, which, by the way, was originally intended to be a week or ten days but has now developed into nearly a month! ...I shall probably be trekking in a few days from now.

your affectionate son,

With time on his hands Malcolm was able to do a great deal of catching up with his correspondence and amongst the letters he wrote at this time was one to his brother Claud in which Malcolm felt able to be considerably more open about his attitudes and opinions than ever he would in his letters home to his parents as indeed he says himself in the opening paragraph of the letter,

Kroonstad, 13th August 1901

My dear Claud,

I must really try and write you a letter with something in it this time for you, for my last to you if I remember right was a mere note. I have told you before I think the reason for my not writing to you oftener, namely that I cannot tell you any pretty little story without it being carefully worded (which would quite spoil some yarns!) as every letter I write to any of the family has I am told to go the rounds of all the family and relations, and if I write an ordinary letter to you it has to go home first and then on to you which is exactly the same as if I wrote to Father or Mother for the letter would go on to you in any case. Well, enough of that. Bertie and I had a great time together down at Bloemfield Bridge and I thoroughly enjoyed my short leave, which was originally intended to be a week or ten days but which has developed in to nearly a month!

I stayed a week with Bertie and then started off for Klerksdorp at the end of the Johannesburg line where I was told I should find my Column, but when I got there I found they had left about three days earlier so then I came round here, which is practically the Headquarters of the Division. I am leaving by the Mail train today for Bloemfontein, as the Division is expected to turn up

A NEW FACTOR IN THE SOUTH AFRICAN LANDSCAPE: BLOCKHOUSES

somewhere near there in a day or two. The rumour is that we are then going to Kimberley, but these facts are naturally never given out publicly so it is most probably an invention on someone's part, especially as Kimberley is not in our district at all, which is the northern ORC.

When I was on my way from Vrede Fort Road to Bloemfield Bridge General Rundle's Division had just reached Standerton, but the only one of your Regiment [East Yorkshires] I saw at the Railway Station was your Quarter-Master but I did not get a chance to speak to him. Bertie will probably see them all as the HQ of their Division is at Harrismith, but I am not sure if he knows anyone in the Battalion. I came across Major Sladen, who commands the 6th MI, while I was with Colonel De Lisle but I did not know who he was then and never spoke to him. Another Officer of your Regiment I came across was Captain Clarke who is the RSO at Elandsfontein, rather an important and worrying billet to be in I should think. He asked me if I was your brother when I went to get a ticket from him, but otherwise we had nothing in common so the conversation dropped and I took my departure. He seemed rather bored and worried I thought. I told you I think about the present CO of your 2nd Battalion who is known by various names beginning with 'Jingle'. He was CSO of General Smith-Dorrien's Brigade when we were in that Brigade from Bank to Pretoria. I hope you won't mind me speaking candidly and telling you the general opinion of him out here. At that time we thought him a good-natured old fool, very fond of showing us guides and markers duties when we had had a hard day's march and not quite the man for CSO to Smith-Dorrien. You have probably heard from brother Officers how he gets on now, so I won't say anything about that, but if you

want to know Bertie will tell you. I wish I had met your battalion, and been able to call on them for as you know there are two or three who were at school or the RMC [Sandhurst] with me. Do you remember Law of Gownboys? Soon after I joined [Charterhouse] he got into the VIth and I remember him well strutting up the aisle of a Sunday in his white tie with a tremendous waddle! He left Charterhouse and went to Cambridge, then when the war broke out he got the war fever and joined the ASC. He is now the Supply Officer of Bethune's Brigade (though still a 2nd Lt) and a right good chap.

You seem to have been having a busy time ever since you went to the Depot but of course an active energetic chap like you does not mind that sort of thing! You have been getting I suppose a devil of a lot of extra pay so you can't grumble – I was rather amused at your account of General Thynne's inspection. When I wonder is the Army going to get rid of these old fools who think far more of a barrack room window being half an inch too wide open than the physical condition and proficiency of a soldier ? I suppose that sort of thing will never be altered.

Poor Bertie Church's12 Regiment, the 7th DGs, are in General Elliot's Division. They are in General Broadwood's Brigade. I have not seen much of them but I believe they are a very nice lot. I have seen a great deal of the 1st KDGs and the 3rd DGs as they have been in Colonel Bethune's Brigade at different times. I don't think much of the latter but the KDGs are the nicest regiment I think I have ever met, they are a capital lot, awfully hospitable, and real good sorts, from their Colonel downwards. I never thought a Cavalry Regiment would be like that.

Here is a little rhyme for you. It is an ode by a Tommy of my Company to an Emergency ration,

THE WEST YORKSHIRES SPENT THE LATTER PART OF THE WAR GARRISONING BLOCKHOUSES LIKE THIS ONE AT STEERPAN

which is as you know is in two parts, one of some dry meat concoction, the other of chocolate. At one time the men used to eat these emergency rations like anything, and to put a stop to it Colonel Kitchener used to give every man who lost his ration 8 days CB [confined to barracks]. This is the ode:-

> Oh! Potted Meat... ...and Chocolate Sweet
> Of you I will sing in Praise
> But should I lose... ...or if I use
> I am sure to get 8 days
>   your affectionate brother,

By 17 August Malcolm was once more with Bethune's column, though Bethune himself (until about 20 August) was on leave and the column was under the command of Colonel Lowe. The column was soon on the march on yet another sweep across the veldt, although there was time, even if just occasionally, for other pastimes, as Malcolm's diary – once more taking up his story after a series of small gaps – reveals:

19 August 1901   Rouse 5.30am by bell. Breakfast 7am. Pack things and put most on Cape cart. Devilish cold. Start 7.30am and trek alongside railway crossing line by Karee Siding. Post pay list at Blockhouse. Try to get De Lisle but no success. Go out shooting in the afternoon with Jorghinsson and about 7 others and walk all the way down to the railway in scrub but it is poor sport. Camping at Roodeheuvel, marched 13 miles.

20 August   Rouse 7.30. Cold morning. Get Colonel De Lisle about 10am. No messages possible. Very hot at noon and I get my face burnt. A lot of sheep and a few horses commandeered. Young Patton-Bethune got a lot of guinea fowl in the afternoon. I go out after duck in the evening and get a teal which falls in the water. Camp at Declfontein. Marched 14 miles.

21 August   Up 5am. Young Betts and I go down to pond. Shoot a duck and teal but both fall in the water. Start trekking at 7.30. Long march. Get De Lisle soon after 8am.

AN ARMED NATIVE SCOUT, ONE OF A SMALL GROUP COMMANDED BY MR WILSON AND ATTACHED TO BETHUNE'S COLUMN.

> *Korannaberg Mountains, South East of Wynburg, 22nd August 1901*

My dear Father,

We are only four days from the line but there is a Convoy going into Wynburg tomorrow to fetch out supplies, so I take the opportunity to scribble you a note.

This trek so far has been rather uninteresting from a warlike point of view. I had not seen or heard a burgher until today and then there were only ten or so, they are not nearly so bold as they used to be. We had a night march last night to try and surround some burghers, but unfortunately they fled before we got near them. I am so sleepy now that I can hardly keep my eyes open or hold my pen straight. The weather is still lovely, sometimes a bit cold at night, but we have had no rains to worry us yet and the days are always nice and warm. There is not much to tell you about of interest. The latest proclamations are being issued rapidly and we hear have already had a good effect in some parts. I have had a little mixed gun shooting lately as we have been passing through country with a great deal of low scrub, and I can generally manage to borrow a gun of some kind so that my Mess is fairly well stocked. No more tonight.

> your affectionate son,

The 26th saw Malcolm particularly busy with signalling, of which the most significant signals were:

Signal/179

Prefix	Time	Location	No Words	Time	Date	Mss No
				20	26.8.01	38

To: Lt Riall From: Capt Watson

The C.S.O. has ridden over to Bethune's camp and has taken message the General wants sending through as soon as you possibly can. They will be sent up to you from your column. We move towards the east end of your hill. Let me know when you get communication with the line.

Signal/180

Prefix	Time	Location	No Words	Time	Date	Mss No
SM				18	26.8.01	39

To: Capt Watson From: Lt Riall

Got messages alright this morning but have no touch with the line yet.

Signal/181

Prefix	Time	Location	No Words	Time	Date	Mss No
					26.8.01	40

To: Chief Pretoria From: Gen Elliott

RH227 Your 6942 to Tucker received here today. Haasbruck with 300 men were reported Korannaberg on 20th I therefore made night march here on 21st occupying Zonnebloem, Mequatlings Nek, Bellevue and Merriemietzie with Broadwood's and De Lisle's Columns sending Bethune to hold line from Bresler Flat with Barker closing the northern line Belmontberg but no sign of Haasbruck hereabouts. Midnight 23rd Broadwood heard of attack on Black Watch at Evening Star and marched at once but arrived too late to be of any use. Last night he moved to Rienzi and will operate from there until rations arrive. CLOCOLAIV is in Rienzi and not as on map. He will advance on line DDDDX LLUME ALLQM KRUQF YTTLV ZYVEB. Am rationing Division as detailed in my 206 of August 15th and clearing country while waiting. Communications difficult last two days raining and no sun. On 21st I shall be PYAZB VQASV ECUYT UEMSE CIVEB MYFYT TLVZY VEBEB inclusive. My intelligence reports about 200 Boers between Korannaberg and Broadwater Basin local commandos of about 50 men each. Prinsloo intelligence agent with Broadwood declares De Wet signature forgery. My last information placed De Wet near Lindley about 17th. Addressed Chief, Pretoria. Repeated Generals Tucker and Knox.

Signal/183

Prefix	Time	Location	No Words	Time	Date	Mss No
XB			50		26.8.01	43

To: D.O.S. Pretoria From: DAAG Gen Elliott, Merriemietzie

Aug 24th AP17 Division leaves here with eleven days rations on DDDMX EVMOI ENEVM PUEAO YVXSV KRUQQ next for rationing hole Division about DDDIE HMETK EUCSC MPPPP I have informed AAG Supplies Bloemfontein accordingly.

Signal/185

Prefix	Time	Location	No Words	Time	Date	Mss No
XB			77		26.8.01	45

To: Int ORC Bloemfontein From: Int Elliott

Aug 23rd S75. Boers left farms Korannaberg on 21st. Rolf Botha with 60 men and womens laager gone east of Belmontberg. Transvaalers have left this for SE ORC. Comdt Steyl has gone SE from Korannaberg passing Fredrickstad farm. VC Fourie with 30 men probably with Botha on Belmontberg. Clearing Berg and vicinity will send full report of captures later.

Signal/190

Prefix	Time	Location	No Words	Time	Date	Mss No
SM			15	10.25am	26.8.01	50

To: Col Bethune From: Lt Riall

We are in touch with Major Pine Coffin and Col Barker.

Signal/191

Prefix	Time	Location	No Words	Time	Date	Mss No
SM			17		26.8.01	51

To: Col Bethune From: Gen Elliott

Have you anything to report. Are you in touch with Broadwood.

Signal/192

Prefix	Time	Location	No Words	Time	Date	Mss No
SB			42		26.8.01	52

To: Gen Elliot From: Col Bethune

ALL THIS TIME THE BOERS WERE STILL BEING ROUNDED UP AND TAKEN OFF THE VELDT. HERE, SOME BOER FAMILIES AND SOME OF THEIR BELONGINGS ARE BEING BROUGHT INTO CAMP

COLONEL BETHUNE LOOKS ON AS HIS TROOPS, THE 3RD DRAGOON GUARDS ARE SHOWN HERE, CROSS ANOTHER DRIFT

I arrived Leyden 5am Trommel 10am about 30 Boers headed east by our troops. This farm has been gutted by Marais and 350 Boers 3 days ago. Am in communication with Barker and Pine Coffin but not with Broadwood.

Signal/193

Prefix	Time	Location	No Words	Time	Date	Mss No
SM			31		26.8.01	54

To: Col Barker and Major Pine Coffin   From: ltl Bethune's Bde

Please leave Koekemoers family on farm Rondehoek as he will be there himself the day after tomorrow.

27 August *Colonel Aspinall and 2 squadrons go out 12.30am. Start 7.30am. Late getting off. Go on with advance guar6d and get in touch with Colonel Aspinall. Reach Trommel 12 noon. Two troops of IY go out to get in touch with Colonel De Lisle and succeed but with difficulty. Camp is at a nice farm though it smells and has been wrecked by Boers. Sleep well. Camp at Trommel, marched 12 miles.*

HAVING TAKEN AWAY THE BOER FAMILIES WITH WHATEVER POSSESSIONS THEY COULD LOAD ONTO A SMALL CAPE CART, THEIR FARM WAS THEN BLOWN UP, THEIR FARM BUILDINGS BURNT DOWN AND THEIR LIVESTOCK EITHER RUN-OFF OR SLAUGHTERED

In amongst all of this, Elliot's various columns did catch sight of the Boers once in awhile:

Signal/194

Prefix	Time	Location	No Words	Time	Date	Mss No
			66		27.8.01	55

To: ltl Bethune's Column   From: Vine Villa Farm Barker's Intelligence Officer

Small parties of enemy have been trekking from mountains with wagons in a NE direction. At Middel engaged 120 at noon killing one, two prisoners they were trekking in NE direction but retired in SE direction. I shall be with right flankers on Varchuontien ridges tomorrow have important messages to pass along line please endeavour to meet.

A HOT MEAL AT THE END OF A LONG DAY WAS ALWAYS WELCOME. THE OFFICERS' COOK WITH HIS WAGGONETTE AND STOVE

Signal/195

Prefix	Time	Location	No Words	Time	Date	Mss No
SB			22		28.8.01	56

To: Major Pine Coffin   From: Col Bethune

Boers reported to have slept here last night and to have trekked to Wonderkop. Have you any news.

The Signals volume does not include Major Pine Coffin's response.

28 August *March 7.30. Bitterly cold. Cloudy morning. Colonel De Lisle's Column bumps into ours soon after starting, but our Convoy gets stuck for two hours at a drift. Nice farm, green forage on side of kopje. Find 12 bags of wheat at the side of the road and burn them. 200 Boer wagons reported ahead. Get communications with Major Pine Coffin at lunch time, lunch with IY, reach camp 2pm. Busy afternoon communicating with Major Pine Coffin and Colonel De Lisle. Night move contemplated. Put Officer's Lamp in touch with DHQ and Colonel Barker. Camp at Braan Bosch Fontein, marched 15 miles.*

Signal/207

Prefix	Time	Location	No Words	Time	Date	Mss No
SB			54	8.30pm	28.8.01	68

To: Gen Elliott   From: ltl Bethune

Some wagons have gone to Witkop via Hartebeestefontein and Driekuil others may have gone to Commando Nek the only other road. Pine Coffin prisoner reports De Wet and Steyn with two Krupp guns and one maxim with Froneman. Prisoner was employed filing rust off dug up shells.

Signal/208

Prefix	Time	Location	No Words	Time	Date	Mss No
SM			15		28.8.01	69

To: Col Barker   From: Col Bethune

Have sent messenger to you will arrive shortly. Please warn picquets.

Signal/214

Prefix	Time	Location	No Words	Time	Date	Mss No
			17			75

To: Major Pine Coffin   From: Col Bethune

All wagons and 250 Boers left here this morning in direction Witkop.

Signal/215

Prefix	Time	Location	No Words	Time	Date	Mss No
			9	9.15pm	29.8.01	76

To: Major Pine Coffin   From: Col Bethune

29 Aug. As some fourteen hundred Boers are reported in or near Witkop I propose tomorrow to move with Col Barker on that place leaving you to move to such a position as to stop a break N or NW say Tafelberg or thereabouts. Your orders should come through Col Barker but I have informed him that I have lamped direct to you. If you do not hear to the contrary move tomorrow accordingly. We move out with two days supplies what will you do.

The diary entries continue:

29 August *Colonel Carr Ellison and 4 squadrons IY go on at 5.30am. main body moves off 7am. Hilly country, bad roads. Wagons still in front. Our gunners fire at Boer Rear Guard at 1pm. In touch nearly all day with Barker and Pine Coffin and part of the day with De Lisle. Walked up to the top of a big hill [in afternoon] but saw no sign of Colonel De Lisle's Column. Busy afternoon. Boers are reported still ahead at Witkop. Get in touch with Major Pine Coffin by lamp. Messages all night.*

30 August *Start of 7am. get Barker and Pine Coffin, both ahead but have left their baggage behind which gets mixed up with ours. Halt from 9 till 12 and outspan. Lunch at 11. Shell Boers out of Witkop. See Major Pine Coffin, got in touch with Barker. Pretty camp. Blows hard all night. Cold. Some natives and Boer ponies captured. Camp at Bloemfontein*

31 August *A Push going out 5am, stopped up 6am. Had breakfast and then climbed up to top of Witkop with 2 helios. Very windy. get in touch with General Elliot and Colonel Barker and get orders etc. Come down about 12. Trek to Rietvlei, Convoy under Colonel Carr Ellison going by a different route. They have one man of their Rear Guard wounded. Smith captures four Boer* *wagons and is shelled by Colonel Carr Ellison.* [There is nothing new about friendly fire!]

The difficulties that commanders in the field faced are shown in the next sequence of signals. They would seem to represent a major alteration to the orders for the current sweep, in order to swing the columns against a concentration of Boer forces; one can almost sense Major General Elliot's exasperation as he endeavoured to get the columns redirected.

Signal/222

Prefix	Time	Location	No Words	Time	Date	Mss No
XB			69	8.30am	31.8.01	83
To: Gen Elliott		From: Col Bethune				

Witkop Aug 31st 8am. Your 302 received. The orders being so conflicting and Barker and Pine Coffin depending on me I am remaining here until I receive definite instructions from you because at present I do not know if you wish Barker and Pine Coffin to march near Rietvlei also. I am in communication with Pine Coffin but not Barker at present.

Signal/225

Prefix	Time	Location	No Words	Time	Date	Mss No
XB			38	9.30am	31.8.01	87

March yourself at one to Rietvlei order Pine Coffin to higher ground near Boschkloof south of Rexford covering Witnek road relying on Barker covering Retiefs and Slabberts Nek. Pine Coffin to communicate with Barker.

Signal/226

Prefix	Time	Location	No Words	Time	Date	Mss No
XB			8	9.45am	31.8.01	88
To: Gen Elliot		From: Col Bethune				

Do I march to Oshoek as per programme. Where will you be tonight.

Signal/227

Prefix	Time	Location	No Word	Time	Date	Mss No
XB			31	10.50am	31.8.01	89
To: Col Barker		From: Col Bethune				

Gen Elliot orders you to cover Retiefs and Slabberts Nek. Pine Coffin to cover high ground near Bosch Kloof south of Rexford. I go to Rietvlei.

Signal/228

Prefix	Time	Location	No Word	Time	Date	Mss No
XB			89	10.25am	31.8.01	90
To: Col Bethune		From: Gen Elliot				

You will not go to Oshoek tomorrow march to Rietvlei with all your baggage will send you orders there. Pine Coffin and Barker will keep their places ordered this morning till fresh orders arrive. We are going to co-operate against commando of 400 reported about Grasfontein. Broadwood marching up from south, De Lisle pushing in from NW. As soon as you arrive at Rietvlei report and be prepared for orders to co-operate and look out for any attempt to break past you.

Signal/230

Prefix	Time	Location	No Words	Time	Date	Mss No
SB			20	1.00pm	31.8.01	92
To: Col Bethune		From: Gen Elliot				

Move on to Rietvlei and examine Witnek for tracks of wagons reported to have gone that way.

Signal/231

Prefix	Time	Location	No Words	Time	Date	Mss No
XB			14	2pm	31.8.01	93
To: Col Bethune		From: Gen Elliot				

any guides that know the roads through Witnek.

Signal/232

Prefix	Time	Location	No Words	Time	Date	Mss No
XB			26	2.5pm	31.8.01	94
To: Gen Elliot		From: Col Bethune				

I captured four natives from the Boers last night who know all this country. With their help my guides can go anywhere.But, as ever, the difficulties of communicating in this rugged country compounded Elliot's troubles:

Signal/238

Prefix	Time	Location	No Words	Time	Date	Mss No
SG			29	1.15pm	1.9.01	2
To: Col Bethune		From: Lt Riall				

THE BRITISH LOST HUGE NUMBERS OF HORSES DURING THE CAMPAIGN IN SOUTH AFRICA. MALCOLM'S PHOTOGRAPHS OF SOME OF THE CAVALRY MOUNTS OF BETHUNE'S COLUMN OFFER AN INSIGHT INTO WHY THIS SHOULD HAVE HAPPENED

I have been trying the country all round for Col De Lisle but so far without answer. The country very broken and it is still hazy.

1 September, Sunday. Woken up at 4.50am. Colonel Bethune and fighting men go out to attack Witnek but Boers have mostly cleared. I climb high hill to get in contact with Major Pine Coffin but it is too misty. Come down at 11.20 and have breakfast and lunch. Captain Smythe comes over from General Elliot's Column. I go out to Kalkoen Krans to try and get communications with General Elliot but without success. Colonel Aspinall goes out to Witnek again; about 100 Boers seen there, stock captured and 2 good stallions but not much good done. Sleep in the afternoon. Get a new Mess tent. Remain at Rietvlei.

Signal/242

Prefi	Time	Location	No Word	Time	Date	Mss No
SB			14	1.5pm	2.9.01	6

To: Col Bethune   From: Gen Elliot

What was your bag yesterday and had you any casualties.

Signal/243

Prefix	Time	Location	No Words	Time	Date	Mss No
SM			5	1.35pm	2.9.01	7

To: Col Bethune   From: C.S.O.

Have you any news of Col Barker or Pine Coffin.

Signal/244

Prefix	Time	Location	No Words	Time	Date	Mss No
			55	2pm	2.9.01	8

To: Itl Elliot   From: Itl Bethune

Casualty list for month of August. Boers killed two, prisoners of war armed eighteen, unarmed 48, Boers wounded 3, ammunition 950 rounds, rifles 24, cattle collected 3904, horses 1700, sheep 7540, refugees 960, wagons captured or destroyed 125, cape carts ditto 95, wheat etc destroyed 2500 sacks, proclamations issued 100.

Signal/245

Prefix	Time	Location	No Words	Time	Date	Mss No
SB		BF PM	97	3.35pm	2.9.01	9

To: C.S.O. Gen Elliot   From: Col Bethune

Messenger sent to you with despatch this morning just returned having been fired on. Could get no touch with Barker or Pine Coffin all yesterday or this morning. Yesterday destroyed ten wagons three cape carts unable to bring them in. About fifty Boers fled NE one Boer killed not gathered. Our casualties one horse. Also captured 127 head of cattle and 230 horses. Am camping tonight at Spreeufontein. Will reach Winburg on 5th. Will make every endeavour to get touch with Barker.

Signal/246

Prefix	Time	Location	No Words	Time	Date	Mss No
SM		Brakfontein	33	7.45am	3.9.01	10

To: Col Bethune   From: C.S.O.

GOC does not wish you to catch up you are rationed up to the 7th therefore take it easy and reach Winburg on 6th by order.

Signal/247

Prefix	Time	Location	No Word	Time	Date	Mss No
SB			26	7.50am	3.9.01	11

To: Col Bethune   From: Col De Lisle

About four miles North of my line today an officer who has just returned says he saw a large mob of cattle.

2 September *Try to climb big hill to get Major Pine Coffin but the Boers are on it and Biggs won't go. Get DHQ [divisional headquarters] all right from a point a mile from camp. Come down 2pm and have lunch. Go back 3pm and send a long message through. Difficult with a three inch and work it myself. Chilly night. Moved to Speen Fontein.*

3 September *Up at 6am and Column marches off at 8am. I remain to send messages and get DHQ again and get some messages from them, all through by 8am. Go down hill by a difficult pass, go by kaffir kraal. Stop short of Brakfontein. Brigade is moving slowly. Try to get a troop to take out to a hill with me but troops too late. Camped at Bredd Glei*

4 September *March 8am. No communications with other Columns. Windy day and rather beastly. Reach camp at 1pm. General Elliot is one day ahead.*

5 September *March at 8am. Get in touch with Winburg at 10am and get all my messages through. De Lisle is camped about 6 miles out of Winburg. We camp close to him on Senekal road. Went out shooting with Jorgensen and get a teal. Camped at Wilge Boom Plaats.*

6 September *March at 8am and go on 6 miles to a place about 4 miles outside Winburg.*

Winburg, ORC. 8th Sept 1901

My dear Mother,

We have only been here a couple of days and are off again tomorrow morning and I have been most awfully busy the whole time, so I regret to say that I cannot explain all you have asked about my duties as Signalling Officer and accounts of treks etc. I am sending you however a rough outline sketch map of the trekking I have done since I joined this Division and I hope that may afford you some satisfaction.

I hope some prints of those photos The King sent you recently are coming along, for of course I have never yet seen them. Please ask The Stores also to hurry up those photos I ordered some time back, as the people I ordered them for are getting impatient and I am getting anxious.

You will see by the map we got nearly up to Harrismith again, but had to turn back to the line for rations etc. We had ripping weather again and I had some good shooting at buck, hares etc but, looked at from a military point of view, I fear the result of the trek

was nil. The heat increases day by day but the rainy weather has not properly set in yet. The proclamation is having a fairly good result in these parts, small parties keep turning up every now and again to give themselves up, so we hope the 15th will mean something after all.

your affectionate son,

THE NATIVE POPULATION RARELY FIGURES IN EITHER MALCOLM'S WRITTEN ACCOUNT OR HIS PHOTOGRAPHS. THIS PHOTOGRAPH SHOWS A HOTTENTOT FAMILY OUTSIDE THEIR HUT. THE TROOPERS HAVE NOT BEEN IDENTIFIED BUT ARE THOUGHT TO BE AN AUSTRALIAN CONTINGENT.

The next day, 9 September, Elliot's division took the field once again for a sweep that would take them from Winburg – in pretty dreadful weather – on the western side of the Orange River Colony back across the veldt to Harrismith. As in the earlier sweeps, this push resulted in the capture of remarkably few Boers, but saw the continued destruction of their farms and the running-off of their livestock.

Malcolm's diary is especially lacklustre for this period as even he appears to be running out of interest in the campaign or perhaps it was all becoming so familiar that finding something novel to record was difficult. Then, on 28 September, Colonel Bethune was ordered to load his troops onto three trains and take them down to Durban and thence onwards to Zululand to repel an invasion by Botha. By the time that Bethune's brigade arrived in Zululand, where they joined General Dartnell's column, Botha's move had been turned by the British forces in southern Transvaal and the invasion scare was over. Malcolm provides a detailed narrative of the deployment to Zululand but, as nothing of any importance occurred, this element of Malcolm's service in South Africa has not been included.

As you will see that far from being 'away from all the fighting' as you rather unkindly put it, I am always well up in it, for whenever there is fighting the Brigadier must be there to conduct operations, and where he goes I go too. I have no ardent desire to be at the head of the Advance Guard every day in order to be sniped at. I can tell you, still when the time comes I am no coward but at the same time I see no use in running unnecessary risks. If I wanted to be shot I should like to have been shot in some big engagement at the beginning of the war and not.

Twenty
BACK TO THE VELDT IN THE ORC

Opposite: The mid-day halt at Molen Spruit near Harrismith

On the 26 October orders were received in which the main part of Bethune's command, along with Malcolm, found themselves ordered back to Harrismith to resume operations with Major-General Elliot's division in the Orange River Colony. Bethune himself had been given three months' leave and the command of his column is given to Colonel Lowe. Lowe's column, as it had now become, arrived back at Harrismith on 31 October where they prepared themselves for the next push into the veldt.

Malcolm was soon busy organising his signallers, replacing defective or lost equipment, and involved in exchanging signals. The signals records show a large flurry of messages — both in the form of telegrams and via heliograph or lamp — being sent as Lowe's column was re-integrated into Elliot's command. Malcolm's first priority was to discover what cipher was in use:

Signal/440

Prefix	Time	Location	No Words	Time	Date	Mss No
SM			19	3.15pm	1.11.01	1

To: CSO Gen Elliot   From: Col Lowe

Have not got this months cypher please PPP.

The response was, almost inevitably, pretty rude:

Signal/442

Prefix	Time	Location	No Words	Time	Date	Mss No
SM			26	3.45pm	1.11.01	3

To: OC Col Lowe's Bde   From: CSO Gen Elliot, Nells Farm

Nov 1st. PPPOC MBRWT AQVBF CTRCK SHQRS XHSNO Your Intelligence Officer is to blame.

And of course we have no idea what the cipher was nor, indeed, what the translated message was as Malcolm, sensible man that he was, took care to ensure that the cipher and the book containing records of signals were kept apart. Other signals concerned the whereabouts of individual officers and men, rations, stores and equipment and the general administration of a military unit. A response to an enquiry from General Elliot's staff concerning feeding strengths tells us the size of Lowe's column,

Signal/459

Prefix	Time	Location	No Word	Time	Date	Mss No
SM			34	1.30pm	2.11.01	20

To: DAAG (B) Gen Elliot   From: Bde Major Lowe's Column

Nov 2nd Nells farm. Approximate feeding strength in event of a trek is as follows. Europeans 1023 Horses 1064 Mules 835 Natives 416.

Of which not all were considered as the fighting strength as a later signal shows:

Signal/472

Prefix	Time	Location	No Word	Time	Date	Mss No
SM			20	3.55pm	5.11.01	3

To: CSO Gen Elliot   From: Col Lowe

Nov 5th fighting strength every available man mounted is 758 not including artillery or officers.

It had been a long time since Malcolm had written home and, despite the fact that he had time enough, he managed only to jot a few lines on a postcard to his mother:

Harrismith. 5/11/01

Feel oh! so naughty. How many Mails have I missed. Fear the worst. Too bad of me. Expect innumerable and lengthy scoldings. No excuse. All my fault. Dare not even write small letter till I have sent long newsy one. Intend make full Diary for month October, so full of change, adventure, and new experiences. trekking out tomorrow. Don't know where or how long. Col B home on three months leave, Colonel Lowe now commanding this Brigade. Rainy season come on with a vengeance, not nice for trekking. Heavy thunderstorm all this afternoon.   MR

Malcolm's diary shows that on 6 November Lowe's column marched out into the veldt:

6 November   *Up at 6am. Move ordered for 8.30am but put off till 9.30am. Good road and a short march. General Elliot goes with General Broadwood and they camp close to Nell's Farm. In touch with Platberg but not General Elliot. Get in about 4pm... 7th DGs have only 3 signallers and 2 heliographs owing to sick men. Camp at Grootgelucht.*

COLONEL LOWE AND THE OFFICERS OF HIS COLUMN

7 November *March at 7am. Breakfast 5.20am. Difficulty at start putting signallers in proper places. Cross Molen Spruit bridge and halt a bit. Guns goof, piston breaks, Mercer angry and wired Harrismith. Very short march. General Elliot goes to our last camp. In touch with him and Harrismith. Pom-pom very busy above camp. In camp by 12. Bath, clean guns etc. Camping at Kaffirstadt.*

In an intriguing sequence of signals sent that day we see a minor operation being carried out, a great deal of huffing and puffing by the column commander – Colonel Lowe – at the lack of alacrity on the part of his subordinates and the highly irritated gunners demanding new parts for their guns,

Signal/478

Prefix	Time	Location	No Words	Time	Date	Mss No
SM			19	8am	7.11.01	39

To: Col Lowe From: Major Thompson

About 50 Boers working round right rear. Your shots nearly a thousand yards over.

Signal/479

Prefix	Time	Location	No Words	Time	Date	Mss No
SM			9	8.5am	7.11.01	40

To: Major Thompson From: Col Lowe

Withdraw your right flank party.

Signal/480

Prefix	Time	Location	No Words	Time	Date	Mss No
SM			13	8.7am	7.11.01	41

To: Col Lowe From: Major Thompson

If I withdraw those I must withdraw from here.

Signal/481

Prefix	Time	Location	No Words	Time	Date	Mss No
SM			25	8.20am	7.11.01	42

To: Col Lowe From: Major Thompson

I propose retiring at a trot on to convoy. Will withdraw post from bluff on left if you command it.

Signal/482

Prefix	Time	Location	No Words	Time	Date	Mss No
SM			12	8.24am	7.11.01	43

To: Major Thompson From: Col Lowe

I will signal to you when to retire.

Signal/483

Prefix	Time	Location	No Words	Time	Date	Mss No
SM			17	8.45am	7.11.01	44

To: Major Thompson   From: Col Lowe

You can retire no necessity to trot as I am covering your retirement.

Signal/484

Prefix	Time	Location	No Words	Time	Date	Mss No
SM			20	8.55am	7.11.01	45

To: Col Lowe   From: Major Thompson

There are some scattered Boers about 800 yards short of your last shot in the open.

Signal/485

Prefix	Time	Location	No Words	Time	Date	Mss No
SM			14	9.10am	7.11.01	46

To: Major Thompson   From: Col Lowe

Why do you not retire as ordered. Retire now please.

Signal/486

Prefix	Time	Location	No Words	Time	Date	Mss No
SM			10	9.15am	7.11.01	47

To: Col Lowe   From: Major Thompson

Was waiting for my right flank.

Signal/487

Prefix	Time	Location	No Words	Time	Date	Mss No
XM			56	9.25am	7.11.01	48

To: CRA Harrismith   From: OC G RHA

Nov 7th Gun carriage just issued to me to replace damaged one is disabled at first round. Piston rod broken at breast of carriage. Please inform Ordnance also AAGRA and Col Flint and ask for carriage to replace first opportunity.

Signal/489

Prefix	Time	Location	No Words	Time	Date	Mss No
SM			52	1pm	7.11.01	50

To: OC CRA Harrismith   From: OC G RHA

7th Nov. My message this morning. On taking to pieces find head of piston rod broken. New piston rod only required no other damage to carriage. Kindly arrange for it to be sent to meet battery first opportunity.

Signal/490

Prefix	Time	Location	No Words	Time	Date	Mss No
SM			21	1.5pm	7.11.01	51

To: Col Lowe   From: Capt Davidson

Have seen about 30 Boers leave here and now on the far ridge almost out of range.

Davidson commanded the Pom-Pom section.

Signal/491

Prefix	Time	Location	No Words	Time	Date	Mss No
SM			18	1.10pm	7.11.01	52

To: OC ADV GD   From: Col Lowe

Send pom-pom into camp. Keep post of twenty men on hill.

Later in the day comes a response to the gunner's request:

Signal/502

Prefix	Time	Location	No Words	Time	Date	Mss No
SM			33	5.15pm	7.11.01	63

To: OC G Battery   From: Gen Elliot's Div

469 Nov 7th. Your helio today. I have asked CRA Kroonstad to obtain you a new piston rod.

8 November *March 6am. Breakfast on eggs, bacon and jam. General Elliot calls up soon after we start and sends Chief's [Lord Kitchener] message about lights at night.*

DAVIDSON AND HIS POM-POM

9 November   *March at 6am. Try for General Broadwood from a hill on the left of road till Rear Guard catches us up. Move on to Newmarket (merely one farm). Get Major Gough of General Spens' Column from there. Try General Broadwood again but still no success. Get General Spens on Hol Kop and exchange some messages. Move on then to Wonderpan where we camp. Cloudy day and helio work is difficult. Padre and I go out shooting doves, blue-rocks and sagaboulos. Get a few doves. Most awful thunderstorm comes on after dinner and lasts three hours. Rain awfully heavy, comes through canvas and along ground. Rimington's, De Lisle's and Damant's [Columns] are about. Camp at Wonderpan.*

Signal/506

Prefix	Time	Location	No Word	Time	Date	Mss No
SB			90	6.35am	8.11.01	67

To: Col Lowe   From: DAAG B Gen Elliot

Nov 7th. The following marked urgent received from Chief begins 8422 Fires and lights should never be used at night by our columns and posts except in case of urgent necessity as they reveal the positions of our troops to the enemy. During the summer months except for cooking purposes lights should be carefully screened from view. Whenever possible cooking operations should be completed before dusk and all lights should then be carefully extinguished for the night.

The diary continues:

Lovely day. Whilst halted 2 Boers come close with a white flag. Cross Cornelius River bridge. Troop of 7th Dragoon Guards hung up. 3 men prisoners and 1 wounded. Colonel Lowe goes to assistance. We burn a farm. Get in about 12. Padre and I walk out with [sporting] guns - nil. Thunderstorm heavy. Brock gets 200 horses and some sheep. Camp at Langbult.

Signal/517

Prefix	Time	Location	No Words	Time	Date	Mss No
SM			14	10.0am	9.11.01	78

To: Col Lowe   From: Gen Spens

What is your news. Have you any information of Boers.

Signal/518

Prefix	Time	Location	No Words	Time	Date	Mss No
SM			96	10.10am	9.11.01	79

To: Gen Spens   From: Col Lowe

A few Boers have been all round me. Boers told kaffirs yesterday that British columns left Harrismith, Standerton and Frankfort on the 6th. Steyn and De Wet are reported to be between Wilge River and Reitz. I have a letter for you ordering you to return to Standerton after the close of these operations. Will send it to you at first opportunity. I camp about 5 miles N W of Newmarket. Have been in communication with Gough this morning. Where do you camp tonight.

Signal/519

Prefix	Time	Location	No Words	Time	Date	Mss No
SM			44	1.30pm	9.11.01	80

To: Col Lowe   From: Gen Spens

S74 Kaalkop 10.35am I am camping tonight at Haarte Beeste Laagte 187. Gough will be at Kalkfontein 184 possibly you could send the letter which you have for me to Gough. Can you tell me where Gen Broadwood's Column is.

11 November, Ox waggons start crossing drift at 6am ...

Signal/520

Prefix	Time	Location	No Words	Time	Date	Mss No
SM			14	4.20pm	9.11.01	81
To: Col Lowe		From: Gen Spens				

Broadwood is due at Waaiwater 678 on Wilge River tonight.

10 November, Sunday *Sergeant Newton and Dungate are both a bit seedy. March at 7am. Brigadier and force strike back to Newmarket, Colonel Aspinall takes Column along. Get message from General Spens before starting from Spitzkop.*

Signal/521

Prefix	Time	Location	No Words	Time	Date	Mss No
SB			88	4.25pm to 7.30am	9.11.01/10.11.01	82
To: Col Lowe		From: Gen Spens				

Nov 9th Rimington reports: begins I can see convoy from Tafelo Kop on left bank of river at Stryjdplaats with large number of cattle moving west. Large herd of cattle about Bonkplaats. We heard reliably that all cattle have crossed Wilge moving west but that majority of wagons have been unable to cross owing to river being up and that they have gone towards Villiersdorp a number of them are hidden in right bank of Wilge. Repeated Col De Lisle, Damant, Intelligence Standerton.

Signal/522

Prefix	Time	Location	No Words	Time	Date	Mss No
SB			24	7.45am	10.11.01	83
To: Col Lowe		From: Gen Spens				

Nov 9th Shall move to Rooikraal 454 tomorrow where Gough joins me. Let me know where you will be.

Signal/523

Prefix	Time	Location	No Words	Time	Date	Mss No
XB			59	8am	10.11.01	84
To: Gen Spens		From: Col Lowe				

My information reports that a large convoy and 200 men partly crossed Wilge River at Bezuidenhouts Drift yesterday going west. In case any have broken back I am taking four hundred men and work towards Uitval 272 and then up right bank. My baggage goes to Kaffirstad where I camp tonight.

Malcolm's diary continues:

…Get Harrismith and a section of General Broadwood's but no answer from him. Collect a lot of stock. Reach Hol Spruit 3pm. Stream too high to cross. [This involved a great deal of signalling between Colonel Lowe and various detachments of his column as well as keeping both Elliot and Spens aware of the situation. It was indeed a busy time for Malcolm as the heliographs winked their messages across the veldt, as, yet again, the British columns found themselves halted by flooded rivers.] *Call back Colonel Aspinall and Convoy from Kaffirstadt where he too failed to cross and we camp at Slabbert's Hoek. Camp at Slabbert's Hoek.*

Signal/533

Prefix	Time	Location	No Words	Time	Date	Mss No
SB			13	6.10am	11.11.01	94
To: Col Lowe		From: Gen Elliot Draaihoek				

Nov 10th Where are you crossing Wilge.

Signal/534

Prefix	Time	Location	No Words	Time	Date	Mss No
XB		FFA	35	6.30am	11.11.01	95
To: Gen Elliot		From: Col Lowe				

11th Nov Unable to cross Hol Spruit yesterday am now crossing at Stolzenfels 133. Hope to cross Wilge today at Bezuidenhouts drift but it is doubtful. Please look out for helio there.

Malcolm's diary entry:

…mule waggons follow 7am. Get General Broadwood from camp about 6.30am. Take a message and get about half way through reply when he departs [but the Signals volume does not reveal any message from or to Broadwood although there are 26 other signals recorded for that day, most of which pertain to the movement of Lowe's column across the river]. *Cross spruit and get his light again but no answer. Move on. Get Major Gough, General Spens and Colonel De Lisle. Wounded Boer surrenders. Get General Broadwood again from new camp station. Cross Wilge River 3pm, 4ft deep, and take photos.*

LAW AND HIS NATIVE SERVANTS AND TREKKING WAGGON

THE BOER WAR 193

Camp opposite side close to a Boer Hospital with a doctor and three nurses. Dine 6pm. Bed early. Sleep sound. Camping at Bezuidenhouts Drift.

Signal/554

Prefix	Time	Location	No Words	Time	Date	Mss No
SM			31	4.12pm	11.11.01	110

To: Col Carr Ellison   From: Col Lowe

Please find out from women in burnt farm whether Dr Boutzma has been on commando or if any men live here who were out on commando.

Signal/555

Prefix	Time	Location	No Words	Time	Date	Mss No
SM			42	4.45pm	11.11.01	111

To: Col Lowe   From: Col Carr Ellison

There are about one hundred and fifty cattle by river two miles North of pom-pom. Women think Dr was with De Wet commando. Women says husbands of women at Hospital was killed Ladysmith name De Jagers two sons living at hospital.

12 November   *Woken up at 1.30am, dress and get pony saddled just in time to start off with night push at 2am. Brigadier and nearly whole force out. Guide Fritz gets muddled and loses his way. Finish up at daylight, 5am, quite close to camp and get slated by Major Thompson of 7th DGs. Move on to Sarie. Get General Spens at 6.30am and take a short message. Columns all around now. We have one man wounded and a horse shot. At Sarie, Colonel Jenner meets Colonel Lowe and we run into General Spens. Sergeant Biggs and I climb steep hill above halting place. Get General Broadwood. More ponies, mules etc caught. Total now of about 1700 head. Work Signalling station with 3 helios. Convoy turns up 3pm. General Spens is camping close by. General Broadwood passes by. Camp 4pm. I spent the afternoon asleep and then to bed early. Camping at Moigelegen.*

Signal/565

Prefix	Time	Location	No Words	Time	Date	Mss No
XB			119	10.10am	12.11.01	121

To: Gen Elliot   From: Gen Spens

S808. Paardenshoek. Nov 12th 9.30am. Dartnell reports as follows commences We saw a few waggons trekking West and some Boers broke back last night. 200 to Valplaats 100 to Leebenburgvlei ends Wilson reports as follows commences Byng is about four miles away on my right Briggs is on his right but a long way off Damant is three miles away on my left De Lisle also about six miles away on my left. Have captured a few Boers and a large number of cattle. Some of the men are now within two miles of Aardenhoek Boers have cleared out NE ends. I am camping near Zonheuvel tonight.

13 November   *March 6am. Padre and I go out on right flank. Dull morning. See Patton-Bethune in distance from hill above Graspan. Brock collects a lot more stock; there are a few animals in every valley and fold of ground. Pass ILH camp close to ours. Get General Elliot about 8am. He has sighted waggons across the river. We halt at Leeuw Spruit for two and half hours. 3rd DGs go on at 12 noon to try and catch waggons, but too slow and no good. ILH in two columns, both come near us at Leeuw Spruit. Start again at 2pm. March through a green oat field. Make for Vinknest, but go eventually to Brakfontein. Family dumped down in a pretty farm there… Camp at Brakfontein, marched 19 miles.*

14 November   *Breakfast at 4.15am, take out 6 men of IY 6.30am to try and get in touch with Colonel Mackenzie. Major Bridges is wounded. We cross the Wilge River and get signals contact with Colonel Briggs…*

Signal/589

Prefix	Time	Location	No Words	Time	Date	Mss No
SB	5.50am		28	6.5am	14.11.01	145

To: Col Lowe   From: Col Mackenzie

Please support me as am pursuing over very extended line and large Boer laager reported between me and Harrismith. Please bring an ambulance.

Signal/590

Prefix	Time	Location	No Words	Time	Date	Mss No
SB			30	6.10am	4.11.01	146

To: Col Mackenzie   From: Col Lowe

Am coming to your support. Orderly has just arrived asking for ambulance as Major Bridges is wounded. Will pick him up and follow you.

THE INTELLIGENCE STAFF OF THE COLUMN AND THE SCOUTS

Signal/592

Prefix	Time	Location	No Words	Time	Date	Mss No
SM			91	7.45am	14.11.01	148
To: Col Briggs		From: Col Lowe				

I started at dawn to support Mackenzie as he believed large laarger to be between him and Harrismith. He started at midnight. He has since helioed that as he is pursuing on a wide front he would like me to continue supporting him. As you are crossing here you can support him and I will march along right bank of river to Majoor's Drift. About a hundred cattle have slipped round bluff a mile to your left and on your side of river.

Signal/593

Prefix	Time	Location	No Words	Time	Date	Mss No
SM			16	7.58am	14.1.01	149
To: Col Lowe		From: Col Briggs				

What direction is he gone. Shall be delighted to support him.

Signal/594

Prefix	Time	Location	No Words	Time	Date	Mss No
SM			23	8am	14.11.01	150
To: Col Briggs		From: Col Lowe				

Mackenzie is about two miles due east but appears to be returning. Would suggest our sweeping towards Harrismith.

Later in the morning, as the various columns close up on each other, Colonel Lowe sends out this warning:

Signal/603

Prefix	Time	Location	No Words	Time	Date	Mss No
SM			22	10.55am	14.11.01	159
To: Col Aspinall		From: Col Lowe				

Push on at once and cross the drift otherwise Broadwood who is close behind you will block you

Malcolm's diary entry notes:

...move up along river bank collecting stock. Get General Elliot and our Convoy. The Brigadier and Colonel Carl Ellison go out and shoot blesbok etc. reach drift about 12 and find nearly all the convoy has crossed. Make camp and sleep. No food except a little chocolate from Dent since breakfast, and next to nothing then. Write letters. Camp at Majoor's Drift, marched 12 miles today.

Majoor's Drift, Wilge River. 14 November 1901

My dear Father,

We arrived here this afternoon and expect to reach Harrismith sometime tomorrow. We are about 18 miles out and as the Mail train leaves at 11am in the morning a Cape-Cart is being sent out early to try and catch it, so I take this opportunity to scribble you a few lines, but only a few as I am very tired after a long day's work and it is now 11pm. We have had a pretty fair trek as treks go nowadays. There was big scheme on and about 14 Columns were out to try and round up some Boers around Reitz but I am afraid the scheme did not altogether meet with the success it was expected to do. However we have all collected a large amount of stock and done the usual amount of devastation to farms and their belongings. The weather, except for one awful night, has been very kind to us and we are returning very sun-burnt but fairly happy and healthy.

We had two most deplorable deaths of Officers, both of them I am afraid through foolhardiness. One of them was a Captain Brass in Claud's Regiment and a very gallant fellow I believe. His Column, General Spens', had arrived at the Wilge River, then in full flood, and was holding a drift and waiting to cross. He was one of the first to reach the river and he spotted a mob of cattle on the opposite bank so he plunged into the stream on his horse at the first place he came to which was not even a drift and tried to reach the opposite bank. The current was far too strong for either him or his horse and though a very powerful swimmer, they say, failed to make either bank and was eventually drowned. It is an awfully sad case. The other Officer was a Captain Williams in the KDGs and one I knew. He was also, I believe, after cattle or something of the sort. He got a long way on in front of his Column, was 'hands-upped' by the Boers, stripped of all his clothes and belongings and then shot in cold blood through the stomach by a young devil of a Boer.

ever your affect son,

15 November *March 6am. I go ahead and send messages through Platberg. Sun is a bit awkward. General Broadwood is close behind us with ILH on our left. Go on a few more miles* and finish message. Camp on town lands, just outside Harrismith, near 'deep hollow' about 11am. Lunch early. Go into town with Wilson. Enquire about Signalling stores. Everything is being sent round via Kroonstad. Very windy. Can't get a shave. Return to camp where I find a parcel of chocolate for me from Mother. Camp at Harrismith, marched 14 miles today.

Signal/628

Prefix	Time	Location	No Words	Time	Date	Mss No
			37	5.20pm	16.11.01	184

To: Bde Sig Off Col Lowe's Bde   From: DSO Gen Elliot

16th Nov. I have three BB lamps you can have them please send over for them. I told Adjt 3rd DGds you could have them.

18 November   *Broadwood and De Lisle move late at night.*

Harrismith. 19th November 1901

My dear Mother,

...at last I am going to make some sort of shape of that long letter I have been promising you so long. I think I told you in my last letter Colonel Bethune is now enjoying three months leave and we have Colonel Lowe of the 7th Dragoon Guards taking his place. So please address my letters to Colonel Lowe's Column now.

You said you wanted to know what regiments were in this Brigade. I will give you instead the regiments etc in the whole Division. There are at present three brigades in the division commanded by General Broadwood, Colonel Lowe and Colonel de Lisle; General Elliot is in supreme command and he and his staff sometimes go with one brigade and sometimes with another – just to see how they are getting on. This coming trek (we march tomorrow at 7am) General Elliot and his staff are coming with Colonel Lowe's brigade and we are starting off in the Bethlehem direction I believe, but where we are supposed to go after that I do not know and am not supposed to tell you if I did. The regiments in the three brigades are as follows:

General Broadwood's: 1st KDGs and 12th IY,

Colonel Lowe's: 3rd DGs, 7th DGs and 4th IY

Colonel De Lisle's: 6th MI and 5th IBC

Each Column has besides four or more 15-pdr Field Guns and a Pom-pom. Each Brigadier or Column commander has his own staff, that is: his Brigade Major, ADC or galloper,

Intelligence Officer with a Staff of a dozen or more guides and scout boys with red bands round their hats, Signalling Officer with two or more HQ Signallers taken from the regiment in the brigade, Provost Marshal with about half a dozen Police (good men taken from regiments in the brigade), Commandeering Officer with a staff of about 70 herd boys and two or three conductors for rounding up stock on the march (in our brigade they wear blue ribbon round their hats for distinction) and perhaps he has a Remount Officer as well though generally one officer does both the Commandeering and Remount business. Then General Elliot has his staff too, called the Divisional staff, that is: CSO, 2 ADCs, a DAAG, a DAAG (B), a PMO, PVO, SO Transport, Provost Marshal, Div Signals O, Div Intelligence O, Div Remount O, and a Chaplain. I forgot to mention that a Brigadier has besides a Supply Officer with a small staff of perhaps half a dozen ASC men for issuing rations etc, a Transport Officer who is in charge of all the transport of the brigade, regimental and other transport and is responsible that it gets along from camp to camp all right, a Veterinary Officer who of course looks after all the animals of the brigade, and a Medical officer who is in charge of a few Hospital waggons and who in conjunction with the Regimental Medical officers looks after the health of the men. I think that is about all to be said about that.

About cigarettes – you sent me the wrong kind of '3 Castles'. The kind I want are made up in green tins of 100 each and are far superior to any other kind of '3 Castles' or 'Straight-Cut'...cigarette...('boy-killers' we call them) of any kind and can't be got out here at any price. I want to buy myself a Christmas present of a good pair of prism Field Glasses but I don't know the address of the makers. Would you please find this out for me, buy the glasses and deduct the amount from my allowance.

You asked me for a list of engagements I have been in with dates. I don't know what engagements you can want or why. I had hoped you were keeping all my home letters for me, to help me make up a good Diary some day, and all the scraps I have been in are in them, but if they are all burnt they are burnt I suppose and there is an end of it. I confess I am a bit disappointed but I hope at all events the bits of Diary and sketch maps have not shared a like fate.

Too sleepy for more now

your affectionate son,

The next morning the remaining British troops push on into the veldt for another sweep against the Boers. It would prove to be Malcolm's last trek in South Africa.

Boer prisoners

20 November *Ox Convoy moves at 5am and the remainder at 6am. We are a bit late. I ride on with message to head of Convoy. We have all sorts of Details and Supply Officers with us… Ground is very soft from recent rain. Cloudy afternoon. Sleep 2-4.30pm. Lights out 8pm. Camp at Ardtully*

21 November *Ox Convoy leaves 5am, remainder at 6am. Colonel Lowe curses us, we think unjustly, for transport being late. Freezing cold morning. I do Galloper mostly. Wear British Warm all day and mackintosh on top part of the day as well. Cross Elands River Bridge. Camp 10.30 in a new formation round a dam. Windy putting tents up. Watson uses a 10" Helio. De Lisle, Broadwood and Dartnell are all on our left. Lights out at 8pm. A drunken Corporal wakes me up about 10pm. Freezing cold. Camp at Uitvlukt.*

22 November *Oxen trek 5am, Brigade at 6am. Our tent is down at 5am. Sharp. General Dartnell shows up at Langberg. Lovely day, the sun is out strong. Big Signal station on Jollykop. A few Boers about till just in camp, then pom-pom and guns play. Capture a few horses. Dartnell has one prisoner and 600 head of cattle. Camp by 12. Padre and I go out on ponies after korahn and bring back a lamb. Camp at Naude's Vlei.*

23 November *March at 6am. Brigadier stays with Rear Guard and takes on fifty Boers, but only frightens them away from ILH who, we hear later, kill 2 and capture 16.*

NATIVE SCOUTS ARMED AND IN UNIFORM

Camp in old spot. Colonel De Lisle already in… Thunderstorm in afternoon. Broadwood comes in about 12 and goes out again at night. East Yorkshires are building blockhouses closeby. ILH have taken 200 away leaving only 200 odd. Camp at Vogelfontein (Bethlehem).

waggon. Camp at Bronkhorstfontein.

26 November *General Broadwood has more casualties at Kaffir Kop. He takes over our Convoy. March all night, very slow. Arrive at Leeuwkop at daybreak, 5am. IY and squadron of 7th DGs gallop after Boers and capture 200 head of cattle… Boers to hold a big meeting on Thursday night. Camp at 3pm.*

24 November, Sunday *March at 6am. Thompson, Padre and I wake up East Yorkshires to say good-bye. Cloudy morning. In camp by 11am. Lunch with IY after riding over to farms for Brigadier… Camp at Zevenfontein.*

25 November *March 6am. Fine day. Go on with Watson to Blaauw Kop to get Bethlehem and other Columns. Fine view. Column gets a few cattle. Get Colonel De Lisle later, he is away above Malan's drift and right out of place having done 50 miles since Sunday morning [no mean feat either !]. Lots of sheep are taken and a great slaughter. In camp by 12 noon and get General Broadwood and Colonel De Lisle from a little kopje by camp. All Observation Posts are now to have heliographs… I write etc. Night push with all mounted men ordered for 12 midnight. We take one tent and one mule*

27 November   *March 6am. Slept well. Breakfast on fried eggs…7th DGs capture a young Boer wearing a bandolier. Another Boer surrenders in the night to one of their posts. Camp about 12. Broadwood goes on a bit to the NW. He has a chance to capture 100 Boers but misses it and KDGs have Eastwood, a Sergeant and 2 men wounded. Try to get Broadwood in afternoon but he is not in sight. Brigadier takes Long to work a Signal Station. Fine night.*

28 November   *March at 5.30. Ox convoy moves at 5am. Move in a westerly direction. Hear that Colonel De Lisle has caught 27 waggons and carts. Broadwood snipes us* [the fact that Malcolm makes no further comment suggests quite strongly that this was no isolated incident, as indeed is his next comment which reflects a frequent practise by senior column commanders who barged across the front of the columns commanded by those officers junior to them] *and then crosses our front. We collect lots of sheep (7,000 odd). We find some Boer families living in old, burnt out houses. Natives sjambokked for ill treating a woman. Find a Cape Cart for Wilson but it is broken up…*

30 November   *We get into camp at Welgevonden.*

BOER 'HANDS-UPPERS': MEN WHO HAD SURRENDERED RATHER THAN FIGHT ON

Kroonstad. 30th November 1901

My dear Father,

This letter will I hope reach you on or some time very close to Christmas Day so I must send my wishes for all my relations and friends to enjoy a real hearty Christmas and be as well as me after mine! I cannot write to all or anything like all of them, I wish I could, so please tell as many as you see that my thoughts are with them and if I could I would be there myself just to see them all again, but it is not to be this year, no nor perhaps for several years to come…

General Elliot is now within 10 miles of Kroonstad and tomorrow we go on another 5 miles closer in. We have had a very pleasant trek, not done anything very wonderful, but still had a pretty good sport. We called at Bethlehem on the way and I saw all the East Yorkshires again. I met Wilkinson for the first time. He is doing Signalling too I see, but having rather a loaf I fancy as his regiment is stuck in block-houses and not moving about. The Railway out to Bethlehem is at last being started and block-houses built all along. Now good-bye and best Xmas wishes to all,

your affectionate son,

A few days later it becomes clear from the entries in Malcolm's diary that Colonel Lowe's column is no longer required for active service and is to be broken up.

Twenty-one

TO THE BITTER END –
DECEMBER 1901 TO MAY 1902

Opposite: Boer prisoners in the midst of Bethune's column

It is a measure of Malcolm's maturity, together with his attention to detail, that we find him left at Kroonstad as almost the sole remaining member of Colonel Lowe's column. His first duty is to square up all the brigade's paperwork as he explains in his next letter home:

Grand Hotel, Kroonstad. 7 December 1901

My dear Father,

Just a line to catch the Mail and let you know I am all right. Colonel Lowe's Brigade has now been broken up completely and I am left here in the Detail Camp with the remains of his Staff. I am trying vainly to take things calmly and get settled down but I am off my head with worry and troubles about getting rations and niggers and horses and all sorts of things connected with the brigade as I am the only Officer of the staff left bar the Medical Officer and the Supply Officer. Colonel Lowe himself has gone home, his Brigade Major has gone on a week's leave to Pretoria, his Intelligence Officer has been sent to another Column, his Provost Marshal, Commandeering Officer and Transport Officer have also been either taken away or gone on leave and here I am left in charge of the Staff, carts, orderlies etc and am also trying to train Signallers from regiments of the Division. Oh! the worry of it all, but things will soon smooth over.

Of the regiments of the brigade - two, 7th DGs and 4th IY, have been sent respectively to General Broadwood and Colonel De Lisle and the 3rd DGs are here by themselves in the Detail Camp and the idea is that a new brigade will be formed including them as soon as two new Cavalry regiments come out, which ought to be soon. Weather just now awfully hot and close. General Elliot is with Broadwood and De Lisle went out in Lindley direction about two days ago.

yours ever,

A few days later Malcolm wrote the letter home to his mother which is quoted extensively at the beginning of this book. After describing a typical mounted column and his duties as signalling officer, Malcolm expresses a feeling then current amongst many officers serving in South Africa, one of frustration mingled with a distinct lack of enthusiasm to be involved in a serious fight at this stage of the war. As he wrote, no one wanted to be wounded or be killed fighting for some ignominious fontein or kop. As Malcolm puts it, it would have been better to have been a casualty in a real battle during the early part of the war. One suspects that this lack of enthusiasm may well have had some impact on morale and the effort put into prosecuting the wars but this would be to denigrate the professionalism of the British military machine in South Africa. It is nonetheless interesting to note from Malcolm's letter the alacrity

with which the officers of Lowe's column departed on leave and curious that Malcolm, possibly because he was the most junior officer, was abandoned to do the best he could, although he had been in South Africa as long as any of them and probably longer than some.

Kroonstad. 14th Dec 1901

My dear Mother,

This is a sweltering hot day. I am sitting in our Mess tent, now an ordinary bell-tent, scribbling away in my shirt sleeves. General Elliot as I told you last Mail went out with only two Columns this time, but they practically contained the whole of the Division. Last night we heard the joyful news that General Elliot was rounding up De Wet with a lot of men and waggons in the area contained by the towns of Kroonstad, Lindley, Heilbron and Wolvenhoek, and as there is a strong line of block-house on three sides of this area we expect great things. Last night all available men from the Details here (200 odd) were despatched off in the Lace mine direction. This is presumably to keep the Boers from turning south again should they manage to cross the line.

Now I must answer questions. First of all I must explain that great stumbling-block of yours 'my duties as signalling officer'...

You will see that far from being 'away from all the fighting' as you rather unkindly put it, I am always well up in it, for whenever there is fighting the Brigadier must be there to conduct operations, and where he goes I go too. I have no ardent desire to be at the head of the Advance Guard every day in order to be sniped at I can tell you, still, when the time comes I am no coward, but at the same time I see no use in running unnecessary risks. If I wanted to be shot I should like to have been shot in some big engagement at the beginning of the war and not ignominiously at some unknown fontein or platz out in the bare open veldt.

your affectionate son,

From now until the end of the war Malcolm's letters and diary entries become ever more irregular and lacking in detail. The only surviving diary consists of a pocket cash book in which Malcolm wrote diary entries from time to time during the earlier part of 1902. For much of this time he was stationed at Kroonstad where he trained troopers and infantrymen, from the various mounted columns belonging to Major General Elliot's division, in the use of the heliograph and other pieces of signalling apparatus. Very occasionally Malcolm himself was engaged in active service signalling at various points along the railway line outside Kroonstad. Malcolm kept no record of the signals he sent or received after Lowe's column was disbanded.

Kroonstad, 27th December 1901

My dear Mother,

The week has come round again, this very quickly, so I must write to let you know how things are going. We had a fairly merry Christmas. I got hold of an Irish subaltern of the KDGs, Reeves by name, and we had our dinner with Brock and another of Colonel Bethune's old staff and a very nice time too we had. After that we went up to the Hospital and had tea with the Nurses and they showed us round the marquees and we saw all the pretty decorations the men and orderlies had made out of coloured paper and what greenery they could get. The latter was mostly tops of plants, bits of mimosa thorn and pretty trailing wild asparagus plant.

your affectionate son,

Malcolm's next letter tells us that he is still in Kroonstad and also tells us more about the organisation of the mounted columns:

Kroonstad, 4th January 1902

My dear Mother,

At last I am glad to say I have got a home Mail. It is the very latest from home...

I am still here as you see, busy instructing Signallers for the Division. I say busy and indeed I am kept pretty busy for as I have told you already I have not the right men to help me and of course that means extra work for me. This camp is as dusty and windy and generally annoying and unpleasant as usual. At this very minute I am sitting in a stifling hot tent fanned gently by a dust storm and after every word or two I write down I have to give a vigorous blow to clear off some of the dust.

I must now get on with answering some of your questions. No 1 is 'What is done with captured beasts when brought into the Line?' I must first of all tell you that at every big town or station along the line there is a properly organised Remount Depot for the receipt and issue of horses; there is an ASC Depot which takes over and issues sheep, oxen and mules; there is an Agent for the Cold Storage Company who used to take over all captured sheep and cattle from Columns and then issue them to the ASC when required but who now only contracts for the civilian population. Finally there is a Government Stock Farm at the nearest small station or siding with good grazing. This last is quite a new departure and was only started a month ago.

What used to be done originally was, the mob of stock was all driven into town, the horses were taken away by the Remount Officer and the remainder was taken over by the ASC Officer. If the ASC Officer had no butcher the Cold Storage Company took over the whole or as much as they wanted of the stock, buying it at live weight. They then took the stock up or down the line to wherever it was required, driving the beasts by day under cover of the block-houses, slew the animals and sold the meat, dead-weight, back to the ASC for issue to the troops. The Cold Storage Coy of course charged a commission for the slaughter and delivery of the meat and that is the reason for the extraordinary rise in their shares. Now that the Government Farms have been started they will no longer supply the troops with the meat but they will still have the contract for the civilian population which is by no means inconsiderable. The stock is now taken over by an Inspector of Government Stock Farms from the Columns, properly looked after on these farms, and the animals are issued to the ASC as required. Frequently the animals have to be sent from point to point by train, but as the trains run all day and night without harm there is room for all this traffic.

Brock of the 5th IBC [? Imperial Bushmen, one of the many Australian mounted contingents)] who was APM, and latterly Remount and Commandeering Officer to our Column, has been made an Inspector of some of these Stock Farms and as this is a very fine billet indeed he is on the high road to success and a good income - lucky devil! I wish I could say the same!! He makes Kroonstad his headquarters; his District is from Wolvenhoek to Brandfort, and he has such a jolly little camp down among the willows and poplars and other shady trees on the river bank and just on the very edge of town. Don't I just envy him. He and old Wilson, our chief guide and intelligence agent to the Column, have taken over our little Mess with its wagonette, chairs, crockery etc (all picked up on the trek!) and set up camp down there.

Oh! this camp is terrible, I am nearly being blown out of my chair in addition to all the other evils! I don't think I ever told you who old Wilson was. When Lindley was taken during Lord Roberts' general advance Wilson was the owner of the biggest and best hotel in the town and Mayor of Lindley to boot. He it was who handed over the keys to the place to General Broadwood. He is a great old card and everyone, Briton or Boer, seems to know him, no matter where he goes, but he is a true loyalist at heart and a very genial, talkative, hearty, old Scotsman. He and I are great friends. I rush out of this abominable camp immediately after lunch every day and spend the best part of the afternoon chatting to the old fellow and his friends in his cool, clean and shady camp. It is awfully jolly down there. I forgot to tell you Old Wilson and I joined Colonel Bethune together at Standerton and stuck to the Column right through till now when we were both cast adrift.

Love to all, Your affectionate son,

8 January *Take Class into 'Park' to try for shade and greater distances. Got turned out. ...Hot afternoon. Nearly all Details sent down to Honing Spruit to hold the line. Lamps as usual* [night time signalling work].

9 January *Stand to from 1.30 till 5am. Sleep from then till 9am. Awfully hot. Send men out to Telegraph poles with Lea at Veterinary hospital but no sun. Return and continue with Flags and Sounder. Feel beastly all day. No appetite, no grub, no sodas. Go to bed early. Wet night.*

Kroonstad, 20th January 1902

My dear Father,

Just a line this Mail. No time for more I regret to say. I have been so busy writing other letters and disposing of other correspondence that I have left your letter till too late. I am so sorry, it is very wrong of me. I will answer Mother's question next Mail. Nothing has happened here of any consequence since last Mail. I came back from Bloemfontein on Monday night (20th). It has been raining pretty well ever since. Horrid weather. I have developed a slight cold. One of the few I have had out here.

your affectionate son,

We hear nothing more of Malcolm's activities until late February and by which time he was ill with dysentery or enteric though when he actually fell ill is not on record in his papers. It is not even clear exactly where Malcolm was by the time of the next entry in his diary but it seems likely he was somewhere on the blockhouse line towards Lindley and still actively engaged in signalling work.

18 February   *Leave about 9.30am with trolley… and reach Lindley about 12.30. No room for me in Hospital so I go on up to Wilson and put up with him.*

19 February   *Stay in bed all day.*

21 February   *Nice morning. Wake early. Elliot's Columns move out to Wilge River. Claud turns up… Thunderstorm all afternoon.*

23 February, Sunday   *Send trolley down for Claud's kit and fix him up in my tent. De Wet tries KP block-house line but finds it too strong. Columns in view to the North of town. Try for them with a lamp.*

24 February   *Fine morning. wake at 4am. Sent Claud out riding on little chestnut pony before breakfast. Barker's Columns come in and camp on north side of town. They have captured 34 Boers.*

27 February   *Breakfast at 9am. Sniping at block-houses close by again. Get up and stay up all day. Feeling much fitter… fine if dull day. Pack up and set off with trolley… reach Kaffir Kop 1.30pm. and sleep through the afternoon. Wet night.*

Although Malcolm would appear to still be suffering from dysentery his diary shows he was still working. He has now reached Kaffir Kop, which was presumably a transmitting station alongside the railway line, where he had a detachment of signallers to look after.

1 March   *A misty morning and drizzles rain. Not feeling well.*

2 March   *Dull misty morning. Still on slops, arrowroot and cornflower. Put Signallers to work on Platform. Fine evening. Sunny. Trolley returns.*

4 March   *Move down to Hospital in afternoon… The wind is down and a fine day.*

7 March   *Hot sunny day with showers in afternoon… Very weak and doze a lot. Communications with Tepman noon SW 12 miles; RN has Rawlinson NE of BM; communication with Pilcher in afternoon.*

8 March   *Heavy sniping all night but no damage however… Get Tepman again but not Pilcher. Rawlinson on lamp. Pass an awful night. Very hot and sunny, heavy shower in afternoon.*

Finally Malcolm is too ill to continue, and on 11 March he is taken to the Kroonstad and found a bed in the field hospital there.

Easter Sunday, 30th March 1902

Dear Father, Mother and Edith,
*   I am writing this in bed as there is a slight dysenteric tendency again, nothing bad. If you have not received a telegram between the date of this letter and the date you receive it you may be perfectly certain I am all right, so please do not get anxious on my account.*
*   Your affectionate son,*

This is the last surviving letter that Malcolm wrote from South Africa and we know nothing of his illness or what happened to him until 14 April when his erratic diary entries show that he had been placed on the sick list and is to be sent down to a major hospital at Wynberg. His brief diary entries later in the month indicate that he was still unwell, mostly from diarrhoea, but was very much better. Soon afterwards he was examined by a medical board which must have passed him medically unfit for further active service and recommended a period of sick leave because:

14 May   *Embark HMT* Dilwara *and sail for England.*

Malcolm arrived back in Ireland in mid-June 1902 where he remained until the early summer of 1903. Then he sailed to India where, in October, he joined The West Yorkshire Regiment's 1st Battalion. Soon enough he would march again – this time to see action on the North-West frontier of India, but that is another story. He never returned to South Africa.

MALCOLM RIALL (1879-1968)

The second son of Commander Arthur Riall, Malcolm was born and raised in Bray, Co Wicklow. After being educated at Charterhouse School and the RMC Sandhurst, Malcolm joined the West Yorkshire Regiment in 1899. After service in South Africa, Malcolm was posted to India where he spent seven years before returning to England. Whilst in India he saw active service on the North-West Frontier. He retired from the Army in April 1914, his term of service having expired, but was recalled to the colours in August 1914 and served through the Great War, spending 1915 in the trenches on the Somme where he was badly wounded. He was invalided out of the Army in January 1919 and awarded an OBE in June 1919. His two brothers, Claud and Bertie, also served in South Africa, in India and through the Great War. All three, like the thirty or so other Rialls who have served in the armed forces over the last three centuries, died at home at the end of long and interesting lives.

(OPPOSITE - MALCOLM RIALL ON THE OCCASION OF HIS BEING PRESENTED AT COURT TO KING EDWARD VII AND QUEEN ALEXANDRA, DUBLIN, 1902.)